SIX MORE DAYS OF GRACE

Other books by G. Derek West

Twelve Days of Grace
The Elevens of England

Six More Days of Grace

by

G. Derek West

Darf Publishers Limited
London
1992

© G. DEREK WEST

FIRST PUBLISHED 1992

British Library Cataloguing-in-Publication Data
A catalogue record for this book
is available from the British Library

ISBN 1 85077 226-6

Jacket designed by Sue Sharples

Printed and bound in Great Britain
by BPCC Wheatons Ltd, Exeter

Contents

v

List of Illustrations

Foreword

AT A TIME when W.G. Grace was occupied with producing the second of his most important full-length books, his thoughts turned once again to all those fellow cricketers with whom he had been associated for thirty years and more. Of their exact numbers he was uncertain, which is hardly surprising, but he settled for an estimate of "a few thousand, more or less, notable men." To have provided a biography of each one of that multitude of team-mates and adversaries would have been a gargantuan undertaking far beyond the capacity of most mortals, not least the Champion, whose ability to ply a pen lagged far behind his remarkable expertise at wielding a bat. Nevertheless, profiting by the assistance of ghost-writers more familiar with the rigorous demands of literary composition, he duly devoted a chapter in two of his books to recording his impressions of many of his most famous contemporaries. These biographical notices range from a few lines to two or three pages for each individual. Such brevity to meet the demands of the publishers placed limits on the amount of information that could be included, and while a thorough exposition of each cricketer's full career was necessarily omitted, the authors were able in some instances to describe the methods of play, adding the occasional anecdote to illustrate personal characteristics.

There was some duplication between the two books, but in all W.G. and his amanuenses dealt with about one hundred-and-fifty cricketers. A few of them have subsequently been accorded full-length biographies by other hands, but the majority still remain without a memorial to their fame. Owing to the paucity of complete information, it would admittedly be impossible to compile an extensive biography of many of them. Some, however, merit a more detailed treatment than W.G. was able to devote to them. In 1989, a book of mine entitled *Twelve Days of Grace* was published as an attempt to provide some filling for the yawning gap. This volume consisted of biographical sketches of twelve leading professionals whose careers were in part or whole contemporaneous with those of W.G. Grace and other members of his family. The present book continues along similar lines by dealing with six more prominent players of the Victorian age – Tom Emmett, Edward Barratt, George Ulyett, W.H. Scotton, Willie

Bates, and Robert Peel. All of them, incidentally, were included in W.G.'s two selections of "notable men."

It was my aim to try to rescue these cricketers from the distant past into which they have receded, to trace their careers, noting outstanding feats and records, and to re-create a picture of their appearance, personalities, and methods of play. It was occasionally possible to find much relevant information about a player's techniques of batting, bowling, and fielding in the published recollections of one contemporary, but this was generally more often the exception than the rule. Some of my descriptions of individual methods of batting and bowling were composed after a collation of the data furnished by several informants, none of whom included every single detail in his account. One example will be found in the attempt to present a visual image of the bowling of Tom Emmett.

Limited-overs competitions were not introduced until long after the days of W.G. and his contemporaries, and certain aspects and features of the first-class game have changed since that time. At the beginning of the Champion's career in 1865, the over consisted of only four balls, the number increasing to five in 1889, and six in 1900. The follow on was compulsory for a deficit of 80 runs, raised to 120 in 1894, and 150 in 1900, when it was made optional, and declarations were not sanctioned until 1889. Six runs off one stroke over the boundary were only allowed for hits clean out of the ground. Tours overseas were organized not by any central body but by private promoters, while at home the teams to represent England were usually chosen for the most part by the authorities at the ground on which Test Matches were played (Lord's, The Oval, and Old Trafford).

In the last third of the nineteenth century, batting and bowling averages were much lower than they are today, largely because of the varying quality of the pitches. The 1883 edition of *Wisden* qualifies batting averages of 23.17, 30.40, and 39.60 as "good," "remarkably good," and "grand" respectively. The top five batsmen in 1882 achieved averages ranging from 34.44 to 31.64, two of them passing 1,000 runs; in 1990, there were over a hundred batsmen with averages higher than 34.44, many of them attaining four-figure aggregates with ten scoring more than 2,000 runs. The top five bowlers playing in more than two matches in 1882 recorded averages ranging from 10.06 (112 wickets) to 11.52 (214 wickets!). Not a single bowler claimed a hundred wickets in 1990, when the first man dismissed his victims at 19.05 apiece and the fifth at 23.16, figures which would have been regarded as verging on mediocrity in the 1880s. Referring once again to the 1883 edition of *Wisden*, one of its contributors declared that if ". . . C. Young can succeed in taking another 28 wickets, *at less cost though than 19.18*, there is every prospect of Hampshire having as good a record in the coming year" (*Wisden's* italics, not mine). Occupying the second place in the national table for 1990, Malcolm Marshall ("Hampshire's player of the season") captured 72 wickets – at an average of 19.18! *Autres temps, autres mœurs.*

By way of explanation, there are a few terms in my text which might be unfamiliar to some readers. Although they enjoyed their heyday in the 1850s and 1860s, some of the "itinerant elevens" were still in existence in the next decade and even a little longer, until they were finally killed off by the ever-increasing spread of first-class cricket. These teams, manned mainly but not always entirely by prominent professionals when they were not required for county contests and the like, travelled round the country, meeting local sides consisting of as many as twenty-two opponents – known as playing against "odds." Although these games were dying out in the old country, many of the fixtures undertaken by the English teams touring in Australia, New Zealand, North America, and South Africa in the nineteenth century were "odds" matches. In order to redress the balance, the local sides in England often engaged the temporary services of one or more professionals, usually bowlers, who were called "Given Men."

Once again, I have relied mainly upon the excellent books compiled and published by the Association of Cricket Statisticians for the details of the score cards in most first-class matches. As regards the career records of individual players, I have in most instances used the monumental *Who's Who of Cricketers* and the county booklets issued by the Association. *Scores and Biographies* and the cricket annuals listed in the Bibliography were consulted for the details of minor contests played at home and abroad. The sketches contain many references to particular matches, and for the convenience of those who might wish to look up the full score I have usually inserted the appropriate place and dates.

I have previously contributed short articles dealing with events connected with some of the six players to *The Journal of the Cricket Society* and *Wisden Cricket Monthly*. To the editors of those publications I must express my appreciation for having granted me permission to include and adapt portions of the material within my longer biographical sketches. References to these articles, where relevant, are given at the conclusion of a chapter.

I owe a debt of gratitude to many persons, who have not hesitated to help me in the course of my researches, in particular to Philip Bailey, who showed matchless patience in advising me on career records and in bringing recently discovered amendments to my attention; Stephen Green, the Curator and Librarian at Lord's, for his guidance in finding source material in the volumes under his charge; David W. Sharp, for information on Robert Peel; H. Webber, for information on Willie Bates; Tony Woodhouse, who has zealously undertaken inquiries on my behalf and supplied the answers with remarkable speed and accuracy; Peter Wynne-Thomas, who has never failed to favour me with information culled from his vast knowledge of cricket; and, finally, the staff of the British Library Newspaper Library at Colindale.

I am once again deeply indebted to Roger F. Mann for placing his expertise and the resources of his collection of photographs at my disposal, and for his kindness in providing all but one of the photographic portraits accompanying the text.

Caversham, Berkshire, 1991   G. DEREK WEST

Note on Money, Weights, and Measurements

Sums of money mentioned in this book are given in the old coinage, one pound consisting of 20 shillings (1s = 5p), and one shilling of 12 pennies.

Weights are expressed in stones (1 st = 6.35 kg) and pounds (1 lb = 0.45 kg), one stone consisting of 14 pounds.

Measurements are given in feet (1 ft = 30.48 cm) and inches (1 in = 2.54 cm), one foot consisting of 12 inches. A yard was 3 feet (0.91 m).

TOM EMMETT
"A Joy for Ever"

MRS EMMETT senior, who had a horror of abbreviations, insisted on calling her son by the complete form of his baptismal name. By the world at large, however, he was always addressed as "Tom" throughout his career and later, and he has been known affectionately to posterity as "Tom Emmett" ever since. A few years after his retirement from the first-class game, it was confidently asserted that there were more anecdotes about him than any other professional cricketer. This claim still holds good today, though another great Yorkshireman (F.S. Trueman) comes pretty close to him in this respect. So far-reaching were the fame and popularity of these two "characters" that they figure in numerous tales, some of them true and some embroidered, while others may be largely or purely fictitious, invented to suit their personalities. A natural humorist with a ready wit, Tom's good temper and ability to laugh at himself as well as others, together with his unfailing keenness on the cricket field, endeared him to all his contemporaries. The stories told by and about him are legion: some of the best, but by no means all, are preserved in his own reminiscences, while others abound in those of his fellow cricketers. Through the medium of cold print, a few of the anecdotes seem to be rather banal when judged by the more sophisticated standards of modern humour, but we are, of course, deprived of the manner in which Tom delivered his witticisms. It may fairly be claimed, however, that his everlasting fame rests as much on his talent for comedy as on his prowess as a cricketer.

Tom was born at Halifax, on September 3, 1841, in a house situated in a road called Crib Lane, which, as he was to observe later, was "not an inappropriate birthplace for an ordinary infant." The development of his interest in cricket during his boyhood followed the fairly normal pattern of numerous games played on the hard surface of streets with the inevitable interludes of broken windows, followed by a panic-stricken flight from the local policeman, whose imposing presence in those days was rendered even more awesome by his tall, silk headgear. The sudden appearance of this top-hatted arm of the law would cause an infectious wave of terror among the budding cricketers, who decamped without further ado – somewhat

1

noisily, one imagines, since at this time and into his late teens Tom's footwear frequently consisted of a pair of clogs.

Of not much more than average height and weight in his manhood, Emmett kept himself in good trim and enjoyed a protracted career in the first-class game. Erect of carriage and neat in appearance, he never ran to fat, and his physique was of ideal proportions to withstand the tasks and strains imposed upon it. In the words of one of his contemporaries, he was "all wire and whipcord, one of the very best bits of stuff a cricketer ever was made of." His light-coloured hair, of which he had no great abundance, was usually hidden under a cap, and his upper lip was covered by a thick moustache. Fair-skinned, one might almost say thin-skinned, he had a complexion that was always remarkable for its rubicund hue. By some ladies he was nicknamed "Mr Punch." This was not, I am sure, an unkind suggestion that he indulged in the deplorable practice of wife-beating, but an allusion to his nasal organ. The most prominent feature of his ruddy countenance, it rivalled Punch's nose in its size and colour. A large, red nose is conventionally – and sometimes rather unfairly – interpreted as a sure sign that its owner is an unmitigated drunk. As far as Tom was concerned, this was a gross calumny. In a team that could boast, if that is the right word, of including only one teetotaller, Tom was known to like his glass at the appropriate time. He freely confessed of one instance of over-indulgence. At Cambridge, on one occasion when Yorkshire were playing against the undergraduates, he spent a convivial evening at Downing College, where his host plied him so liberally with champagne that when Tom plunged his face, nose foremost, in the wash-basin the next morning, "it made t'watter fair phizz."

It was Tom's proud boast, however, that drink never made him unfit to play, and consequently the appearance of his nose was a source of embarrassment to him on more than one occasion. Stationed down at long-leg once, he heard a spectator with a penetrating voice call out, "Bah gum, there moost 'ave been a powerful lot of stooff go down that throat to make that norze *thaat* coolour!" Even worse was a conversation he had with a Yorkshire supporter at a time when the County was in the doldrums. The unknown wasted no time in telling him that things were going wrong because "You're all doing too mooch of thaat." Emmett failed to understand what he was getting at, and back came the accusation that too much beer was to blame. "Who told you so?" asked Tom, only to receive the blunt reply, "Your nose." Tom was so incensed that he came near to throwing a punch at his outspoken tormentor. Controlling himself with difficulty, he snapped back, "Then mah nose is a bloody liar!" and stamped away to cool off.

A genuine all-rounder, though admittedly not the top-notcher of his time, Tom was no passenger in the field. Keen, energetic, and adaptable,

Tom Emmett   *Courtesy Roger Mann*

it was not in his nature to remain rooted on one spot or to amble about at a sedate pace. "Lackadaisical" was not a word that featured in his vocabulary. Be it a short distance or a long trek into the out-field, he always used to run to his allotted post between overs. His original position was cover slip (second slip), but on the whole he was seen at his best in the covers or in the deep, where "he would cover miles of ground." He exhibited the highest standard of professionalism in his approach to fielding. Left-handed in all things, he found this placed him at a marked disadvantage. For all the good it was, his right arm might just as well have been tucked inside his waistcoat. Concluding that a fielder, to be successful, ought to be ambidextrous, he set about the task of remedying the situation. Having equipped himself with an india rubber ball, he spent countless hours of practice hurling it against a wall and catching it with either hand, according to the direction of the return bounce. This devotion to the fine honing of his skills as a fielder paid dividends with his discovery that he was able to hold catches with his right hand as well as with his left. Tom was not the only Yorkshire cricketer who strove to achieve a certain degree of ambidexterity, and here again there is a link with Fred Trueman, who was naturally right-handed. There may be some readers who can clearly remember, as I do, the sight of Fred occasionally using his left hand to send a long, accurate return to the wicket-keeper.

Generally safe and ever agile even when he was past forty years of age, Tom held 276 catches in his first-class career. He missed some, of course (who after all does not?), the most spectacular instance occurring in the contest between Gloucestershire and Yorkshire at Cheltenham, on August 22 and 24, 1878. With the second day wiped out by heavy rain, the home side did not begin their first innings until shortly after play had been resumed on the 24th. Batting in adverse conditions with the ground extremely wet, W.G. Grace's innings was short (c Lockwood b Emmett 10). It ought to have been even shorter, since he returned the simplest of sitters to Tom, who had opened the bowling with Willie Bates. It was too simple, as it turned out, since the butter-fingered bowler suffered the humiliation of spilling the greasy ball on to the sodden turf. The misery and frustration caused by his failure to secure the most desirable wicket of all in such unbearable circumstances was too much for the hapless bowler. I don't know if he gave voice to his agony, but if he did, you can be sure that the language was as highly coloured as his nose. His physical reaction was visually dramatic. Snatching off his cap, he hurled it on to the ground and trampled it into the mud. Then, seeing the offending ball lying near his feet, he gave it a powerfully savage kick, which sent it speeding on its way to the boundary, adding four runs to his opponent's score. Once this rare tantrum was spent, play was resumed and, in the words of a member of the Yorkshire team, "Tom spent the rest of the day apologising to W.G. Grace."

It is always particularly galling to see a bowler's best efforts wasted by the negligence of his team-mates, but such a situation, when chance after chance went begging, provided the origin of one of Tom's most famous witticisms. As the ball fell through a fielder's nerveless fingers for the umpteenth time, he gravely informed all those around him that "There's an epidemic 'ere today, but it ain't bloody catching!"

As a batsman, Tom was not the best left-hander of his day, but he played many a useful knock, practising a "pleasant habit of getting runs when no one else could stop the bowling." His nearest approach to a four-figure aggregate was recorded in 1881, when he totalled 858 (average 19.95), but twice he fought his way into the top twenty of the national batting averages (1869 and 1873). It was a matter of intense satisfaction to him that he marked his highest ever score and solitary century in first-class cricket off the bowling of the Grace brothers and their allies. This feat he achieved in the contest at Clifton, on August 14, 15, and 16, 1873. Going in first in Yorkshire's second innings, after the follow on, he notched 104 runs, including a 5 and ten 4s, by far the highest figure on his side.

There were occasions, in times of dire necessity, when Tom would curb his natural instincts and settle for defensive tactics, though defence was not his normal game. To describe his technique as orthodox would be miles wide of the truth. Once you saw him stepping briskly towards the crease, you could be sure that the field would wake up and, if only he stayed in for a while, you would be rewarded with a generous measure of free entertainment. Anxious, perhaps, to open his account and push the score along, he would keep calling upon his partner for seemingly impossible runs during the first few overs, for then and at all times he was an inveterate run-stealer. At the non-striker's end, he would back up so far that the rattled fielders were goaded into making a wild shy at the wicket – and usually missing it, just as Tom calculated they would, and as often as not the risk taken was justified by the outcome. His judgement of a delivery was somewhat bizarre, a characteristic shared with some of his Yorkshire team-mates, and there seemed to be no recognized principle to his batting. A couple of full tosses, half-volleys, or long hops, or any permutation from these three, would be treated with extravagant respect and played quietly back to the bowler, whereas most other batsmen would have been only too grateful to accept these gifts and smite them lustily to the boundary. Should the bowler, however, send down a delivery of immaculate line and length, it was by no means unusual to see Tom hit the ball back hard and high over his opponent's head. Some of his strokes were not calculated to please the purists, but nobody could deny the extraordinary ferocity of his cut, particularly square of the wicket, and on at least one occasion he felt it only fair to issue a warning to the fielder crowding in on him at point ("If Ah were thee, mester, Ah'd stand a little farther back, because when Ah 'its theer, Ah 'its adjectival 'ard!").

There were still a few lob bowlers about at this time, but Tom reckoned nowt to such infantile trundling and used to pride himself as a champion smiter of the "slows." Assisting England against Gloucestershire at The Oval, on August 15, 16, and 17, 1878, he was presented with a golden opportunity to demonstrate his mastery of the under-hand delivery. Going in at number eight, he had scored a couple of runs when he found himself confronting the Gloucestershire amateur, Frank Townsend. Congratulating himself on his good fortune, Tom took his guard and waited for his natural prey. The slow, curving trajectory of the lob gave him a split second to make up his mind whether to play forward or back. In the end he did neither, choosing to shoulder arms and offer no stroke. It was a fatal decision. Townsend's length was perfect, and the ball, deviating unexpectedly from the pitch, broke the wicket. Appalled at this public humiliation after all his boasting, Tom tried to put a brave face on it by replacing the bails on the stumps, tapping his bat on the block hole, and saying, "'Ere, Mr Townsend, joost let me 'ave that wun over again, will you, please?" The Gloucestershire team laughed, and Tom set off back to the dressing-room, his emotions a mixture of anger and self-disgust. His actions in picking up the bails and resuming his stance at the crease once more had puzzled the crowd, and as he was approaching the entrance to the pavilion, one of the spectators called out:

"Tom, how was it?"

"Don't Tom me," snapped the unhappy victim.

"Well, Mr Emmett, how was it?"

"Don't Mr Emmett me," was the savage rejoinder.

"Then what shall I call you?" asked the ill-used spectator.

"Call me a bloody fool!" hurled Tom over his shoulder as he vanished inside the dressing-room.

Looking back to Tom's days of glory, a journalist observed that "it was perhaps as a bowler that Emmett was chiefly a joy for ever," though such a description fitted the man in all respects. If his batting, to put it mildly, often bordered on the patently unorthodox, his bowling could best be set down as starkly eccentric. A fast left-hander, he developed his action in the old round-arm days, and even though bowling above the level of the shoulder became legal in 1864 when he was in his early twenties, the position of his arm hovered somewhere between the horizontal and the perpendicular. He usually delivered round the wicket from the extreme end of the bowling crease, approaching off a fairly long run with "an odd, corkscrewy sort of action," his left elbow rotating frantically and his whole torso lurching about from side to side. These ungainly contortions

F. Townsend

became much more pronounced if his footing was rendered hazardous after rain, and on one occasion when he was slipping and writhing about, one of the crowd at Bramall Lane shouted, "'Ere, you chaps, send that booger 'ome, or else 'e'll twist 'issen in two!" Had line and length been the principal characteristics of his methods, Tom would have been one of the best bowlers in the land. As it was, he was very good. Appearing in twenty-three seasons in first-class cricket in England, he attained a place in the top twenty of the bowling averages fifteen times and the top ten on eleven occasions. Not too many of his contemporaries could make a similar claim. His besetting sin was a lack of accuracy. Two or three balls would fly wildly out of the batsman's reach, followed by a virtually unplayable one pitching around the line of the leg-stump and whipping across to the off, as often as not terminating the batsman's innings. Tom delighted in this pet delivery, which, for reasons known only to himself, he called his "sostenutor," sometimes adding, "Why, what else could you call it?" It has to be admitted that in his time he sent down an inordinate number of wides, but he persisted in his off theory throughout his career. There was a certain craftiness about his operations on those occasions when, having placed most of his fielders on the off, he would launch several very fast deliveries to leg as a means of unsettling the batsman. This process of perplexing his opponent was completed by a sudden reversion to off theory, often with fatal results. If statistics be taken as some accurate measure of success, then his technique assuredly paid rich dividends: at the end of his career he had taken a stack of wickets at a remarkably low cost.

During his teens, Tom earned his living as a mill hand, and on his days off he played in local cricket matches. Engaged by the Halifax Club for a nominal fee, he turned up at the ground with his flannels wrapped up in a newspaper and still wearing his clogs. Subsequently, he spent some three years as the professional of the Keighley Club, and in the 1870s, several years after the beginning of his first-class career, he held an appointment at Middlesbrough, which now and then prevented him from assisting his County. At one time or another, he turned out for most of the principal itinerant elevens, as well as appearing against them as a "Given Man" hired for a match fee by various local clubs.

Tom made his first-class debut at Trent Bridge, on August 2 and 3, 1866, when Nottinghamshire secured a comfortable victory over Yorkshire by nine wickets. The newcomer was far from disgracing himself. Going in at number ten, he was undefeated twice, but more importantly he was Yorkshire's most successful bowler, taking five for 33 and the only wicket to fall in Nottinghamshire's second innings. This was his sole appearance of the season, but in 1867 he played in six of the County's seven fixtures. His opportunities for bowling were initially somewhat limited, since the recognized opening attack consisted of Luke Greenwood and George Freeman, but by the time the season was drawing to its close he had more or less ousted Greenwood and established his famous partnership with Freeman. Tom had an excellent match in Yorkshire's heavy defeat of Lancashire at Old Trafford, on June 27, 28, and 29. Notching the top score of all (61), he also captured eight wickets. Immediately before this, against Surrey at Bramall Lane, he recorded an astonishing analysis – his best of the season – in the visitors' second innings (12–8–7–6).

At the end of August, the Surrey Committee arranged a match for the benefit of their old wicket-keeper, Thomas Lockyer, with a combination of Surrey and Sussex contending against England. The opposition was not at full strength, but the team contained some good names, and Tom made his first association, destined to be prolonged over the next twenty years, with W.G. Grace. The latter's batting powers were, comparatively speaking, still in the burgeoning stage, and since he was dismissed for only 12, he probably left no instant impression on the young Yorkshireman. The future Champion's bowling, however, was a different matter, and in both innings he opened the England attack with Emmett. W.G. captured eight wickets in the match, but Tom's return, with ten victims all told (5–52 and 5–26) was even better. In seven matches that summer, he took forty-eight wickets at an average of 7.66 and came second in the national bowling table, an astonishing performance for any bowler in his first full season.

Tom's first-class appearances increased to eight the following year. His first contest was the annual match between the All England Eleven and the United All England Eleven, in which he opened the United bowling with George Freeman, an ideal combination of fast right at one end and fast left at the other. Freeman, one of the most handsome cricketers in England, was regarded by many, including W.G., as the finest fast bowler they had ever encountered, though Tom at this time trod close upon his heels as a pitiless destroyer. Their celebrated association, probably the most lethal in England for a few years, was short-lived, since Freeman decided that his best long-term interests lay in the business of auctioneering at Thirsk, and apart from a thin scattering of appearances he was lost to first-class cricket from the early 1870s onwards. While they flourished in unison, each provided the perfect complement to the other, either sharing the wickets between them or one in the ascendant while his partner supplied a deadly support from his own end. They bowled unchanged throughout the entire match in two of the Yorkshire fixtures of 1868, a feat which was repeated in 1869 (twice), 1870, and 1871.

With sixty wickets at an average of 8.80, the left-hander came third in the bowling table and for the second consecutive season occupied one position higher than his partner. The next three years saw Freeman in advance, though Emmett's record was not so different and in one instance superior as regards the number of victims. It was in 1868 that Tom produced one of his most memorable performances with the ball. When Nottinghamshire came to Savile Town, Dewsbury, on July 27, 28, and 29, Freeman (6 wickets) and Emmett (4) dismissed their opponents for 162, though they conceded 127 runs of the total between them. Freeman was out of luck the second time round, and one man was run out. The other nine all capitulated to Emmett at a personal cost of only 34 runs, but the Yorkshire batting failed for a second time, and the heroic Tom ended up on the losing side.

Nine wickets for 34 runs, you might say, must surely be the best analysis ever achieved by Emmett in the whole of his first-class career. Not so. The feat was surpassed in the following season, when Yorkshire overwhelmed Cambridgeshire, at that time a first-class county, at Hunslet, Leeds, on July 12 and 13, 1869. Cambridgeshire fielded quite a strong team, including their three "crack" batsmen (John Smith, T. Hayward, and R.P. Carpenter), but an illness, which eventually proved mortal, prevented the appearance of George Tarrant, their best bowler, who had enjoyed considerable success against Yorkshire in previous seasons. His presence was sorely missed, when Yorkshire won the toss and elected to bat. Their innings lasted into the second day, with Roger Iddison, the captain, contributing 112 to the total of 352 (second top scorer, at number eleven, was Tom Emmett, with 47 not out). This massive handicap seems to have thoroughly demoralized the visitors, including the three "cracks," when Freeman and his partner went to work. Operating unchanged throughout the remainder of the day, they swept aside the puny resistance of their opponents, dismissing them for 40 and 46, with only one double figure in each innings and the "cracks" nowhere, scoring but 28 between them. On this occasion, it was Freeman who played the supporting role, taking three for 16 and one for 15, while Tom's return of seven wickets for 15 runs was followed by nine for only 23! Thus, in one and the same contest, he registered his best analysis in an innings (9–23) and his best match figures (16–38) for the whole of his career. These statistics, incidentally, are better than any to be found in Freeman's first-class record.

At The Oval, on June 24, 25, and 26, 1869, Emmett made his debut in the series Gentlemen v Players. As a result of various disputes and grievances, some of the leading northern professionals refused to assist the Players for some five years from the mid-1860s onwards, and Tom probably owed his selection as much to this boycott by others as to his exploits with the ball. In spite of the absence of the northern "cracks," this turned out to be a very even match, in which the Players were defeated by only 17 runs. With four for 76 and four for 78, Tom was the most successful bowler on his side, and he had the satisfaction of dismissing W.G. for 43 in the first innings. Omitted from the team for the next seven encounters, he returned for the Oval fixture of 1872, and from that date as far on as the three matches got up in 1881 he was regularly chosen to assist the Players. All told, between 1869 and 1885, he appeared in twenty-five matches. His record was no more than modest, but in this he was not alone, since there were other cricketers who failed to live up to the reputation they had acquired in county matches and other contests. He scored 675 runs at an average of 15.69, with a highest score of 57. As a bowler, he was far from being a success, capturing only thirty-eight wickets at 29.73 each, a mediocre average by the standards of the time. His best figures with the ball were, strange to say, those marked in his debut match of the series.

Since W.G. appeared in all but two of the contests between the Gentlemen and the Players in which Emmett participated, this may have contributed in some measure to Tom's disappointing results in the bowling department. The Yorkshire left-hander was opposed to the Champion in two other matches in 1869, both of them fixtures between the North and the South, and it was, perhaps, significant that George Freeman assisted the North on both occasions. At The Oval, on June 3 and 4, W.G. was a comparative failure – run out for 19 and caught off Freeman's bowling for 14. Handsome George took six for 12 and three for 43, while Tom had three for 26 in the second innings. Possibly the Yorkshire pair were lulled into a sense of false security by their formidable opponent's low scores, but W.G. was about to run into form. Shortly after his meeting with Emmett in Gentlemen v Players, in which he notched 43 and ominously 83, the Champion entered a purple patch with three centuries. For MCC he scored 138 not out, and 48 and 121, against Surrey and Nottinghamshire respectively, while for Gentlemen of the South v Players of the South he went on the rampage with a mammoth contribution of 180.

The return of North v South took place at Bramall Lane, on July 26 and 27, and some days earlier Tom was chatting to the Rev E.S. Carter, a prominent supporter of Yorkshire cricket and an occasional player for the County. During the course of their conversation, Mr Carter said, "What do you think of this W.G. Grace who is making such big scores?" It may be assumed that Tom's mind was occupied with the memory of the Champion's low scores in the first North v South match, a recent failure against Lancashire, and above all the quality of the trundling opposed to him when he helped himself to two of the three centuries. Tom's reply was a classic: "It's all very well against this South coontry bowling. Let 'im coom oop to Sheffield and plaay against me and George, and we'll show 'im summat different." This attitude is by no means unique: similar sentiments were once expressed to me by a Yorkshire

C. E. Green

professional of a later date ("They don't know how to play cricket down there!").

Came the great day with the South winning the toss and electing to bat. There were nine single-figure scores from numbers three to eleven, but the final total was 173, thanks to W.G., whose share was a magisterial 122. He was bustled out for only 7 the second time, but when the North went in again, one of those southern bowlers, of whom Tom had no very high opinion, created a panic among the batsmen, and the South enjoyed a satisfying revenge for their earlier defeat at The Oval. Only one of the North's bowlers succeeded in maintaining his high reputation – George Freeman, who clean bowled the Champion twice and captured thirteen wickets in exchange for only 86 runs. Emmett, by contrast, played a much less distinguished part in the proceedings: he conceded nearly as many runs (79) in far fewer overs and accounted for only one of the despised southerners. Not long after this chastening experience, the downcast left-hander had another conversation with Mr Carter. "Well, Tom," said that reverend gentlemen, "you've had him at Sheffield: what do you think of him now?" "Mester Carter," came the reply in a semi-serious tone of voice, "Ah call 'im a nonsooch: 'e ought to be made to plaay with a littler baat."

Early in the next season, at Lord's, on May 30 and 31, there was another famous battle between the Yorkshire pair and W.G., when MCC went down by one wicket. Bowling unchanged on a hard, dry wicket, Freeman with six victims and Emmett the other four put out the home side for 73. According to one spectator, the former achieved a rare and spectacular dismissal of W.G.'s opening partner by knocking out all three stumps! With the "kicking" wicket more dangerous and fiery than ever, MCC would have fared even worse at their second attempt but for a long and courageous partnership between the Champion and C.E. Green, later famous as the patron of Essex cricket. Battling manfully against the rearing expresses, W.G. made 66 – considered to be one of his very finest innings, given the conditions – and Green 51. They carried the attack into the enemy's camp, but at the fearful cost of considerable physical punishment. The memory of this experience was still fresh in Mr Green's mind and on his body many years later: "We were both cruelly battered about; indeed to this day I carry a mark on my chest where I was struck by a very fast rising ball from Freeman." Tom, who had the honour of being at the crease when Yorkshire pulled off their narrow victory, had five scalps in MCC's second innings, and an additional frond to his laurels was the dismissal of W.G. Grace. In fact, throughout his career, he proved to be one of the Champion's most formidable adversaries, claiming his wicket thirty-five times, including ten clean bowled. Doubtless, on occasions, the "sostenutor" was responsible for administering the quietus.

It was unfortunate that the fearsome partnership of Freeman and Emmett should have been terminated prematurely by the virtual retirement of the former, though some of the leading English batsmen might have heaved a sigh of relief at the possible prospect of less bruising moments at the wicket. Fate, however, had not dealt so scurvily with Tom as might be supposed, since a worthy replacement for Freeman surfaced in the person of Allen Hill, who developed much of his cricket in the unofficial Yorkshire nursery at Lascelles Hall. Though not so terrifying as Freeman, Hill was formidable enough to suit anybody's tastes with his talent for scattering the stumps. On May 18, 19, and 20, 1874, the All England Eleven were playing against Fourteen Undergraduates of Oxford on the Christ Church ground. The AEE had engaged both Emmett and Hill for this occasion, and the latter was revelling in the uncertainties of a fiery pitch. Top scorer for the undergraduates in their first innings was Lord Harris, but Hill subjected him to a particularly torrid time. One delivery, pitched short of a length, rose steeply, whizzed within an inch of the aristocratic nose, and came to rest at first bound in the hands of the long-stop. At the end of the over, which the batsman thankfully survived, Emmett walked past him and, with a twinkle in his eye, observed, "Ah reckon you smelt 'er." This was the first but by no means the last meeting between his lordship and Tom.

As the 1870s unrolled and reached out towards the next decade, there was a seasonal increase in the programme of first-class fixtures. Hitherto, only the best ground bowlers employed at Lord's could count on a summer more or less filled by appearances for MCC and their counties, supplemented by a handful of representative contests, such as North v South and Gentlemen v Players. The augmentation in the number of matches yielded more opportunities for bowlers like Emmett to distinguish themselves, and in 1874 he topped a hundred wickets for the first time, capturing 107 at an average of 11.61, with five or more in an innings ten times and ten or more in a match twice. His current partner Hill kept him company with 101 victims at 11.44 apiece. They bowled unchanged throughout a match twice in this season, a feat they recorded five times in all during their association.

The events of the contest between Gloucestershire and Yorkshire at Cheltenham, on August 17, 18, and 19, 1876, remained engraved on the tablets of Tom's memory for all time. Having won the toss, W.G. elected to bat on an excellent wicket, and the unfortunate visitors were condemned to suffer one of the most miserable days of their existence. The total at close of play stood at 353 for the loss of only four wickets. It must be assumed that the law-makers at Lord's were in complete ignorance of Tom's heartfelt wish that the Champion should be compelled to use "a littler baat," since the Gloucestershire captain had been in all day and had reached 216 not out. That night, the Stygian gloom enshrouding the dog-tired, dejected Yorkshire side was temporarily lightened by an immortal remark from Tom, which inevitably found a place in the folklore of cricket. His wisecrack to his weary team-mates, when rendered more suitable for those with tender ears, ran something along the lines of "Damn it all, it's Grace before meat, Grace afterwards, and Grace all day, and Ah expect we'll 'ave more Grace to-morrow."

This prognostication could hardly have been more accurate: Gloucestershire eventually made 528, with W.G. carrying out his bat for 318. Morale was at zero among all the Yorkshire side, and once, before the fall of the final wicket, even Emmett forsook his normal state of ebullience by collapsing into a sitting position on the pitch with a plaintive cry of "Get out!" Throughout the latter part of his prolonged innings, the Champion was secretly amused to observe how Ephraim Lockwood, the somewhat ineffectual captain, was experiencing considerable difficulty in persuading some of his team-mates to have another go at "the big 'un," the principal offender being Allen Hill, whose share of the 210 overs sent down by eight bowlers amounted to only sixteen. Tom, predictably the most willing and overworked of the lot (51 overs), grew more and more exasperated at Lockwood's bumbling incompetence and the attitude of some of the team. Turning on the long-suffering Ephraim, he snapped, "Why don't you make 'em? Ain't you captain?" Up spoke the insubordinate Allen Hill, taunting Tom with being "as mooch afeerd o' t'big 'un as Ah am!" This stricture was too much for Tom. Grabbing the ball, he addressed first the offender and then the rest of the team, yelling, "Get out o' t'way, and look out i' t'long-field. Ah'm going to finish 'is innings!" This rash promise was not fulfilled, and according to W.G., "he favoured me with three monstrous wides to begin with, and laughing was general all over the ground." The match, by the way, ended in a draw, when a violent thunderstorm and torrential rain prevented Yorkshire from completing even their first innings.

Tom was nettled when he saw W.G.'s accusation in print, which, typically, he insisted was "'wide' of the mark," and his irritation was well founded. True enough, he was guilty of giving away three wides in the whole match, but they were delivered in three separate overs. The Champion evidently became aware of Tom's displeasure, since he modified his remarks in a later description of the incident. Although he eliminated the earlier calumny of the "three monstrous wides," he defended himself by expatiating on Emmett's inaccuracy on that and many another occasion, claiming that umpires were always too lenient and often refrained from signalling a wide against him.

However sensitive Tom may have been on the subject, there is no doubt that W.G. was justified in his animadversions on the left-hander's lack of precision. The wildness of some of his deliveries arose out of his perpetual attempts to bowl his off theory by pitching the ball a fraction wide of a batsman's normal reach, and his inability to maintain a constant line told against him time after time. Records covering the whole span of his first-class career are not always complete in such matters as indicating to which bowler the wides should be credited. Nevertheless, a rough count demonstrates that Tom delivered *well over six hundred wides*, averaging around one per innings in which he was put on to bowl. There were some real horrors standing against his name in the ledger. In one match in 1880, the first four-ball over of his spell produced three wides and fifteen from the bat, including one 6 dispatched into the blue by his old friend, Lord Harris. Playing for the All England Eleven against the United North of England Eleven at Bolton, on July 20 and 22, 1871, he operated unchanged throughout the match with J.C. Shaw, another fast but much more accurate left-hander. His figures were four for 56 and six for 14, but in the first innings he gave away eight wides, with three more in the second. Appalling as that may sound, it was not his highest tally. Towards the end of his career, in the county fixture at Gloucester, on June 30, July 1 and 2, 1887, Tom surpassed himself by delivering *eight* wides in the first innings, followed by *seven* in the second!

During part of the second half of the nineteenth century, it was often the custom on some of the larger cricket grounds, such as The Oval, to give public recognition of meritorious deeds, especially to batsmen scoring a half-century or more. The reward for amateurs was the presentation of a new bat, for professionals usually a sovereign or half-sovereign, known as talent money. In the middle of one season, after the future Lord Hawke had taken over the captaincy of the Yorkshire team, he consulted the score-book, shook his head, and admonished his jovial senior professional, pointing out that he had already delivered over forty wides. Far from hanging his head in shame or shuffling his feet in embarrassment, Tom came back with an instant rejoinder: "Good; then joost gi'e me t'ball, sir, and Ah'll soon bring 'em oop to fifty and earn talent money."

Instead of mildly hibernating and recruiting his energy for the coming season, Tom spent the winter of 1876–77 far from home as a member of the team taken out by James Lillywhite, junior, to tour Australia and New Zealand. One of five Yorkshire professionals in the party, among them his bowling partner Allen Hill, he had an enjoyable time on the whole, in spite of suffering from bouts of seasickness and encountering some primitive conditions of travel and accommodation that would have shattered the nerves of any modern cricketer touring down under. Most of the fixtures were against local teams of "odds," but there were three first-class matches, one against New South Wales, and two against Australia, subsequently recognized as the first Tests between the two countries.

Lillywhite's Twelve was an ill-balanced combination, since it included only one genuine wicket-keeper, who, as it turned out, was not available for the Test Matches, and too few specialist batsmen. On the other hand, it was top heavy with bowlers, and although he captured quite a few wickets in the "odds" matches, Tom was largely an also-ran in the three first-class contests. Treated as no more than a change bowler, he was put on in only three of the six innings, delivering a mere twenty-nine overs in all and obtaining no dismissals. He did not arrive back in England until the first week of June, and at the end of the season he squeezed into the twentieth place in the bowling averages, with sixty-nine wickets at slightly under 15 runs apiece.

After Joseph Rowbotham, a short, tubby man with an ever expanding girth, relinquished the Yorkshire captaincy in 1875 and all but retired from first-class cricket, the Committee arrived at an odd decision in appointing his successor. Since there was still no amateur available to play on a regular basis, the duties would have to be entrusted to yet another professional, and the position was conferred upon Ephraim Lockwood. This choice, on paper, seemed reasonable enough. Ephraim was the best batsman in the side as well as being a more than useful bowler, and he possessed an extensive knowledge of the game. You cannot help wondering, however, how much or how little the Committee really knew about him as a person, and whether they had ever taken the trouble to study his general demeanour. Good-natured in the extreme, convinced apparently that the be-all and end-all of leadership consisted in trying to please everybody, easily imposed upon – witness that match against Gloucestershire in 1876 – and exuding an air of gormlessness, Ephraim was out of his depth. His batting in county matches deteriorated, and after two seasons he was relieved of the captaincy. As his successor, the Committee nominated Tom Emmett, who was in any case the most senior man in the side, with a longer service than Lockwood. You might well ask, then, why he was not given the appointment when Joe Rowbotham retired. Perhaps the deceptive hue of that famous nose had proved to be a stumbling-block to an earlier promotion.

Tom was the official Yorkshire captain from 1878 to 1882, and he continued to act as the skipper in the first half of the next season, until the Hon M.B. Hawke was available to take over the duties. Thereafter, during Hawke's absence, the acting captaincy usually devolved on Louis Hall. Tom was by no means a bad captain. He possessed a rare talent for placing the field, and he found it easy to work with the rest of the team. Leading by example, "he not only proved an able general, but batted with more success and in better form than usual, fielded smartly himself, and kept the rest of the field alive." The only fault to be found in him, at least in his honeymoon season, was a certain aspect of his management of the bowling, which gave increasing cause for concern in subsequent years.

When Tom was newly appointed to the leadership, he was summoned to appear before the Committee to receive some instructions in the nature of his duties. That puritanical streak not uncommon then and later in the old West Riding surfaced on the other side of the table, when certain members held forth at length upon the discipline to be imposed on the boisterous professionals under his charge. They were particularly obsessed by the subject of card-playing and hoped, it appears, that the new captain would put a stop to what they considered to be a nefarious practice. Tom would have none of that. He was always glad, he informed them, to relieve the tedium of a long railway journey to a distant away fixture with a hand of cards. At the same time, he hastened to add that he would do his utmost to prevent his team-mates from staying up late at night to play innumerable games of cards, and with this undertaking the Committee had to be content. He also endeavoured to keep temptation at bay and would politely but firmly refuse a thoughtless but well-intentioned offer from a spectator to stand drinks all round to the team during the course of a match.

The principal reason for Tom's removal from the captaincy, even in the absence of the Hon M.B. Hawke, was that long-standing complaint about the way in which he handled the Yorkshire bowling. Some skippers, taking advantage of their position, will put themselves on for lengthy periods. Tom erred in the other direction, often betraying a marked reluctance to turn over his arm, which was a decided drawback, considering that he was one of the principal trundlers of the Yorkshire side. In a review of the fledgling skipper's first season at the helm, one of the cricket annuals declared that "he has been wonderfully modest, in putting himself on to bowl, and yet has been very successful in that line." This mild rebuke seems passing strange, considering that he came fourteenth in the bowling averages, with 107 wickets at 11.77 each. Only once more during his tenure of the captaincy, however, did he ever approach a tally of a hundred victims. Perhaps he felt that a man of his mature years, whose pace was becoming nearer to medium, and who had extra responsibilities, was entitled to pass some of the burden on to others. Nor should it be forgotten that this period also saw the emergence of Edmund Peate, the slow left-arm genius, as the keystone of the Yorkshire attack.

It is just possible that Tom's mental attitude in the matter of putting himself on to bowl may have been exaggerated by events at the start of his years of leadership. His first outing as the Yorkshire captain occurred in the away fixture with Cambridge University, on May 20, 21, and 22, 1878 – hardly an auspicious occasion, since the result was a victory by ten wickets for the home team. Of the eight bowlers given a turn in the first

Ephraim Lockwood

innings, however, the captain was by far the most successful, taking five wickets for only 31 runs. He put himself on as first change and delivered 34.3 overs – more than anybody else, indeed more than the combined efforts of four of his team-mates. This might have contributed in part to the anecdote, doubtless invented or at least embroidered to illustrate Tom's lack of familiarity with the mechanics of his new role. The story tells that, on one occasion in the infancy of his period of captaincy, he took the ball and bowled without relief until the luncheon interval. When play was resumed, he continued wheeling away at his end, but with a diminishing air of enthusiasm. Finally, at the conclusion of an over, he limped off to his place in the field, chuntering away at the unfairness of the world, and those within earshot heard the burden of his complaint: "Why doesn't t'owd booger taak me off?"

The season of 1878 saw not only Tom's first year of captaincy but also his benefit match, the fixture with Gloucestershire at Bramall Lane, on July 29, 30, and 31. He received a little less than £620, a reasonably good sum for the time, but not perhaps an overly excessive amount, considering his immense popularity. In view of the friendly rivalry existing between the beneficiary and W.G., who obliged with the top scores for his side (62 and 35), a thumping Yorkshire victory by 244 runs could have added to the enjoyment of the occasion. George Ulyett and Ephraim Lockwood played their part in the celebrations by making centuries, but Tom did little out of the ordinary with the bat, scoring 15 and 18. He put himself on in the visitors' first innings, conceding 41 runs in taking two wickets, but one of his victims, appropriately, was the Champion, dismissed by a caught and bowled. His analysis, by the way, showed the addition of two wides!

The Melbourne Cricket Club had been negotiating with I.D. Walker, the Middlesex amateur, to take out a party of English gentlemen to Australia in the winter of 1878–79. As it turned out, circumstances prevented I.D. from completing the arrangements and accompanying the team on its voyage down under, and the management of the whole affair and the captaincy of the side were eventually assumed by Lord Harris. Nigh insurmountable difficulties were experienced in the selection of the party, which never came near representing England's real strength, one of the principal snags being the dearth of first-rate bowlers among the amateurs accepting the invitation to go on the tour, and the final solution was the decision to add two professionals to the team. The pair selected for the primary purpose of doing most of the bowling were Tom Emmett and George Ulyett. As far as the former was concerned, this was a very satisfactory arrangement, giving him plenty of opportunities with the ball, far more in fact than on any other tour in which he participated. The choice of Ulyett to share much of the trundling with his fellow Tyke, however, was not entirely a happy one as regards the needs of the team as a whole.

Though an effective bowler in certain conditions, Ulyett rightly considered that his major talent lay in batting. This, again, was something that worked to Emmett's advantage.

The voyage, at least at the beginning, was a period of prolonged misery for Tom. Confined to his bunk during the first few days by constant attacks of seasickness, he could only curse the fate which made his particular stomach so susceptible to the motion of the sea and the ship. After an especially rough crossing of the Bay of Biscay, the fury of the waves was stilled, and the surface of the water became somewhat calmer. Thinking that a little fresh air might prove beneficial for the condition of his churning internal organs, Tom crept out of his cabin and nervously mounted the companion-ladder. The first sight to meet his gaze on deck was scarcely conducive to an improvement in either his morale or his physical discomfort. There stood Lord Harris, apparently impervious to the recent turbulence of wind and weather, a cigarette jutting out beneath his splendidly curled moustache. At other times and in other places, Tom welcomed the soothing influence of tobacco, but such a sight at that very moment would have been almost too much for the sufferer without the aid of his ingrained sense of humour. Lord Harris was the first to speak, saying, "Glad to see you out, Tom; but you don't look very well." "No, my lord, Ah don't feel very bright," came the reply. Then, after a brief pause and a shaky glance overboard, he heaved a sigh, adding, "Ah don't think they've 'ad t'eavy roller on, my lord." Tom has always been credited with having originated this famous and lovingly treasured witticism, but he was not in fact the first cricketer to come up with the idea of a connection between the roughness of the sea and the noblest game. A similar remark was attributed to John Wisden en route for a tour of North America in 1859.

The programme of the tour consisted of thirteen matches, of which five were against first-class opposition. Considering the weakness of Lord Harris's party, which was at times cruelly exposed, it was surprising that the Englishmen were not repeatedly overwhelmed. Their performance in the five important contests was rather disheartening – two victories but three defeats. No blame could be attached to the captain's favourite Yorkshireman ("Tom Emmett carried us in the bowling department"), who far outstripped all his fellow trundlers, including Ulyett. In the five first-class matches, he was put on in nine of the ten innings, taking forty-four wickets for an average of only 11.63. Six times he captured five or more in an innings, and in two of the matches his overall tally exceeded ten. His best performance occurred in the notorious encounter – of which more later – with New South Wales at Sydney, on February 7, 8, and 10, 1879, when his figures were eight for 47 and five for 21. Against Victoria at Melbourne, on March 7,

8, and 10, his match figures were eleven for 109 (6–41 and 5–68). In the solitary Test Match, played at Melbourne, on January 2, 3, and 4, England were heavily defeated by ten wickets, which was rather a let-down for Tom. His analysis in Australia's first innings (7–68) was his best in international contests.

In the course of taking those seven wickets, he was credited with no less than an equal number of wides! His tally for the five first-class matches amounted to twenty. At one stage in the tour, an Australian journal of humorous content (the *Melbourne Punch*) invented a dialogue, which poked fun at two of Tom's essential attributes:

"Which is Lord Harris?"

"Him with the moustaches."

"And which is Lord Emmett?"

"Him with the pale face a-bowling the wides."

The tour, however, was not without its more serious moments, and there was an extremely unpleasant incident in that fixture at Sydney, in which Tom registered his best match figures. Batting first, the English Eleven ran up a good total of 267, and New South Wales, with a deficit of 90, were obliged to follow their innings. With the total at 18, W.L. Murdoch was adjudged to have been run out and, without any sign of dissent, set off for the pavilion. The official giving this decision was G. Coulthard, a Melbourne professional, whom Lord Harris had engaged to accompany the team as umpire. Coulthard had already stood in the Test Match at Melbourne and the first contest against New South Wales at the end of January, both of them ending as victories for the home sides. In this return fixture, however, New South Wales had a desperate struggle for survival on their hands, and since a great deal of rivalry existed between Melbourne and Sydney, the dismissal of the favourite Murdoch on the word of a Melbourne man caused wholesale resentment throughout the ground. D.W. Gregory, the captain of New South Wales, told Murdoch he was not out and ordered him to return to the wickets. This was followed immediately by an invasion of the pitch by a thousand or more spectators, who surrounded the English team, with Lord Harris one of the principal targets of their animosity. One of the larrikins, intent on physical violence, struck out wildly at his lordship with a whip or stick. Arming themselves each with a stump, the two English professionals moved forward to protect their skipper, but while the latter was persuading them not to inflame the ugly situation by offering overt violence in return, Nemesis in the shape of A.N. "Monkey" Hornby overtook the assailant. Strong, stocky, with a physique toughened by countless tussles on the rugby field, the Lancashire amateur seized the culprit by the collar, forced his way through the milling crowd, and arrived almost shirtless at the pavilion to hand over his prisoner to the authorities. So monstrous was the disorder that play had to be abandoned for the day, much to the detriment of the home side's chances. On the morrow, rain followed by hot sunshine rendered the pitch unplayable, and the batsmen were skittled out by Emmett and Ulyett for 49, leaving Lord Harris's team victorious by an innings and 41 runs. It is to be hoped that those betting men who, it was alleged, had been responsible for fermenting the trouble, went home with empty pockets.

One of the members of the touring team, Mr F.A. Mackinnon of Kent, had a favourite deck-chair, and since he was travelling back to England by a different route, he entrusted it to the guardianship of Tom Emmett. The latter, I am inclined to think, did not take on this new responsibility as seriously as he ought to have done. When Kent went north to play against Yorkshire at Bramall Lane, on June 16, 17, and 18, 1879, the chair had still not been returned to its owner, and Mackinnon determined to tackle his man on the subject at the earliest opportunity. Tom succeeded in talking his way out of a tight corner with marvellous aplomb. He had, he assured Mackinnon, looked after that chair with loving care, letting nobody else use it when he was about, and storing it "oop top o' t'deck-'ouse every night." Somehow, unfortunately, either from the rolling of the vessel or the clandestine use of it by "soom 'eavy chap," it became so rickety and dilapidated that the ship's quartermaster declared it was a perfect disgrace and refused to tolerate its unwelcome presence on deck any longer. "So Ah 'ad to chook it overboard," explained Tom, "boot Ah poot a label on it wi' your address, and there was a good breeze aft, and Ah thought you might 'ave got it be now!"

The Yorkshire captain had an indifferent season with the bat in 1879, but he captured sixty-three wickets at 9.87 each (seventh position in the table). His batting and bowling averages were, in fact, almost identical. At the end of the season, surprisingly for anybody so susceptible to the buffeting of the waves, he accepted an invitation to join the team for Richard Daft's brief tour of Canada and the USA. The party, made up of professionals from Nottinghamshire and Yorkshire, played twelve matches, all against "odds," winning nine and losing none. Most of the bowling was done by Alfred Shaw and Fred Morley, the Nottinghamshire pair, but Tom managed to obtain forty-two wickets at 3.21 apiece. Exactly half of this tally was secured in the contest against a Picked Twenty-two of Canada at Toronto, on September 15 and 16, when he registered match figures of twenty-one wickets for 43 runs. When not actually engaged on the cricket field, some members of the party passed the time taking the mickey out of their team-mates or playing practical jokes on each other. Tom was a victim during an outing to Niagara Falls. He had seen a snake in the vicinity, which made a great impression upon him, and he went on talking about it for several minutes. The weather being rather hot, he sought some relief by removing his boots and socks and dabbling his aching feet in the cooling water. While he was engaged in this innocent pastime, one of the team stealthily stuffed one of his socks with some slimy worms. When Tom resumed his footwear, he gave a piercing shriek, convinced that his toes had come in contact with another snake.

From time to time, Tom was called upon to stand as umpire in various matches. It was not a role he relished much at first, since he dreaded making a fool of himself by giving wrong decisions, but even this activity was the source for a little humour. While on the tour of North America with Richard Daft's team, he was intrigued by the local custom of giving guard to a batsman. Instead of using the terms "off" and "leg," the umpires used to say, "A little more east," or "A little more west." Tom was determined to give this a try in one of the matches played at Toronto, and when one of the Canadian batsmen asked for his guard, he assumed that middle was required and called out, "A little east." This instantly revealed a basic weakness in the standard procedure: Tom had lost his bearings and did not know which was east and which west. Seeing daylight between the bat and the stumps and thinking that the batsman had not heard him properly, he repeated his directions, only to see the batsman retreating further in the direction of square-leg. A hasty switch from "east" to "west" set matters aright, otherwise, "Ah should 'ave 'ad t'man on t'ɓoundary."

Although he occasionally used the points of the compass in fixing the exact position of a fieldsman, umpiring was a different matter, and it is fair to assume that Tom decided to revert to the normal English idiom in the first important match in which he officiated, a contest between Yorkshire and the Australians at Bradford, on June 25, 26, and 27, 1888. The visitors won the toss and took first innings. As the opening pair were on the way to the wickets, he made a mock solemn announcement to the home side, saying, "Now, gentlemen, there's wun thing Ah want you to bear i' mind, and that is that no wun moost appeal unless t'wickets are clean bowled."

There is another story about Tom's antics as an umpire, this time in a minor match in the neighbourhood of Rugby. The tale is told by W.E.W. Collins, an author and mainly a country-house cricketer, though he did make a few appearances in the first-class game. Tom liked hearing jokes as well as telling them but, observed Collins, "after a cricket luncheon his perception was sometimes a little hazy." The proceedings, it must be admitted, bore a distinct resemblance to that ancient music-hall routine, in which the straight man, endeavouring to deliver a little recitation to the audience, is constantly interrupted by the comic asking him a conundrum of excruciatingly feeble humour ("I say, I say, I say . . ."). Collins approached his quarry and posed the question: "Why aren't they going to have the umpire's coats at Lord's any longer, Tom?" The latter replied with something like the equivalent of "I don't know. Why, etc?" to which came the rejoinder, "Because they are long enough already." It is the type of witticism that survives today only in Christmas crackers, and Collins confessed that "There was not much in it after all." It was, however, far too subtle for Tom after his cricket luncheon. Instead of uttering the time-honoured, classic retort of "I don't wish to know that!" he gave a sickly smile, affected to laugh, and took up his position in the field. Throughout the next hour or so he was unusually silent, wearing a perplexed look and surreptitiously examining the cut of his coat. Suddenly his brain began to clear, the penny dropped, and he collapsed in helpless laughter. This, unfortunately, coincided with a request for a two-leg guard from a somewhat bucolic batsman, who not unnaturally concluded that Tom was laughing at *him*. Advancing belligerently down the pitch, he threatened to belabour the supposed offender with his bat. Luckily Tom managed to regain his feet in time, and after some fast talking and a quick run-through of the conundrum he succeeded in smoothing the matter over for all concerned.

The season of 1880 saw an improvement in Emmett's record as a batsman but a decline in his performance with the ball – only forty-three wickets at an average of 17.46, and only one instance of five wickets in an innings. A team of Australians under the captaincy of W.L. Murdoch was on tour in the old country, and just before the season closed the first Test Match played in England came off at The Oval, on September 6, 7, and 8. Putting aside the unpleasant memories of the infamous riot match at Sydney, Lord Harris consented to lead the England team, but it has been said that two or three members of his touring party, including Emmett, refused invitations to play in the Test. This allegation, as far as the left-hander is concerned, is open to question. He was not worth a place in the side on current performance, and he was certainly not averse to meeting the Australians elsewhere, appearing in four matches against them. An excellent tourist down under, Tom was never chosen to assist England in a home Test Match.

A considerable improvement in all-round performance attended the Yorkshire captain's efforts in 1881. With an aggregate of 858 runs, the best of his whole career, he obtained an average of very slightly under twenty (19.95) and reached the half-century or more on six occasions. Against Middlesex at Lord's, on May 26 and 27, he made 89 not out ("a sample of clean, hard and brilliant hitting"), by far the best exploit with the bat in the whole match, and it included "a tremendous drive to the on for 6." It was not Middlesex, however, but another southern county that suffered even more from Emmett's prowess. At The Oval, on August 11, 12, and 13, Surrey made 224, to which Yorkshire replied with 256, the highest figure being 61, an "admirable innings" by the skipper, going in at first wicket down. At 3.45 p.m. on the final day, the second having been rained off, Surrey began their second innings. After the loss of an early wicket, they prospered for a time. Since Peate and one of the changes were unable to make a breakthrough, Tom was persuaded by his team-mates to try his luck. The second wicket fell at 54, and the remainder of the play provided one of the biggest sensations of the season. In little more than an hour after the start of the innings, Surrey were put out for 66. Almost unplayable on the rapidly drying pitch, Tom returned figures of 11–9–22–8, and at one period, in the space of three overs, he dismissed five batsmen without conceding a single run! The visitors knocked off the deficit for the loss of only one wicket. On looking back over his eventful career, Tom felt that this was the bowling performance of which he was most proud.

Among the crowd at The Oval on that red-letter day was a small contingent of Yorkshire supporters, who resolved to honour their hero by carrying him off in triumph to the pavilion. Tom's discomfort was as huge as his embarrassment, and when they hoisted him up, he cried out in dismay, "Nay, for goodness saak chaps, doan't shoulder me; Ah've me pockets full o' brass, and if you lift me oop it'll all roll out!" Since "brass" is usually a matter of great moment to many Yorkshiremen, they relented and put him down. As he made his way to the pavilion, he congratulated himself on the efficacy of his quick-witted excuse. There was, in fact, hardly a single penny piece in his pockets.

Tom missed his Christmas dinner at home in 1881. A glutton for punishment, and notwithstanding the misery of earlier years, he agreed to join the touring party visiting Australia and New Zealand in 1881–82. Thirty matches constituted the fixture list, most of them against "odds," but there were seven first-class contests, including four Tests. From Tom's point of view, it was a repetition of the state of affairs obtaining on the tour of 1876–77: the party contained several first-rate bowlers, whose opportunities with the ball were far more extensive than his. Now aged forty, he made no more tours abroad, possibly for two main reasons – the emergence of younger trundlers and the perpetual bouts of *mal de mer*. He did not go so far as St Govan who, according to tradition, almost expired from seasickness and blamed his condition upon his ship-mates, who had been gormandizing when they should have been fasting! Nevertheless, Tom felt bitter about his fate. Green with envy as well as green from an overwhelming queasiness, he found it galling to see Ted Peate strolling unconcernedly on the deck and polishing off all his meals ("breakfast, tiffin, dinner, ditto-repeato," according to the sufferer), while he was hanging helplessly over the side feeding the fishes. Later, with a wry smile, he gravely expressed his opinion in a somewhat unsavoury jest that, in view of his "liberal contributions" to the waves, he ought to have had his fish for the table supplied free.

In the second Test at Sydney, on February 17, 18, 20, and 21, 1882, Tom was the butt of a witticism from a member of the crowd, which he was never allowed to forget during the rest of his final trip down under. Since the weather was very hot, the English team were all wearing thin silk shirts. Tom, as ever, had been running energetically to and fro in the field, and all that exertion caused his shirt tail to work up out of the back of his trousers and float out behind him like a miniature balloon. This incongruous sight gave rise to a good deal of laughter among the players as well as the crowd. Tom was not amused. He guessed that they were all laughing at him but not why. Finally, just at the moment when he discovered the cause of the general mirth and was angrily stuffing his shirt back into his trousers, a voice from the crowd shouted, "Tom, your swag's out!" Throughout the remainder of the tour, his team-mates never stopped asking him, "Tom, have you got your swag out?"

In spite of his comparative under-employment on his final tour and his veteran status, there was no sign of any abatement in Tom's boyish zest for the game, and in 1882, the last full season of his tenure of the Yorkshire captaincy, he gave ample evidence of his value to the County as an all-rounder. A slight diminution in the level of his batting (average 17.14, with only one half-century) was more than outweighed by his performance in the other departments. "The Life and Soul of the Yorkshire Eleven" and a shining example to his younger brethren in the field, he held twenty-four catches – his highest seasonal figure – and there was a signal revival in the quality of his bowling. His answer to any criticism that he did not put himself on often enough was an aggregate of ninety-five wickets at an average of 10.98, securing for him the seventh position in the national table. Eight times he recorded five or more victims in one innings, and ten or more in a match thrice. His best performance was reserved for the end of the season in Yorkshire's contest against MCC at Scarborough, on August 31, September 1 and 2. The captaincy of the home side was, significantly, transferred to the Hon M.B. Hawke, who opened his attack with Emmett (on throughout most of the match) and Peate. One of Tom's loose ones received dire punishment from Mr C.I. Thornton, who unleashed an enormous on drive, smiting the ball far away through one of the upper windows of a house situated outside the ground. Such grievous maltreatment would have cowed the soul of many a trundler, but Tom was made of sterner stuff. He went back to work undismayed, and not long afterwards he had the sweet satisfaction of clean bowling the aggressor. Thornton, however, was not his only victim. Sweeping through the remainder of his opponents, who could only total 115, he bagged eight wickets in all at a cost of 52 runs. Following on, MCC fared worse at their second attempt. Denied the opportunity of even one mighty swing with his bat, Thornton was trapped leg before for a blob by Tom, who shared the wickets equally with Peate, and Yorkshire romped home to a prodigious victory by an innings and 70 runs. All in all, an excellent match for the veteran – top scorer with "an admirable innings of 51 (including eight 4's)," and figures of thirteen wickets for 83 runs.

Apart from that disgraceful riot match at Sydney, Tom was never backward at taking on a boisterous crowd. "He was," in the words of one journalist, "a born actor," and he had no hesitation in calling a halt to the proceedings in the middle, raising his voice to full pitch, and delivering a dramatic harangue, interlarded with appropriate witticisms, much to the delight and amusement of both the spectators and the fielders. Sometimes his orations struck a more serious note ("'Oo knows better, you or me?" "Tha does, Tom."), as on another occasion during the Scarborough Festival in the early 1880s. Joe Hunter, the regular Yorkshire stumper and a local man to boot, had been replaced by an amateur called G.A.B. Leatham. Some of the spectators expressed their resentment by barracking Leatham, until Tom walked over to the most vociferous section of the crowd and quelled the boos and catcalls with an appeal to their better instincts. "Nah, laads," he said, "Scarborough 'as allus 'ad a reputation for being respectable. Don't loss your character." This exhortation had its desired effect, and from that time onwards Leatham was allowed to keep the wickets in peace.

It may well have been at the Scarborough Festival also that Tom used to renew his acquaintance with one of his female admirers. Lady Londesborough, whose husband was one of the leading patrons of Yorkshire cricket and the Festival, derived much amusement from Tom's sprightly conversation, always delivered in a broad dialect, and she would often send a message asking him to come and talk to her in her carriage. The pleasure was mutual, and he was always highly gratified to receive the invitation. Other people, however, had some misgivings about these meetings, feeling that there was a distinct possibility that he might offend against good taste by employing a vocabulary too colourful for the delicate ears of an aristocratic lady. On being taxed with this rather bluntly on one occasion, Tom, as usual, had a ready answer:

"Well, you see, it's this way. Ah tries to suit mesen to me coompany, boot if Ah joost drops out a flowery thing or two, 'er leddyship only

smiles the more affable, which sets me at me ease like. And thaat's
'ow we gets on so well together, she and me."

Although Tom actually improved on his place by one notch in the
national bowling table for the season of 1883, his tally of wickets fell
to fifty-five, while his average rose to 14.23. He also bowled in fewer
innings, one of the reasons being that the County had discovered a new,
very fast right-hander in G.P. Harrison. The latter, some twenty years
younger than Emmett, took a hundred wickets in his debut season and
seemed set for a regular place in the side for several years to come. As
things turned out, the newcomer failed to live up to expectations to such
a marked degree the next year that he was dropped from the team. At
the beginning of the season of 1884, Emmett was engaged for nothing
but the Colts' match at first and looked to be on the way out. Far from
it. At an age when, in cricketing terms, he might have been considered
as having one foot in the grave, he experienced an extraordinary period
of success. As though miraculously revived by the turn of events, he
carried the main burden of the Yorkshire bowling in partnership with
Ted Peate, another individual who seemed to have forfeited some of the
Committee's confidence. Both of them passed the century of wickets
in all matches. This was the third time in his career for Tom and, a
curiosity, his tally was 107 for the third time. The cost in 1884 was
11.68 apiece which, in the list of bowling averages, made him the fourth
best trundler in England. There were, it is true, some forty wides to
testify that he was at times as erratic as ever, or even more so, but
his record of five wickets in an innings (10) and ten in a match (3) was
the best of his whole career. One of his most outstanding performances
occurred when he turned out for a team got up by C.I. Thornton, his
old adversary, in a match against Cambridge University, on May 22,
23, and 24. The ground was in excellent condition for batting, yet
the veteran gave the undergraduates a hard time in their first innings,
while three of his Yorkshire team-mates were doing little with the ball.
Only 39 runs were scored off him, and his victims amounted to eight.
Although he gave away four wides in the second innings, he was the
most successful bowler once more (5–54), achieving his finest match
figures of the season. For Yorkshire against Sussex at Bramall Lane, less
than a month later, he marked his best performance in a single innings.
Louis Hall was acting as the deputy captain by now, and he opened
the attack with Peate and Emmett. The deeds of the other Yorkshire
bowlers were insignificant beside Tom's, for he captured eight wickets
for only 32 runs. At one time, his trundling proved so "puzzling" to
the Sussex batsmen that, in one spell of eleven overs and three balls,
including nine maidens, he took six wickets at only one run apiece!

When the Yorkshire Committee appeared reluctant to offer him much in the way of regular employment at the beginning of the 1884 season, it was hardly surprising that their elderly reject should have looked around for some alternative means of maintaining his livelihood. From 1884 to 1886, Emmett seems to have held a tenuous and not clearly defined engagement as a member of the ground staff at Lord's. The lists of MCC ground bowlers published in *Wisden* for those years are confusing and contradictory on this point. In the 1884 edition, the roll of employees for that year does not include Emmett's name. The next issue, however, gives him as one of the ground staff for 1884 and 1885, whereas the succeeding edition excludes him for 1885 and 1886! The indications are that he may have been appointed after the original list for 1884 had been established, at a time when he may have thought his days with Yorkshire were numbered – though eventually, as we have seen, he was fully employed by his County throughout that season. Nevertheless, he did assist MCC twice in first-class contests. At Canterbury, on August 6, 7, and 8, 1885, he played against Kent, who emerged as easy winners by an innings and 48 runs. This match did little to enhance his reputation. He scored 14 and 2 and got through an enormous amount of work with the ball for a man in his forty-fourth year, but with little to show for all his strenuous efforts: in 91 overs, of which 54 were maidens, he took only two wickets and conceded 83 runs, on top of which were five wides! He had much better luck the next season at Cambridge, on May 31, June 1 and 2, though he was on the losing side again. Nobody, however, could have pointed an accusing finger at Tom, who made 13 and 34 (with five 4s, the second top score), opened the bowling, took seven wickets for 62 in the first innings and finished with match figures of ten for 110 – and six wides.

It would perhaps, be unreasonable to expect that an old stager of forty-four going on forty-five should maintain the standard he had achieved in 1884, and in the next season Emmett was not so successful as of yore. His aggregate of wickets fell to eighty, while his average shot up to 18.22. That fatal propensity for delivering wides was, alas, only too self-evident, and his total was well in excess of sixty. He had his good days, capturing five or more wickets in an innings five times, his best analysis (7–50) occurring in the Roses match at Old Trafford, on June 18, 19, and 20, 1885. For sheer stamina as well as all-round play you would have to give the palm to his doings in the drawn contest between Yorkshire and Nottinghamshire at Bramall Lane, on June 29, 30, and July 1. The home side had only one innings, and Tom, batting at number eight, shared a stand with F. Lee which increased the total from 127 to 237. After a shaky beginning, in which he survived two chances, the senior partner stroked his way confidently to 57 before being trapped out of his ground by the stumper, his leg-hitting and off-driving being "especially brilliant." This, however, was not his only contribution to the action. The most prominent of the Yorkshire bowlers, both in employment and results, he returned match figures of 91–56–92–9. It must be added, however, that his line and length went astray at times, with an overall tally of eight wides.

On the basis of probability and bearing in mind that Tom was now midway between forty and fifty, you would have felt justified in the belief that he would have reached the stage of easing himself into a well earned and honourable retirement, when the season of 1886 was getting under way. With Ted Peate's powers on the wane, Bobby Peel's not yet fully developed, and the veteran entering his twenty-first year of service with the County, Yorkshire's bowling resources looked depressingly thin on the ground. As though rejuvenated by the fires of eternal youth, the evergreen senior professional accepted the challenge. When younger team-mates, for one reason or another, failed to live up to their potential, the elder statesman of the side was not found wanting. His dedication to the task before him and his boyish enthusiasm to overcome all obstacles never deserted him, and his unremitting labours were richly rewarded. The season of 1886, in terms of deadliness to the opposition, was his most successful with the ball. Fifth in the bowling averages, with over a hundred victims for the fourth time, he captured 124 wickets, the highest aggregate of his career, at 12.83 each. Once again he bagged five or more in an innings ten times, and twice he secured ten in a match. One of these feats, mentioned previously, was for MCC v Cambridge University, but Middlesex at Bradford, on August 16, 17, and 18, provided his finest return of the season (10–91). The old enemy at Old Trafford, on July 8, 9, and 10, proved particularly vulnerable to him in their first innings, when he achieved his best performance by conceding only 33 runs in taking seven wickets. Two more victims fell to him in the second innings, but his overall success in this encounter was slightly marred by the black mark of six wides. In this respect, he committed an even greater offence at Hove, on August 23, 24, and 25, by presenting Sussex with seven extras in one innings and one more in the other. Though not so profligate in yielding free runs to the opposition as he had been in the previous season, he still passed the half-century in 1886.

"Long may he flourish!" was the sentiment expressed in one cricket annual on the veteran's exploits in 1886, while another was even more specific, saying, "It is to be hoped he may have several more seasons of first-class cricket before him." These expressions of good-will, unfortunately, were not destined to be realized. The years finally began to take their toll even of the seemingly indestructible Tom, and 1887 was the final season in which he held down a regular place in the Yorkshire side. No longer capable of bowling for such lengthy spells with telling effect, even though he had reduced his pace to medium years ago, he managed to dispose of five opponents in an innings only twice, and his seventy-three wickets were obtained at an average of 19.21. This decline in his striking powers was accompanied by a signal augmentation in his tally of wides, rising to the giddy heights of over seventy. Maybe the Yorkshire Committee felt that the team could no longer afford the luxury of giving away so many extras to the opposition and decided to replace him with a younger man. He participated in only three first-class matches in 1888, not one of them against another county. His eleven wickets (best 5–15) cost 11.36 runs each and, ironically, earned him the twelfth position in the national bowling averages. At Scarborough, on September 3, 4, and 5, he made his final bow, assisting Yorkshire against MCC. He took one wicket for 14 runs in each innings, securing his ultimate victim with a catch held by his captain. It might be supposed that, in keeping with the solemnity of the occasion, Tom was on his best behaviour: in twenty-five overs he delivered not a single wide!

There was a distinct lack of warmth and finesse in the means adopted to inform the veteran that he would no longer feature in Yorkshire's plans for the future. It was, at best, an example of the traditional northern bluntness of speech combined with a misguided attempt at heavy humour. At worst, it was one of those instances when a Yorkshire player's notice to quit is served upon him in a manner marked by a cruel absence of any sensitivity. The memory of the treatment he received still rankled with Tom several years after the event. He asked "some one in authority," whom he declined to identify (Hawke? the County Secretary?), if he would be wanted again and received the wounding reply, "No, we don't want to see you any more." Tom was prepared to concede that this might have been meant to be a joke, "but it was not well put; indeed, after my long service to the county it seemed to be in bad taste, and I felt it."

Like many another professional of his day, Emmett would sometimes earn a useful supplement to his wages by obtaining a few weeks of temporary employment as a coach at a public school. He was evidently accompanied by his wife on one occasion when he went to fulfil an engagement at Stonyhurst College. His keenness, sense of humour, and ability as an instructor endeared him to his pupils, who in those days practised the charming custom of expressing their appreciation by presenting their coach with a plate of strawberry tarts. The quantity of tarts was in direct ratio to the popularity of the recipient, and Tom was handed a dish piled high pyramid-fashion with these delicacies. As he moved away, precariously balancing his prize, one of his pupils suggested he might need some help in transporting the tarts to their destination. Tom, however, was in no need of assistance, replying, "Ah'll joost taak 'em 'ome to t'missus." It is to be hoped that Mrs Emmett enjoyed a fair share of the goodies.

After his retirement from the Yorkshire scene, Tom served for several years as the permanent cricket coach at Rugby. In securing this plum appointment, he was fortunate in obtaining the support of Lord Harris, one of his oldest cricketing friends as well as his captain on that tour of Australia in 1878–79. His lordship, in recalling the incident, paid a glowing tribute to the qualities of his favourite Yorkshireman:

> In his latter days I was happy to be instrumental in getting for Tom the situation of professional bowler at Rugby, and of being able to recommend him, not only for his eminent capacity as a cricketer, but also because I'd never heard him say, or seen him do, anything that would bring the least harm to boys.

These words were written some thirty years after the event, but you almost have the feeling that Lord Harris might have fished out the old, yellowing copy of his original testimonial and copied part of it practically verbatim into his memoirs.

One of Tom's pupils at Rugby was Plum Warner, who recollected that his good-humoured coach preferred the boys to hit the ball hard and play easily rather than imposing a cramping confinement on their style – which, when you think about it, bore some resemblance to the Yorkshireman's own batting technique. He did, however, insist on certain basic principles, such as avoiding a two-eyed stance, and he instilled into his charges the correct method of playing forward and back. The forward defensive stroke was taught to the graphic command of "Smell 'er, sir, smell 'er!" When it was a question of jumping out to drive the ball, he had no patience with a batsman who could not make up his mind and dithered at the crease. Tom tended to become a little irritable at such times and, remembering the old adage about the sheep and the lamb, always shouted, "If you coom to 'er, coom. You may as well be stoomped be two feet as be wun inch!"

After relinquishing his position at Rugby, Emmett obtained an appointment as a ground bowler with the county club at Leicester. A serene old age would have been an appropriate reward for an old player, whose talents, sunny disposition, and boundless enthusiasm for the game had made him one of the most popular cricketers of his day, but it was not to be. A fate, as malevolent as it was unjust, overtook him, and his health began to fail. *Wisden*, in its obituary notice, stated that "His closing days were, unhappily, rather clouded, but on that point there is no need to dwell," without giving the reader any further enlightenment – an irritating habit not confined to this particular passage. The end, when it came, was sudden and unexpected. Although he had been ailing for some time, he had felt well enough to go along to the ground to watch the final day of the match between Leicestershire and Worcestershire. The former, his adopted county, came from behind after trailing badly on the

first innings and pulled off a remarkable victory. Perhaps the excitement
was too much for Tom. At his home the next morning, on the last day of
June 1904, he was smitten down by an apoplectic seizure from which there
was no recovery.

Few would deny the claim that Emmett was one of the leading all-
rounders of his time, though it must be admitted that there were better in
some respects. Notwithstanding his ability to play many a useful innings,
his overall performance with the bat fell below that of some of his more
versatile contemporaries among the all-round men of the Victorian age. He
scored 9,053 runs, with one century and twenty-four half-centuries, but
his average amounted to no more than 14.84, which was not particularly
high, even by the standards of his day. With the ball, however, it was an
entirely different story. His first-class career spanned twenty-three seasons
– the first and last containing only four matches – and three tours, during
which he captured 1,571 wickets at an average of 13.56, a record with
which nobody could find fault. R.G. Barlow, William Barnes, and Willie
Bates all achieved a higher aggregate of runs and a much better batting
average, but none of these three came anywhere near Tom in the column of
wickets taken, nor at a lower cost. His feat of obtaining a hundred or more
dismissals in four seasons was superior, and he was also far in advance of
them in the number of times he took five wickets in an innings (121) and
ten in a match (29). There was, of course, the matter of the "monstrous
wides" sent down to W.G. and so many other batsmen, but this should
not be allowed to detract from his ability to bowl with that sustained and
relentless hostility which brought him eight or more wickets in one innings
on twelve occasions, including nine victims twice. If he had hardly ever
scored a run, he would still have been worth his place in any team for his
bowling, his performance in the field, and his good-fellowship. Of him it
was once said, "He hits hard, bowls hard, runs hard, and works hard."
What more could one want in a cricketer?

NOTE.– Some of Tom Emmett's personal characteristics and the details
of his encounter with W.G. Grace at Cheltenham in 1876 were treated in
my article, "Tom's Three Atrocities," *The Journal of the Cricket Society*,
XI, 3 (Autumn 1983), 14–17.

EDWARD BARRATT
The Forgotten Man

A ROBUST, left-arm medium-pacer, whose massive moustache would probably have made his contemporary, Field Marshal Lord Kitchener, gnash his teeth with envy, Frederick Martin, a stalwart of Kent and the MCC ground staff, once found himself thrust into the limelight. The selectors of the England team to meet Australia in the second Test at The Oval, on August 11, 12, and 13, 1890, were presented with an awkward problem demanding the most urgent solution. On the same dates, Yorkshire had a fixture with Middlesex at Bradford, and when the amateur A.E. Stoddart chose to assist his county rather than his country at The Oval, Lord Hawke retaliated by refusing to release the professionals Bobby Peel and George Ulyett for duty with England. In the normal course of events, the selection committee would have been able to call upon the services of an excellent replacement for Peel in the person of his principal rival, Lancashire's Johnny Briggs, but the latter was temporarily incapacitated by an injury. So, in the absence of those two left-handed wizards of the north, Fred Martin was hastily appointed to fill the vacancy.

The selectors, as things turned out, had more than ample grounds for congratulating themselves on their late choice. Delivering at a pace slightly quicker than that of his two celebrated contemporaries, and exploiting to the utmost degree the advantages created by a diabolical pitch saturated by rain, Fred Martin far outshone the performance of his principal bowling partner, George Lohmann, and emerged as the chief architect of England's victory by two wickets. His figures were more than remarkable by any standard. In Australia's first innings, he disposed of six batsmen for only 50 runs, and in the second his analysis was six wickets for 52, eight of his victims being clean bowled.

The final Test in the summer of 1890, scheduled to be played at Old Trafford, on August 25, 26, and 27, was abandoned without a ball being bowled, but in any case Martin had been replaced by Johnny Briggs in the nominated list of the England team, which had been chosen by the local committee, as was the normal practice in those days. Although he was the first, and for many years the only bowler

Frederick Martin

to take twelve or more wickets on his Test debut – a record which was not surpassed until Australia defeated England at Lord's in 1972 ("Massie's Match") – Martin played only once more for England, or rather England's Second Eleven, as it were. While Peel and Briggs were representing their country in Australia in the winter of 1891–92, the hero of The Oval took part in the tour of South Africa and appeared in the solitary Test at Cape Town, on March 19, 21, and 22, 1892, taking two wickets for 39 runs in the second innings. As far as international contests were concerned, there could be no doubt about the pecking order: Fred trailed behind Peel and Briggs, who were also both superior all-rounders.

Fred Martin was merely one example of a cricketer doomed by an accident of birth to the unequal task of having to compete with rivals regarded, with justice in some instances, as possessing greater skills. We have only to call to mind the melancholy fate of two such splendid batsmen as Andrew Sandham of Surrey and Percy Holmes of Yorkshire, who scored 107 and 67 first-class centuries respectively, but who were nevertheless condemned to the necessity of an almost perpetual existence in the shadow of Jack Hobbs and Herbert Sutcliffe. Consider also, in more recent times, the case of two fine, left-handed, opening batsmen, whose claims were or have been largely ignored by the selectors, who extended their preference to other candidates. The doughty Alan Butcher, of Surrey and, at the time of writing, a notable stalwart with Glamorgan, has so far been capped only once. With the captain, Mike Brearley, dropping himself down the order for the Oval Test against India in 1979, Butcher was brought into the side as Geoff Boycott's opening partner. He scored 14 and 20, and he has never been recalled to the colours. Even more striking was the neglect of that other Glamorgan hero, Alan Jones, who scored more runs in first-class cricket (36,049, with fifty-six hundreds) than any other non-Test player, but whose nearest approach to supreme honours at the highest level was a single appearance for England against the Rest of the World in 1970. Yet Andy Sandham and Percy Holmes both appeared for England a few times, and Fred Martin and the two Alans were all accorded a brief moment of fame in exalted circles, whereas there have been others who were denied a complete recognition of their merits. One such, whose career coincided with the inception of international contests between England and Australia, never played in a Test, never went on a tour abroad, and was chosen to assist the Players against the Gentlemen on only one occasion. No matter what outstanding feats he performed, the circumstances were, in one way or another, never propitious.

Born at Stockton-on-Tees, on April 21, 1844, Edward Barratt stood a little over the medium height of those days and weighed between eleven and twelve stones. A mild, somewhat diffident man in most things and in no way remarkable for any pronounced strength of character, his outward appearance was nevertheless far from being insignificant. Ever meticulous in the matter of hirsute appendages, he took infinite pains to cultivate a neat, modified version of the martial style rendered famous by Ambrose Burnside, the intensely loyal but bumbling general of the American Civil War, remembered today more for the impressive luxuriance of his whiskers rather than his ability to command large bodies of troops. Above his smooth, clean-shaven chin, Ted Barratt's close-clipped sideburns merged with his carefully barbered moustache to form a continuous line of facial adornment running from one ear by way of his upper lip to the other.

A zealous fielder in his youth, especially when stationed at cover-point or slip, Barratt was also a forcing left-handed batsman, whose hard-hitting powers far exceeded his conception of scientific defensive play. His talents in these two departments of the game, it must be added, tended to deteriorate with the passage of time. An excellent slow left-arm bowler on his best days, with a considerable break from leg to off, he was never averse to dispensing the occasional straight, fast delivery and the "Chinaman" by way of variety. Often effective on both wet and dry pitches, he seems generally to have cared little for the satisfaction of hitting the sticks, preferring to drop the ball on or outside the off-stump with the intention of luring unwary batsmen into giving catches to the packed off-side trap or rashly running out of the crease. A good proportion of his tally of wickets was secured with the co-operation of his fieldsmen and the wicket-keeper.

Ted Barratt might well have been considered fortunate in the location of his place of birth, since Stockton-on-Tees was one of the most famous and thriving centres for cricket in the north of England at that period. He was already turning out in local matches while he was still a teenager, though cricket was not really his main concern in those days. Ted was trained as a plumber, a trade which he only gradually relinquished as cricket began to absorb more and more of his time. Bearing in mind the financial benefits accruing from both occupations in the twentieth century, you have the feeling that if he had been living today, Ted would probably have stuck to his plumbing and let the cricket go.

A spirit of adventure, perhaps, or maybe the opportunity for self-advancement persuaded Barratt to seek his fortune beyond the boundaries of Stockton-on-Tees, and by 1868 he had obtained a position at the Railway Works at Swindon. There, on May 25, 26, and 27 of the same year, he took his first important step towards achieving fame on the cricket field. Chosen to assist Twenty-two of the Great Western Railway Club (or New Swindon) against the itinerant United South

Edward Barratt   *Courtesy Roger Mann*

of England Eleven, he did little as a batsman, scoring o and 8, but he captured seven wickets in the match. No analysis is available, but since at least four bowlers were put on and only 177 runs were scored from the bat, it is no more than reasonable to suppose that Ted's bowling cannot have been particularly expensive. The home side won this contest by 30 runs, and if you care to examine the score card, you can have little difficulty in reaching the conclusion that he made a signal contribution to this notable victory. W.G. Grace, who was assisting the United South in this match, was already stamping his indelible mark on the cricket scene as the most merciless destroyer of the majority of bowlers in England, but on this occasion he was able to make only 10 runs in each innings. Moreover, it could be confidently maintained that the inhibiting presence of twenty-two opponents in the field against him had little to do with his early departure for small scores. The modes of dismissal? Caught and bowled Barratt on both occasions. W.G. was favourably impressed, and so, possibly, was his younger brother Fred, who also gave a return catch to the same bowler to end his second knock.

On May 10 and 11 of the following year, Ted Barratt made his first appearance at Lord's in a twelve-a-side match between the Colts of the North and the Colts of the South. In a low-scoring contest – the highest total in one innings was only 83 – he was the top scorer with 12 in the northerners' first attempt, but he achieved little success with the ball. Towards the end of the season, the United South of England Eleven had their revenge upon the Great Western Railway team at Swindon, on August 26, 27, and 28, winning by ten wickets. I do not know if Ted was able to achieve much in the way of spin in this match, but it would probably be an error to maintain that he "toiled not," seeing that Henry Jupp and Thomas Humphrey contributed 135 and 65 respectively to the visitors' total of 283 in their first innings.

While still at Swindon in the early part of 1870, Ted Barratt took some time off to play in the inaugural match of the newly formed United North of England Eleven at Dewsbury, on June 6, 7, and 8. As the opening bowler for the opposition (Sixteen Colts of England), he claimed six wickets for only 40 runs. With the bat, unfortunately, he registered a "pair." During the course of the season, he appears to have bade farewell to Swindon by accepting a professional engagement with the Longsight Cricket Club, at Manchester. Earning an occasional fee as a "Given Man" with local sides, he assisted Twenty-two of Rotherham against his old adversaries, the United South of England Eleven, on June 20, 21, and 22. W.G. was absent (playing for MCC), but brother Fred was in the opposing team again and was one of Ted's four victims on first hands. In the second innings, the "Given Man" gave excellent value in return for his wages, claiming no less than eight wickets with only 55 runs coming from the bat.

At the end of July 1871, Ted had yet another encounter with the United South of England Eleven – and the two Graces – when he turned out for Eighteen of the Manchester Broughton Club. In an unfinished match, the visitors had only one innings, during which he bowled unchanged to reinforce W.G.'s highly favourable opinion of his skills by capturing six wickets for 45 runs. The Champion, according to his own testimony, put in a good word for Ted at Lord's, and in 1872 the latter accepted an engagement as a member of the MCC ground staff.

Shortly after appearing in a minor match at headquarters, in which he took five wickets, including W.G.'s, Ted Barratt made a sensational debut in first-class cricket. Selected as a substitute for Alfred Shaw, the slow to medium-pace right-hander, to represent the North against the South at Prince's Ground, on May 16, 17, and 18, 1872 – torrential rain, in fact, limited play to the first day – he was designated to open the bowling for the North in partnership with J.C. Shaw, the fast left-hander from Nottinghamshire. Slow or medium left-arm bowlers of Barratt's type were by no means common in the early 1870s, and doubtless the novelty of his delivery contributed something towards the demoralization of the southern batsmen, only three of whom got into double figures. Ted "paralysed the South," and by the time they had all been dismissed for 186, the newcomer had achieved one of the most remarkable successes on a first appearance – eight wickets for 60 runs, including the last three in four deliveries. Strange to say, the two batsmen who eluded his twisters were W.G. and G.F. Grace, who both succumbed to the pace of Jemmy Shaw, but by now the two famous brothers had probably become largely accustomed to the Barratt methods in those earlier United South matches.

In the equivalent fixture at Lord's, immediately afterwards, Ted was out of luck in the South's first innings, but he came back to restore his newly earned reputation in the second, claiming seven wickets in return for only 18 runs. Another North v South contest took place at The Oval towards the end of July, in which he was given only five overs and conceded 20 runs. He played four times for MCC in first-class matches, but he distinguished himself only in the away fixture with Cambridge University, on May 23 and 24. The visitors batted first, scoring 234, and then Ted "came off with a vengeance" when the undergraduates went to the wickets. He opened the MCC bowling with Alfred Shaw, and this formidable partnership "established a panic as the shades of evening were falling." By close of play, the home side had lost seven wickets for 24 runs, and the second day saw MCC pulling off a comfortable victory by an innings and 35 runs. Ted's share of the spoils in the Cambridge first innings was six for 29, but he was less successful in the other three MCC matches, in which most of the bowling was entrusted to Alfred Shaw and George Wootton, another more senior member of the ground staff. His record at the end of the season was twenty-five wickets at an average of 13.48. One of the cricket annuals expressed some disappointment that he had been unable to repeat "his extraordinary exploits in the early matches between North and South." Though failing to come up to the mark as a bowler with any consistency afterwards, he earned lavish praise for his admirable fielding and for proving himself to be "a resolute batsman of the 'slogging' persuasion."

It was possibly the lack of opportunities for bowling that brought about Ted Barratt's decision to quit his post at headquarters. In 1873, he was engaged as a ground bowler at Prince's Cricket Ground, the scene of his initial triumph for the North against the South, and the following year found him occupying a similar position at The Oval. Having moved from his home at Stockton-on-Tees, he set up house in the Battersea Park area in London and concentrated on establishing a qualification to play for Surrey County by residence. In making these rapid changes of employment, Barratt could in all probability claim a wellnigh unique record: I can think of no other professional bowler who held appointments on the ground staff of the three principal cricket grounds of London in the 1870s, certainly not in so short a space of time.

As far as first-class cricket was concerned, the period encompassing the seasons of 1873 to 1875 saw Ted Barratt in a state of eclipse. He was not, of course, idle: apart from fulfilling his duties as a ground bowler and doing some umpiring, even at the highest level, he also turned over his arm in numerous minor matches for Prince's Club and subsequently the Surrey Club. Interspersed between these fixtures came occasional engagements as a "Given Man" to assist various local teams, sometimes against one of the itinerant elevens in the north, and once or twice he played for his native county of Durham. By 1876, he was qualified to appear for Surrey, for whom he made a somewhat inauspicious debut (0–33) against Cambridge University at Cambridge, on May 25, 26, and 27.

The three years of enforced absence from the more intense and demanding conditions of first-class cricket exerted a temporary adverse effect upon Barratt's bowling powers. He logged thirteen matches, in which he captured thirty-six wickets at 19.38 apiece, which was a fairly high average for those days. His most notable exploit occurred in the contest with Yorkshire at The Oval, on August 21, 22, and 23, 1876. Assisted by the presence of some moisture in the pitch, he bowled unchanged throughout the visitors' first innings in partnership with the "evergreen," veteran off-breaker, James Southerton, and marked a return of five wickets for 37 runs. Figures of five for 65 in the second gave him the feat of claiming ten wickets in a match for the first time in his first-class career. It would by no means be the last.

A brief moment of highly unlikely glory occurred in Surrey's nail-biting fixture against Middlesex at The Oval, on August 10, 11, and 12, of the same season. Though completely unsuccessful with the ball (0–20 and 0–25), Ted Barratt surpassed all his previous efforts with the bat. A respectable score of 31 in Surrey's first innings was followed by a splendid display of heroics in the second. Casting caution to the winds and completely unruffled by the sight of several chances going to ground, he employed the long handle with such untrammelled exuberance that only six runs were required for victory at the fall of the ninth Surrey wicket. A few minutes later, Ted's luck finally ran out when he tempted fate once too often, and cover-point thankfully held on to a simple catch. According to the figures displayed on the telegraph board, Middlesex were the winners by 1 run, but on re-examining the official books the scorers announced that an error had crept into their calculations and that the result of the match was, in fact, a tie! The improbable hero was the most successful batsman in Surrey's second innings – a feat he very rarely achieved – and his score of 67 was the highest of his first-class career. Although he indulged in some useful swinging of the bat on occasions in future seasons, he never again quite equalled his performance of that historic tie with Middlesex.

By now, Ted Barratt had completely identified himself with the fortunes of Surrey by taking up residence in Bowling Green Street close to The Oval. His adopted county was in poor fettle at this time in its history, being particularly strong in neither batting nor bowling, and Ted and his career statistics were destined to suffer under the crushing burden of an inordinate amount of bowling for several seasons. His tally of wickets in all first-class matches in 1877 showed a sizeable increase from 36 to 92, but at the slightly higher average of 20.03, and although he captured five wickets in an innings six times, his best match return was nine for 86. This season, however, contained one highlight as far as Ted was concerned, when he was selected – probably as a substitute for the ailing Alfred Shaw – to assist the Players against the Gentlemen at The Oval, on June 28, 29, and 30. A high-scoring contest ended in a predictable draw, with the Players totalling 405 and 119, and the Gentlemen 427 in their only innings. As far as batting was concerned, Ted failed to trouble the scorers – no very unusual experience for him, on the whole – but of all the seven bowlers who laboured so manfully for the professionals on a perfect run-getting pitch, he was by far the most successful with four wickets for 116 runs, and it was doubtless some consolation that one of his victims was G.F. Grace.

Taking full advantage of a predominantly wet season in 1878, Ted Barratt emerged as one of the select handful of bowlers to take a hundred or more wickets in all first-class matches. His victims numbered 135, and he recorded the most economical seasonal average of his career (14.04), apart from his first in 1872. He claimed five or more wickets in an innings fifteen times, and on five occasions he captured ten or more in a match (best 12–141). This was the year when D.W. Gregory's Australian team were on tour in England, and perhaps they grew to dread the appearance of the bewhiskered Barratt, whom they encountered in seven innings in four first-class matches, as well as one or two minor affairs. It would be charitable not to linger too long over Ted's performance with the bat – eight runs in six innings with a highest score of three – but his bowling record against the colonials was nothing short of phenomenal. He captured thirty-seven wickets at an average of 9.35, with five or more in an innings on four occasions, and thrice he achieved match figures of ten or more victims. His most extraordinary feat, which earned him a permanent place in the record books, occurred in his third encounter with Gregory's team while assisting the Players of England at The Oval, on September 2 and 3. Four bowlers were put on in the first innings, with three of them having nothing to show for their pains. Ted, however, registered the best bowling in one innings of his whole career by returning the astonishing analysis of *10 wickets for 43 runs!* As a perfect illustration of his system of bowling, the modes of dismissal speak volumes – seven caught and three stumped. His failure – if you can use such a term when discussing such a startlingly splendid performance – to clean bowl a single one of his victims was described by one of the cricket annuals as "the greatest curiosity of the season."

Unable to live up to his impossibly high standard, Ted took no more than one wicket in the second innings, though he conceded only fifteen runs. The Australians managed to scrape home by the narrow margin of eight runs, thus achieving a somewhat hollow victory. To designate the defeated side as "The Players of England" was a misnomer if there ever was one. "Eleven English Players" would have been far more accurate, since the team was in no way representative of the full professional strength of England. There was bad blood between John Conway, the Australian manager, and some of the English professionals who had taken part in the tour down under in 1876–77. At one stage in the programme, some of the colonials, as they were then called, had declined to take part in a match got up for the benefit of the English party unless they were guaranteed a fee of £20, which was regarded as an excessive sum in those days. Now, in 1878, some of the Englishmen concerned and several others declined to assist the Players in the fixture at The Oval for anything less than the same amount. This demand was rejected, and what was not much more than a scratch team, described in one of the cricket annuals as "a comparatively second-rate Eleven of Players," provided the opposition for the tourists. Ironically, had the Players fielded all their best men, Ted Barratt might not have been an automatic choice.

Relieved, no doubt, that his boys had not suffered a humiliation at the hands of rather moderate opponents, John Conway was perhaps easily persuaded to make a magnanimous gesture. Summoned to his presence in order to hear his congratulations, Ted Barratt was then presented with the more tangible reward of the ball he had used in performing his splendid deed and a five-pound note. The money was doubtless the most acceptable of all, but he ought to have received far more. In those days, it was customary on some grounds, especially The Oval, to call upon the crowd to show their appreciation by making donations in recognition of an outstanding individual performance with bat or ball. On this particular occasion, two persons, claiming that they were representing the ground authorities, circulated among the spectators, making a collection ostensibly on the hero's behalf. Not a penny of it, unfortunately, found its way into Ted's pockets, since "The pair proved to be members of the light-fingered fraternity, and decamped with their spoils undetected." Lady Luck, more's the pity, rarely smiled upon Ted.

So, with his "dodgy bowling," aided by some excellent fielding and catching by his team-mates, Ted had been able to take full advantage of the sticky wickets on which he had frequently operated in 1878. "Barratt's 'all sorts'," observed one of the cricket annuals, "paid wonderfully well." A tribute to his versatility, perhaps, but, as will be seen, there is a slightly disturbing ring to this description of his system of bowling as "Barratt's 'all sorts'." Having scaled the heights with 135 wickets in 1878, he ignominiously plummeted to the depths in the following season. His complete loss of all recognizable form, characterized as an "unaccountable decadence," materially weakened the Surrey bowling and limited his appearances in first-class cricket to only seven matches. He took no more than ten wickets at great expense (average 31.50), and for the first time in his career he failed to record five victims in an innings.

The Australians were touring England again in 1880, but Barratt was given no opportunity to pit his wiles against them. His loss of form continued in the early part of the season, and he was omitted from the Surrey team until the beginning of June. Failing to produce anything as startling as his performances of 1878, he "was shunted for a time

E. M. Grace

injudiciously as it would appear." To treat the unfortunate left-hander as virtually the sole cause of the County's ill-success at this period would be grossly unfair. There was a dearth of first-rate performers with the ball in those days, and there were numerous occasions when the Surrey bowling seemed to be floundering helplessly and hopelessly in the Slough of Despond. Absent for much of July and the following month, he was recalled to the side for Surrey's fixture with Lancashire at The Oval, on August 23, 24, and 25. After failing to avoid the follow on, the representatives of the Red Rose succeeded in winning the match by 60 runs, thanks to some inept fielding and missed catches, but the responsibility for Surrey's defeat could scarcely be laid on Ted's shoulders. All his old powers returned to him, as he produced one of the best bowling performances of his career, taking eight wickets for 53 runs in the first innings and five for 108 in the second. These statistics gave a considerable boost to his record for the season, showing twenty-nine victims in six matches at an average of 17.65 – a noteworthy improvement on his figures for the previous season.

Ted Barratt turned out fourteen times for Surrey in 1881, very much in the role of an over-burdened work horse. His aggregate of wickets rose to eighty-two, but he conceded 1,605 runs in taking them, at an average of 19.57. He was especially expensive in his first five matches of the season. Delivering in eight innings, he claimed twenty-four victims, but these cost him 727 runs, and five times the "runs against" column ballooned into three figures. In the defeat by an innings inflicted upon Surrey by Yorkshire at Huddersfield, on June 2 and 3, the home side's score card showed two centuries, and Ted received a merciless drubbing (4–158). As if to add to this humiliation, Yorkshire's Edmund Peate, who bowled unchanged with Allen Hill throughout Surrey's two innings, gave him an object lesson in the art of slow left-arm trundling with match figures of fourteen wickets for 77 runs.

Surrey's next fixture was a home match with Gloucestershire, on June 9, 10, and 11, resulting in yet another daunting defeat, and although his figures in the first innings (5–120) were eventually more respectable than those of the Yorkshire match, Ted had another unhappy outing. His chief tormentor on this occasion was Edward Mills Grace, the Champion's elder brother, and years later W.G. was able to recall some of the details of the massacre. Keen-eyed and batting in his usual unorthodox style, E.M. hit up a rapid 77 ("a thoroughly characteristic display"). His method of dealing with Barratt's good-length deliveries consisted of a liberal use of his notorious pull, and whenever the hapless bowler dropped the ball short, E.M. dismissed it vigorously to the boundary with an even more enormous heave. As a variant to his favourite stroke, he employed a manoeuvre which found no favour in his victim's eyes. Of this feature of E.M.'s batting one of the cricket annuals observed that "his three back-handed hits from Barratt for four were a little distasteful to that bowler." A late cut, perhaps, or even a reverse sweep?

After his first five disastrous matches of the season, all of them resulting in overwhelming defeats for Surrey, Barratt contrived to bowl a little more economically, and in the contest with Sussex at The Oval, on August 1 and 2, 1881, he recorded a signal triumph. This occasion, sadly, marked the final appearance for Surrey of the veteran batsman Harry Jupp, but Ted Barratt was largely responsible for giving him a good send-off. The home side won by eight wickets and, on a pitch affected at times by rain, Ted achieved match figures of fourteen wickets for 103 runs (7–45 and 7–58) – his finest performance in one match for Surrey and, for that matter, the best of his whole first-class career.

As a result of injuries, Barratt's appearances for Surrey were limited to fourteen matches in 1882. His "bowling was sadly missed," and, to add to the once all-conquering County's tale of woe, he was not the only bowler to break down during the season. Denied the opportunity to confront Sussex once again in the match at The Oval, on July 17, 18, and 19, his absence was particularly unfortunate for Surrey, "as he has always been singularly effective against Sussex batsmen," to wit his marvellous performance in the equivalent fixture of 1881. With Barratt away, the visitors did much as they liked with the mediocre efforts of the seven trundlers employed by the Surrey skipper and won the match comfortably by five wickets.

Barratt's greatest exploit of the season came off in the contest with Oxford University at The Oval, on June 19 and 20. The pitch, rendered dead by recent rains, could scarcely have suited him better: his "bowling puzzled the Oxonians considerably, and indeed chiefly contributed to their defeat." He registered yet another "pair" with the bat, but with the ball in his cunning left hand and the scales weighted heavily against the batsmen, he captured five wickets for 34 runs in the first innings and no less than eight for only 39 in the second.

The old enemy from down under, captained for the second time by W.L. Murdoch, were in England once more in 1882, and Ted Barratt was involved in two confrontations with them in the course of the season. For Surrey at The Oval, on May 25, 26, and 27, he was on the losing side by a margin of six wickets and, in conditions which ought to have favoured his twisters, he suffered from a lack of competent support from his team-mates in the field, performing no more than adequately with match figures of five for 98. This, however, was a princely return compared with his analysis in the second match,

which, ironically, followed shortly after his notable triumph over the
bewildered Oxonians. Engaged to assist W.G. Grace's United Eleven
at Chichester, on June 26, 27, and 28, he found himself in a situation
that could hardly have been less auspicious. The Champion and his
henchmen had experienced considerable difficulties in raising a team
– there were three other first-class matches on the same dates – and the
final make-up of the United Eleven was far too weak to do battle with
the powerful tourists. When play was due to begin, several of the United
men had not yet arrived on the ground – one, in fact, never turned up
at all – and although he won the toss, W.G. felt obliged in such a
dilemma to give his opponents the first innings. Taking full advantage
of a splendid wicket, the Australians "did exactly as they liked with the
weak bowling," piling on the agony to the extent of totalling 501 runs.
Then Spofforth and his coadjutors shared the wickets between them to
secure a gargantuan victory by an innings and 263 runs. It was in no
way a match for Ted to cherish in his memory. His undistinguished
contribution to the proceedings consisted of scores of 0 and 4 not out,
and one hugely expensive wicket at the cost of 153 runs!

In spite of all the vicissitudes inflicted upon him by the fates in 1882,
Surrey's sorely worked trundler (almost 1,000 overs delivered, plus 67
for the United Eleven) ended the season with quite creditable figures.
His 94 wickets – his highest aggregate since 1878 – were obtained at the
quite respectable average of just under 17 runs apiece. Better things,
however, lay in the offing, and in the following year the inscrutable
goddess Fortune elected to turn her Wheel in Barratt's favour.

It was ordained that Ted Barratt should enjoy what was in many ways
his most successful season in 1883. This was rather unusual to some
extent, since for much of the time hard, true wickets, favouring the
batsmen and often placing the slow bowlers at a disadvantage, were the
order of the day. Barratt, however, succeeded in exercising his craft no
matter what conditions were imposed upon him by the vagaries of the
climate. The sum of his victims totalled 148 – the best achievement of
his first-class career and the highest tally by any bowler in the English
season of 1883 – and these were bought at an average of 15.90. Yet a
further dimension of his success was to be found in another personal
record: he obtained five or more wickets in an innings eighteen times,
which figure was nearly half the number of innings in which he bowled,
and ten or more in a match on six occasions! His season was not entirely
free from physical problems, since he was a victim of severe lameness
for a while, and considering the enormous amount of bowling he
was required to get through (over 1,400 overs delivered) with little
consistently effective support at the other end, "his performance was
most creditable."

There were many good things for Ted Barratt to savour in 1883. He recorded his usual success against his favourite "rabbits," the Sussex batsmen, both home and away. At The Oval, on July 2 and 3, the visitors won the toss and took first innings on a perfect pitch, "but none of the eleven could do anything against Barratt's bowling," and they were summarily dismissed for the meagre total of 80, thanks largely to the Surrey left-hander, who bowled unchanged, achieving an analysis of eight for 48. He picked up two more wickets in the second innings and claimed seven victims in the return fixture at Hove, a week later.

Gloucestershire, too, felt the sting of his scourge in their two meetings. At The Oval, on May 31 and June 1, he took five wickets in the first innings but came in for some stick in the second (0–86). At Cheltenham, on August 20, 21, and 22, however, he did much better, with twelve victims for 121 runs, "a great performance against such a batting side." As usual, he failed to lift W.G.'s scalp, and he was, in fact, singularly unsuccessful against the Champion in grand matches, taking his wicket only three times in first-class cricket. In more ways than one, this fixture at Cheltenham proved quite eventful for Ted. One of the nominated unpires failed to turn up, and with Surrey taking first knock, Barratt was called upon to officiate in the absentee's place until his turn came to bat – at number eleven, of course. For the record, he scored 5 not out, and Surrey won by nine wickets.

It was the Somerset batsmen, however, who qualified for the undesirable distinction of being the principal martyrs at Ted's hands in 1883. Although the western county fielded what was considered to be a strong side for the match at The Oval, on August 2 and 3, "none of them played Barratt with any confidence." Winning the toss and batting first on a "splendid wicket," the visitors were all at sea, and their resistance crumbled before the Surrey attack. Dismissed for a total of only 84, they fared rather better at their second attempt, but they nevertheless crashed to a massive defeat by an innings and 213 runs. Barratt's tally for the match was thirteen wickets for 105 runs (7–39 and 6–66), his best haul of the season.

In the return fixture at Taunton, a fortnight later, he was almost as ruthlessly devastating. On this occasion, the Surrey batsmen, apart from the amateur W.W. Read in both innings and his professional namesake J.M. in the first, were neither particularly consistent nor productive, and at one time it looked as though the home side might have had a chance of avenging their abject humiliation at The Oval. Surrey, however, eventually registered yet another victory, and "it was the very effective bowling of Barratt which pulled them through at the finish." His match figures of twelve wickets for 115 runs included his best ever performance for Surrey (8–28) in Somerset's second innings. After several years in the wilderness, Surrey were beginning to assume a prominent position in the world of cricket once more, thanks in part to Ted Barratt's bowling, which "contributed in no small degree to the general success of the season."

As a result of the experience he had gained on the hard wickets of 1883, Barratt might have claimed that he had virtually mastered the art of having to perform in conditions generally adverse to a bowler of his type. More often than not, the weather in the summer of 1884 also tended to favour the batsmen. Although he was not quite so effective as he had been during the previous season, he still found a place among the top ten wicket-takers. His tally of victims went down from 148 to 121 and, with an average of 18.17, he proved to be more expensive. Surrey's bowling resources were still rather slender at this time, though he had found a most useful ally in the amateur, Mr C.E. Horner, a fast-medium right-hander, who was enjoying the best season of his short first-class career by taking over 100 wickets. This pair, between them, got through an enormous amount of work for their County, and one of the cricket annuals felt that the slow left-hander's bowling "demands something more than passing notice."

After an interval of two years, the Australians under W.L. Murdoch were touring England again, and Ted Barratt had one encounter with the old enemy, when Surrey took them on at The Oval, on May 19 and 20, 1884. The visitors cruised to a comfortable victory by eight wickets, but Barratt acquitted himself with the ball far better than any of his team-mates in the Australians' first innings, registering an analysis of five wickets for 93 runs. This, in fact, was to be his last performance of any intrinsic merit against the hard-hitting batsmen from down under.

In previous seasons, it will be remembered, the Sussex batsmen had proved themselves to be especially vulnerable to Barratt's bowling, and over the years he had claimed five or more of their wickets in an innings no less than nine times and ten or more in a match thrice – his best record in this respect against any opposing side. Yet, strange to say, his favourite victims managed to escape comparatively unscathed in 1884, both home and away. Not so the undergraduates of Cambridge University, who in the past had more than once become enmeshed in his snares. At The Oval, on June 19, 20, and 21, they fell into the trap once more, giving the scheming left-hander his best match return of the season (13–136) and Surrey a victory by 148 runs.

The summer of 1884, as it turned out, was destined to be Ted Barratt's last full season in first-class cricket. Over-bowled throughout much of his service with Surrey, he was no longer nearly so lethal in the following year, when there were some welcome reinforcements in the ranks of the County's bowlers. The brilliant George Lohmann, right-arm medium-fast, who had made a modest debut in 1884, claimed well over 100 wickets in 1885, ably assisted by John Beaumont, a fast, right-handed import from

G. A. Lohmann

Yorkshire, whose aggregate of victims also ran into three figures. Waiting in the wings to support these two was a very fast man, Tom Bowley, who was tried in five matches for Surrey in 1885. Mr C.E. Horner, Barratt's partner of 1884, was still available off and on, but he was not selected for more than about half of the fixtures and took only a small number of wickets. With the advent of Lohmann and Beaumont, Ted was becoming surplus to the County's requirements, and he made his final appearance for Surrey against Lancashire at Liverpool, on July 16, 17, and 18, 1885. One of eight bowlers put on, he did little to suggest that he had any claim to a place in the side, taking one wicket for 40 runs in eleven overs. His record for the season, in which, of course, his opportunities were limited, was far from encouraging – only fifteen wickets at an average of 26.40.

There was one final first-class match to come in the next season, and the opponents, appropriately enough, were the Australians. Ted Barratt was engaged to make one of the team got up by Mr C.I. Thornton to meet the tourists at Chiswick Park, on July 2 and 3, 1886. The home side was in no way remarkable as any kind of representative eleven, since six counties, MCC, and Oxford University all had fixtures on the same dates. Amassing 345 runs on the first day, the Australians had captured six wickets in the second innings of Thornton's team, when this two-day game ended in a draw. Barratt, who actually notched his highest ever score (13) against the Australians, had opened the bowling in partnership with Alec Hearne, of Kent, who performed fairly well in taking three wickets for 67 runs in 37 overs, including 16 maidens. Ted, however, "proved terribly expensive," with figures of 34.3–4–115–3! As had often happened in the past he owed his wickets to the collaboration of the stumper. All told, he played against the Australians on eight occasions in first-class matches, achieving his greatest triumph in 1878, and ending up with a creditable record of fifty-one wickets at an average of 16.15. A breakdown of the modes of dismissal secured in taking these wickets yields a perfect illustration of the Barratt system of attack. Only ten of his victims were clean bowled; exactly the same number were stumped; and the remainder consisted of no less than thirty caught and one caught and bowled!

So, Ted Barratt passed from the scene of first-class cricket, never to return as a player. Throughout his career he took 790 wickets, averaging 17.54 each, and three times he captured over a hundred in one season. On sixty-nine occasions he claimed five or more victims in an innings, and his tally for ten or more in a match amounted to eighteen. To this may be added his feat of capturing eight or more wickets in an innings eight times, six of them for Surrey. His career was comparatively short, merely twelve seasons, and in only half of them was he fully employed. Time and again he was called upon to turn over his arm for incredibly long stints of bowling, such as 91 overs in a single innings and 88 in another, while several times he logged more than a hundred in a match, two of these feats occurring in consecutive fixtures. Throughout those twelve seasons, covering 153 matches, he delivered slightly in excess of 8,200 four-ball overs, which represents an enormous expenditure of sweat and energy, most of it in the service of his adopted county.

A belated benefit was granted to Barratt in the contest between Surrey and Yorkshire at The Oval, on August 18 and 19, 1887. This match, from Ted's point of view, was a success in most ways, apart from lasting only two days, since there was a good attendance, and Surrey won easily by an innings and 10 runs. From time to time, during both his playing days and afterwards, he held various coaching engagements at Cambridge University and elsewhere. He was also employed as an umpire, standing in four of the contests in the series Gentlemen *v* Players, and he officiated on the county circuit on a regular basis in the seasons of 1889 and 1890, when he was one of the pair of individuals nominated to the official list by Surrey. Umpiring and coaching were not his sole sources of income from 1889 onwards. In that year, he became the landlord of *The Duchy Inn* in Bowling Green Street in close proximity to The Oval and, in addition, his services as a member of the ground staff were retained by the Surrey authorities. He was not, unhappily, destined to make old bones. Although he was able to carry out his duties as an umpire in at least nine first-class matches in the summer of 1890, he was coming to the end of the road. His health suddenly deteriorated rapidly, and he died of consumption on February 27, 1891, at the early age of forty-six.

The reasons for Ted Barratt's exclusion from the highest honours the game had to offer in his lifetime are not too difficult of explanation. First of all, he was an eternal victim of unfavourable circumstances. In 1878, when he proved so successful against D.W. Gregory's Australian team, there were no Test Matches, in what was his second most prolific year (135 wickets), nor, it may here be added, were there any in 1883, when he achieved his highest tally of victims (148). He was not in contention for a place in the England side in 1880, when his appearances in first-class cricket were severely limited by his loss of form, and the selectors prudently gave preference to the slow bowling of Mr A.G. Steel and Alfred Shaw. In 1882 and 1884, the automatic choice for England against Australia was Yorkshire's Edmund Peate, who was undoubtedly a superior exponent of slow left-arm bowling. Peate's incomparable command of line and length gave him the edge over Barratt as much as his infinite capacity for controlling the amount of break to be applied to the ball. It was the same story, too, when it came to the long-running series of Gentlemen *v* Players – a single appearance on Ted's home ground, The Oval, in 1877, when Shaw was absent through illness. W.G., who had a soft spot for Barratt, felt that he "might have been chosen oftener," though the Champion conceded that Shaw, for example, was the greater bowler. More than once, Barratt was called upon to take Alfred's place, when the latter was out of the reckoning for one reason or another. One instance occurred in the contest between Gloucestershire and England at The Oval, on August 15, 16, and 17, 1878. In its brief report of the match, one of the cricket annuals observed that "A. Shaw could not come, so Barratt, the usual 'odd man,' was secured." Such, it seems, was Ted's lot in life when it came to the selection of teams for grand matches: he was all too frequently cast in the role of a substitute for somebody else.

The second reason for Ted Barratt's failure to reach the topmost rung of the ladder of fame was his inability to maintain a perpetual mastery of his craft, and this blemish condemned him to an existence in the ranks of the second best. His pace was slow; in fact, the big hitter C.I. Thornton remembered him as "one of the very slowest left-hand bowlers I ever met," and this characteristic, as will be seen, often worked to Barratt's disadvantage. Mr Thornton, however, freely admitted that he never really enjoyed his confrontations with Ted, "for there was no one who had so much twist on the ball." In addition, the left-hander's bowling habitually broke away from a right-handed batsman, and Thornton, a mighty hitter to leg, usually found himself much more at home against the off breaks of James Southerton, which he frequently pulverized with impunity.

Some of the old cricket annuals published in the nineteenth century made a habit of devoting several pages to diagrams showing how the field should be placed for different types of bowlers, and for several years Barratt's name was cited at the appropriate place as "a good specimen of the slow left." This particular diagram often has all the fielders stationed on the off side, apart from the men at short-leg and mid-on. With Barratt's own blend of off theory, however, the field setting could be even more extreme on occasions. One of the annuals once asserted that Ted's bowling was much the same as ever, adding that "he has nine fields on the off side, and bowls nearly every ball that side with every variety of pitch." His stock delivery was an enormous break from leg, which often spelt destruction to any adversary who was too timid to go on the attack. For those, however, who could not resist the temptation to fling the bat thoughtlessly at anything off the wicket, he had a pet delivery. Relying upon the natural impatience exhibited by some of his opponents, he would bowl the ball slightly beyond the normal length, pitching as much as almost a foot wide of the stumps and breaking away with the aim of inducing a spooned-up catch to the packed off-side field. It must at the same time be conceded that Ted's deliberate choice of leaving a vast, unguarded expanse on the leg side constituted an open invitation for a quick-footed, hawk-eyed batsman to chance his arm at exploiting the pull stroke.

During the first few years he spent as a member of the ground staff at The Oval, it is by no means unlikely that Ted Barratt would have been influenced to a certain degree by the bowling methods of the above-mentioned Jimmy Southerton. The latter, a redoubtable veteran of many a hard tussle in the service of Surrey and one of the most successful wicket-takers of the Victorian age, was a slow right-hander, who tended to place more emphasis on delivering prodigious off breaks rather than maintaining a perfect line and length. Barratt seems to have been a zealous disciple of the gospel according to the venerable James Southerton, whereas his two other great contemporaries Shaw and Peate were dedicated apostles of the creed of pin-point accuracy and a much less extravagant amount of break.

From the point of view of developing his skills, it would, perhaps, have been far more beneficial for Ted Barratt if he could have served a longer apprenticeship at Lord's, where he would have had ample opportunities for observing the technique of Alfred Shaw, one of the principal bowlers on the MCC ground staff. From Alfred he might have discovered that accuracy and an immaculate length are more infallible deceivers of batsmen than an enormous twist from leg to off or vice versa. If you delivered the ball at the same slow pace as Ted Barratt, you could not afford to ignore the cardinal virtues practised by Shaw and Peate. Unfortunately, the Surrey trundler went his own way, and consequently his principal and fatal failing was a lack of consistency. A sterling performance in one match would sometimes be followed by the most dismal of displays immediately afterwards, giving rise to sternly admonitory remarks, such as "Barratt is the most disappointing of bowlers. On one day . . . he can bowl splendidly on a perfect wicket, while on the next he will vary slow long hops with full pitches." The frequent recurrence of his notoriously "very bad ball" was often reflected in the "runs conceded" column of the bowling analysis with a prodigality matching that of the twist he applied to the ball. No amount of break will regularly compensate for deviation in length and pitch, and on several occasions his bowling was described with such comments as "destructive but expensive."

To be fair to Barratt, it must be remembered that in many matches the captains of the Surrey team often kept him on for far too long – for the simple reason that there was probably nobody else in the side good enough to relieve him. There was even one awe-inspiring occasion when he opened the bowling at the beginning of the match and was still wheeling away with the same partner at the close of play. When the innings finally came to an end the next day, his bowling figures were five for 102 and his share of the 166 overs delivered was 81. This excessive employment may be attributed to the lack of experience in leadership betrayed by the County's temporary skipper, but there were similar

Alfred Shaw

I. D. Walker

examples of over-bowling in other matches. The natural consequence of these prolonged spells of trundling was that the batsmen were liable to get set and start flogging the tiring Ted's deliveries to all quarters of the ground. Added to this was the far from adequate service he received at times from his fielders, and, apparently not possessing any great strength of character, he was apt to become easily disheartened and give like offence. Keen and active at stopping and catching the ball at the outset of his career, his willingness and expertise in this department of the game were outstanding, and he received the welcome accolade of "fine field" in one of the cricket annuals. After the passage of several seasons with their burden of disappointments and the inordinate amount of bowling imposed upon him, he became, perhaps, somewhat embittered with the course of events, and that laudatory comment was replaced by the qualification "good field when he likes." Another annual was less disposed to treat him so lightly and showed no hesitation in describing him succinctly as an "uncertain field."

On his bad days, which were sometimes depressingly all too frequent, Ted Barratt often suffered severe punishment, particularly when he found himself confronting some of the leading amateur batsmen, who were familiar with his style of bowling and far too experienced to succumb easily to the devious wiles of his off theory. W.G., admittedly one of the earliest to encounter Barratt, soon worked out the best way of dealing with him. Instead of hitting out wildly at the ball pitching outside the off-stump and veering away, the Champion would step back and calmly cut it. The alternative method was to run out of your crease and hit the ball before it pitched, though this stroke was rather more risky than the cut. Young Fred Grace might not have been always entirely at home in countering Barratt's slow twisters at one time, but as we have seen, they presented no terrors to his more belligerent brother E.M. In that stirring contest between Surrey and Gloucestershire at The Oval, in 1881, when E.M. succeeded in destroying the unfortunate bowler's length and confidence, Barratt weakly capitulated with the plaintive cry, "It's no use now; my little game is over. Help yourselves, gentlemen!"

The Grace brothers were not the only leading lights of the amateurs to relish an encounter with Ted Barratt. Around this time, the opening pair for Middlesex consisted of I.D. Walker, the County captain and probably the greatest batsman of all that illustrious band of the famous Walker brothers, and his youthful partner A.J. Webbe. The former was frequently seen at his best when contending against slow left-arm bowlers, and his particular favourite of the breed was Barratt, especially on those occasions when Ted was doomed to suffer the unhappy experience of having one of his bad days. Although Webbe candidly confessed that he also was very partial to an encounter with the Surrey trundler, he always deferred to his skipper's wishes by going to the non-striker's end whenever Barratt was delivering the first over of the Middlesex innings, "feeling sure that at the least a couple of fours would result from it."

It was all too evident that Donny Walker did not adhere to W.G.'s recommendation on the best method of dealing with a widish delivery pitching on the off side and breaking away, since he seldom used the cut against Barratt, or anybody else, for that matter. His tactics were seemingly more dangerous to his survival, though infinitely more spectacular to behold. Employing a stroke then regarded as virtually unique – indeed, he is often credited with having introduced it to first-class cricket – he would step across and unleash a mighty off drive or cover drive. Now, it must be admitted that on rare occasions he would miss the stroke altogether, but when, as was most often the case, he made contact with the ball, it was always with the middle of the bat, lofting it into the blue high over the heads of mid-off and cover-point.

Perhaps Donny Walker was the batsman who was once inflicting such a pitiless trouncing to the squirming Ted, that the latter was heard to blurt out a hopeless cry, as pathetic as it was revealing of the bowler's character. Realizing the woeful inaccuracy of one of his deliveries, the victim called down the pitch, "Don't hit her, sir! *I'll give you four!*"

Therein, of a certainty, lay the fatal flaw in Barratt's make-up. Excessive amounts of bowling and a succession of dropped catches are enough to turn any cricketer sour and take the heart out of him for a while. When it came to the crunch, however, Ted Barratt seems to have given way to black despair more easily than others, and in this mood of hopelessness his spirit quailed, and he allowed himself to be intimidated by opponents made of sterner stuff. Men of iron resolution like Alfred Shaw and Edmund Peate, or Wilfred Rhodes of a later generation, would never have knuckled under and stooped to pleading abjectly with a batsman for mercy.

When he came to record his reminiscences of some of the cricketers with whom he had played since the beginning of his career, W.G. Grace took particular pains not to forget his erstwhile protégé, whom he had once helped to make his way into the world of first-class cricket. The Champion devoted a full page and a half to Barratt, whereas R.G. Barlow, an all-rounder with a much better record (over 11,000 runs, more wickets at a better average, and seventeen England caps), was accorded only half a page, much to the indignation of *The Manchester Guardian*, which dismissed Ted as "a third-rate bowler and a tenth-rate bat!"

Another elder statesman of the game, much more accustomed to using the pen than W.G., also retained a graphic recollection of the Surrey left-hander. In the summer of 1888, after he had retired from first-class cricket, Barratt was employed as a coach at Rugby. One of his pupils was the future Sir Pelham Warner, who practised his batting against his tutor in the nets, encountered him in a match, and was impressed by his ability to bowl the "Chinaman." The visual image of Ted was still fresh in his former pupil's mind some fifty years later. "I recall his bowling vividly to this day," said Plum, "as I do his mutton-chop whiskers."

GEORGE ULYETT
"Happy Jack"

THE poor benighted "Southron folk" were flummoxed by his name at first. Some of them got the spelling wrong by doubling the "l", whilst others couldn't pronounce it properly and would persist in referring to him as "Yuleyett." Any self-respecting Yorkshireman could have told them, and probably did in no uncertain terms, that the first syllable of the name rhymes with the Yorkshire city of Hull. Yorkshiremen were as proud of him as he was of being a Yorkshireman. And Yorkshire he was through and through in many ways with his bluntness of speech and salty humour, and yet he was much more jovial and exuberant than the typical Yorkshire cricketer, or what has come to be regarded as the uncompromising model of the species. As far as he was concerned, "every match was simply a jolly game," and one of his captains felt that he would have been an even greater asset to the Yorkshire team if only he had learnt to take his cricket a little more seriously. Seriousness, however, both on and off the field, usually took a back seat in Ulyett's attitude to life in general. The enjoyment he derived from merely playing cricket was so patently obvious that he established an enduring bond with the people beyond the boundary ropes. One of the supreme crowd-pleasers of all time, he brought joy and happiness to young and old alike, who in their gratitude accorded him a generous measure of hero-worship. His legion of adoring admirers in his home county lovingly dubbed him "Our George," but he was more universally known as "Happy Jack," a nickname bestowed upon him not long after the beginning of his first-class career. The story tells that Yorkshire were on course for a heavy defeat, and the general atmosphere of gloom pervading the dressing-room affected ten members of the side. The exception was Ulyett, the only man to present a cheerful face to the turn of events. "Look at George there," said one of his team-mates, "he's the only jovial man of the company; we shall have to call him 'Happy Jack'." There was, it should be said, an authentic Jack Ulyett, the youngster's elder brother, but George was perfectly willing to accept the sobriquet, which clung to him thereafter throughout his career, both at home and abroad, and he was known to introduce himself as "George Ulyett, commonly known as 'Happy Jack'."

George Ulyett   *Courtesy Roger Mann*

GEORGE ULYETT   63

Ulyett was born at Pitsmoor, Sheffield, on October 21, 1851, the same day and month as another celebrated representative of the White Rose, Geoffrey Boycott. Apart from both being opening batsmen in their heyday, Yorkshire pride and the identical birthday were about all they had in common. In their approach to cricket they were poles apart, yet each was able in his own way to achieve undying fame. Though capable of occasional stints of hard grafting at a pinch, "Happy Jack" was far more inclined to live up to his nickname by demonstrating his pleasure and gratification to all and sundry. He took risks and gloried in them, accepting setbacks and failures as part of the inevitable price to be paid, and he was always getting in and out of various scrapes with charm and a ready turn of wit. Time and again he found himself in hot water but usually succeeded in talking his way out of difficulties. A natural comedian and a born actor with the ability to assume any facial expression appropriate to the circumstances, he could range over the whole gamut, feigning horrified dismay one moment and round-eyed innocence the next. Mock seriousness and straight-faced leg-pulling formed essential ingredients of his repertoire, and he was an accomplished *raconteur*. His favourite subjects were usually humorous incidents involving himself with, admittedly, a minimum of adherence to the plain, unvarnished truth. As Alfred Shaw observed, "Happy Jack's" stories "gained in breadth and colouring with each narration."

By the accepted standards of any age, Ulyett was a fine figure of a man, the beau ideal of a cricketer. Erect of carriage, not much below six feet in height and weighing around fourteen stones in his prime, with burly, broad shoulders and sturdy limbs, he was built like a champion prize-fighter – and, it may be added, he was not without some skill in the noble art. He wore his hair short, brushed flat with a centre parting, and his fresh, ruddy countenance was adorned with a dark moustache of impressive depth and density. A spark of that famous sense of humour seemed to lurk in the corners of his eyes as they met your gaze. All the same, if you took a closer look, you would probably have decided that he was not a man to meddle with in certain situations.

During his late teens, Ulyett was employed as a metal worker at a rolling-mill. This was not, I imagine, an occupation that appealed to him as much as cricket, which became and remained his absorbing passion. His attendance at the mill was anything but regular during the summer months, when he made a habit of skiving off to take part in matches in the neighbourhood. The inevitable consequence of such flagrant dereliction of duty was dismissal from his job. One can only conclude that the youngster was already capable of making full use of his winning ways, since, it seems, his employer would always relent and take him on again at the works. In 1871, at the age of nineteen, he obtained an engagement as a professional with the Bradford Club, and in the last season of his three-year stint he had the good fortune to pull off a quite remarkable feat for an unknown. Selected to play for Eighteen of Bradford against the United South of England Eleven on June 23, 24, and 25, 1873, he opened the bowling and managed to capture six wickets in the match, which ended in a victory for the home side. The youngster made a vital contribution to this success by dismissing W.G. Grace for 2 and 27, clean bowled in both innings.

Tidings of his exploits soon came to the attention of the Sheffield authorities, and not long afterwards Ulyett was drafted into the Yorkshire Eleven, making his debut in the contest with Sussex at Bramall Lane, on July 14 and 15. Batting at number eight in his only innings, he could manage no more than eight runs, but match figures of four wickets for 41 secured him a place in the team for the return fixture at Hove, a week later. His second appearance for Yorkshire was almost his last, for he succeeded in "getting into a scrape." One evening, in the hours of darkness, he met two members of the Bradford Committee who were in Hove, and who persuaded him to go back to their hotel for some jollification. Returning to his lodgings after midnight, Ulyett found himself locked out, and he had to borrow a ladder and climb up to the window of his room. The details of this escapade were somehow leaked to the Committees of Sheffield and Bradford, and he was given a severe tongue-lashing for being out so late during the course of an important match. With his usual plausible manner, the youthful sinner contrived to talk his way out of the threatening situation by pointing out that he had been in the company of those two eminently respectable gentlemen from Bradford, with the result that all was forgiven. The incident, however, was not forgotten by some of his team-mates, who made a habit of addressing him for some time afterwards as Jack Sheppard, after the criminal notorious for his ability to escape from tight corners. Perhaps this also contributed to his more permanent nickname of "Happy Jack."

Apart from one fixture, Ulyett retained his place in the side for the remainder of the season. He accomplished little of moment with the bat, but his bowling yielded an average of 13.18, and his sixteen wickets included one haul of five for 17 against Nottinghamshire at Huddersfield, at the end of August. In 1874, he logged twelve first-class appearances, all but one of them for Yorkshire, and once more his record with the bat was very mediocre (201 runs at an average of 9.13), whereas his bowling gave rise to expectations of possible prominence in the future. His tally of victims was exactly trebled, with only an infinitesimal increase in his average. On no less than five occasions, he claimed the wickets of five or more batsmen in one innings. He marked his best performance in the match between Yorkshire and the United South of England Eleven at Bradford, on June 22, 23, and 24, taking seven wickets for 82 runs in the first innings. With three more for 25 in the second, he achieved one of the best match performances of his whole career. One of his victims in the United South's second innings was W.G. Grace, whom he clean bowled for the only time in first-class cricket.

During these first two seasons, Ulyett presented the appearance of being a useful bits-and-pieces man. In his youth and throughout his career, he was an excellent fielder, especially at a distance from the wickets and, in his latter days, the less demanding position of point. Possessing an exceptionally safe pair of hands, he rarely missed a catch, and his statistics in that department of the game finally peaked at a total of 368 dismissals. As a bowler, he was distinctly fast, employing a high delivery, and on a bumpy, kicking pitch he was a dangerous adversary, inflicting bruises and aching bones on many an unfortunate batsman. Now and then, in his first two or three overs, before he had settled into a better line and length, he would unintentionally cause the ball to swerve in the air from the off to such a degree that the fielder at long-leg was given a busy time saving the extras. Sometimes he succeeded in achieving a lethal combination of pace and break-back from the off with the ground to help him, but in general he was apt to keep pounding away, relying chiefly on sheer speed with a minimum of skill and subtlety. Occasionally, of course, in conditions ideally suited to his methods, he came off with a vengeance, but in the long run he usually fulfilled the role of a useful change when more talented trundlers were frustrated by the batsmen or required a rest from their labours.

When "Happy Jack" came on the first-class scene, Yorkshire already possessed two good fast men in Allen Hill and Tom Emmett. Since neither showed any sign of yielding his role or place in the side, it is possible that Ulyett might have realized there was not much future for him as a bowler who could also bat a little on occasions. The Yorkshire side at this time could boast of only one really first-rate batsman in the ranks (Ephraim Lockwood), and it is possible that Ulyett might have concluded it would be more advantageous for him to pay more attention to the development of his own skills in that department of the game. At any rate, his bowling was much less successful in 1875 – only thirteen wickets at almost twenty-eight runs each, and only one outstanding performance (1–12 and 7–40) in the contest with Surrey at Bramall Lane, in the middle of June. On the other hand, there was some improvement in his batting, and in the match against Lancashire at Old Trafford, on June 24, 25, and 26, he registered his first half-century, scoring exactly 50. A week later, he made his debut in the series Gentlemen v Players at The Oval, though he achieved little with either bat or ball, and he was not selected for the equivalent fixture at Lord's. The next season followed a similar pattern. Although his bowling showed a tally of twenty rather expensive wickets, he scored rather more consistently with the bat. This was, perhaps, a foreshadowing of things lying in the not too distant future, for the burly Yorkshireman was about to come into his own with the willow.

In his conception of the art of batting, George Ulyett was a sort of Victorian Ian Botham. A punishing hitter, convinced that the best form of defence was attack, he exploited all the natural advantages of his magnificent physique. There was no prodding and poking about the block hole when he was at the wickets, and even when he was forced into playing a defensive stroke, he would hit the ball hard rather than letting it come limply on to the bat. Caring little for the pace of the bowling, for slow and fast alike were grist to his mill, he exulted in his physical powers, revelling in the exhilaration of smiting the ball into the far reaches of the ground. No mere slogger, but a scientific batsman and a rapid scorer, he forced the run rate with all the strokes – *all*, since he amassed his runs all round the wicket with drives, cuts, and leg-hits. Above all, it was his driving that entranced the spectators, and in those days when you had to send the ball clear out of the ground to score a six, he was famous for hitting sixes. His method, then, was based on a splendid combination of keen eyesight, timing, and physical strength, and a determination to enjoy himself at all costs. Those last few words expose the flaw in his temperament. Time and again, his innings would come to an abrupt end through sheer recklessness, and on one occasion one of the cricket annuals castigated him with the remark that his batting average "would be even greater if an insane impatience occasionally did not cause him to lose his wicket." These failures, fortunately, were offset by many a sterling deed that made him one of the most exciting and attractive batsmen of his time. All the same, the spectators never knew quite what to expect, and, looking ahead, one of the most striking instances of this feature of his batting occurred in one short week in the summer of 1880. Yorkshire defeated Nottinghamshire by five wickets at Bramall Lane, on August 9, 10, and 11, but although he captured one wicket, his personal contribution to the home side's victory was minimal, since he was dismissed for a "pair," clean bowled in both innings. An encounter with Surrey at The Oval took place immediately afterwards, and "Happy Jack" bounced back with a vengeance. As though to silence any criticism of his recent failure, he scored a splendid century, which "fairly broke the Surrey bowling." His innings, one of the most perfect he had ever played until then, was worth 141 runs, his highest to date, but his tactics had been much more circumspect than usual. In a stay of about three and a-half hours, he struck two mighty drives for 5 and nine 4s, but his score also included fifty-nine singles, an extraordinarily large proportion for him. Another almost unparalleled feature of this performance was a complete absence of any chance given to the field.

As a member of the team managed and led by James Lillywhite, junior,

Ulyett made his first visit to Australia and New Zealand in the winter of 1876–77. In the "odds" matches, which constituted the bulk of the programme, it might be conjectured that he did not take himself too seriously, since his performance with the bat was anything but consistent, and in the contest against Fifteen of New South Wales at Sydney, on January 12, 13, and 15, 1877, he suffered the mortification of being dismissed for a "pair" by F.R. Spofforth. In the three first-class matches, however, he achieved the best record for the whole team with an average of 48.60. Against New South Wales on even terms, following immediately after his humiliation in the "odds" affair, he played "a dashing innings for 94," the highest figure attained by any English batsman throughout the tour. His scores in the first Test at Melbourne, on March 15, 16, 17, and 19, were nothing out of the ordinary (10 and 24), but he captured three wickets for 39 runs in Australia's second innings. In the first, he had no official victim, though he did manage to dispose of the home side's champion batsman, Charles Bannerman, who had made 165 when he was obliged to retire hurt with the middle finger of his right hand "split . . . in all directions." England, defeated in the first encounter, were victorious in the second contest at the same venue a fortnight later, and Ulyett was in excellent form. Apart from taking three wickets at a cost of 16 runs each, he was England's top scorer in both innings, making 52 in the first and 63 in the second, during which he "hit the bowling to all parts of the field."

The final match of the tour was an "odds" affair against Twenty-two of South Australia at Adelaide, on April 14, 16, and 17, 1877, and "Happy Jack" distinguished himself in more ways than one. Top scorer once more, he made 17 and 58, his second knock being "the grandest exhibition of hard hitting which had ever been seen in Adelaide." His treatment of the bowling while practising was even more severe, and after several doughty blows he ruined the face of the blade. Examining it critically, he made a magnanimous gesture which won the heart of a youthful admirer by handing the bat to him and saying, "Ah doan't think mooch o' t'baat, laad. Taak it away." The astonished youngster asked what he should do with it, and back came the reply, "Taak it yoursen, laad. Ah doan't want it!"

The success which crowned his efforts with the bat down under seems to have spurred Ulyett on to even greater efforts. Far from being jaded by the demands of the tour, he began striding to the forefront of England's leading batsmen in his most successful season to date. With an aggregate of 844 runs, he registered an average of over twenty (24.11) for the first time on home soil. Another first was his maiden century in first-class cricket while assisting the Players against the Gentlemen at Prince's, on July 5, 6, and 7, 1877. Top scorer for the professionals with 53 at his first attempt, he more than doubled this figure in the second innings, logging fourteen boundaries in hitting up 118, though luck was on his side in the matter of missed catches.

From 1877 as far on as 1892, Ulyett was an almost automatic selection for the Players. All told, he appeared in thirty-seven matches, in at least ten of which he held the captaincy from the early 1880s until his final encounter with the Gentlemen at Hastings, on September 12, 13, and 14, 1892. His record as a batsman in the series was one of the best of his age. Going to the wickets sixty-five times, he attained an aggregate of 1,791 runs and, without the assistance of a single not-out innings, marked an average of 27.55. He passed the half-century twelve times, and twice he reached three figures. His best performance occurred at The Oval, on July 3, 4, and 5, 1884, when he remained at the crease nearly three hours, scoring 134, including no less than twenty-one 4s. The Gentlemen had every reason to dread the appearance of Ulyett that season. In the fixture at Lord's, immediately afterwards, he scored 94 in the first innings and 64 in the second, opening his broad shoulders to smite the ball into the pavilion several times on both occasions.

With his predilection for using long-handle tactics, there was always the distinct possibility that Ulyett would run the risk of sacrificing his wicket by sheer impetuousity and a lack of judgement. In the two Gentlemen v Players matches of 1878, his tally in four innings was only 52 runs, with a highest score of 24, and three times he was dismissed by catches. One of these occurred when he essayed one of his favourite drives, failed to get hold of the ball properly, and holed out in the deep to a fielder stationed in front of the pavilion. Later, while strolling round the ground, he happened to walk past Lord Londesborough's carriage, in which the nobleman's wife was seated, watching the play. Lady Londesborough, it may be remembered, had a soft spot for Yorkshire cricketers, deriving considerable amusement from their natural, unpolished modes of speech, which would without question have shocked many another high society dame in those days. As Ulyett hove in sight at the side of the carriage, she immediately engaged him in conversation and asked him how he managed to get out from that particular ball. There was nothing disrespectful in his demeanour nor any intention of deliberately giving offence. On the other hand, he made no attempt to mince his words in answer to the question, saying, "Ah meant to poot t'booger over t'pavilion!" There was no mistaking the meaning, but at least the delighted Lady Londesborough had one more Yorkshire "pro" tale to add to her collection.

Progressing from strength to strength in 1878, Ulyett registered two more personal records. For the first time in his career, he achieved a four-figure aggregate, amassing 1,270 runs at an average of 27.02, which gave him the fifth position in the national table at the end of the season. The contest between Yorkshire and Gloucestershire at Bramall Lane, on July 29, 30, and 31, had been designated as Tom Emmett's benefit match, and it would be tempting to think that Ulyett made a special effort to do old Tom proud. In Yorkshire's second innings, in which he shared a long stand with Ephraim Lockwood, the visitors' bowling "was mercilessly punished." Shrugging off the sight of several chances going to ground, Ulyett raced to a rapid century, notching 109, which included two huge 6s and eleven 4s. He was particularly severe on Mr R.F. Miles, whose slow left-arm trundling went unrewarded at a cost of 86 runs. Sixteen of these (the two 6s and a 4) came off one four-ball over, and it would be reasonable to assume that Ulyett bore the chief responsibility for destroying the amateur's length, accuracy, and confidence in equal proportions, since Mr Miles conceded nine wides in the innings. All in all, Tom Emmett's benefit match was an event to treasure throughout the broad acres: the home side won by 244 runs; Ephraim Lockwood also made a century (107); the beneficiary caught and bowled W.G. in the visitors' first innings; and Willie Bates captured eleven wickets.

This was the only hundred appearing against Ulyett's name in 1878, but his uninhibited desire to knock the cover off the ball yielded nine hard-hitting half-centuries. As a bowler himself, he achieved his highest tally of wickets so far, with 53 dismissals at 17.45 each. His best performance occurred in the contest against Surrey at Bramall Lane, on July 15 and 16. Having knocked up 67 runs with ruthless ease, he opened the Yorkshire attack. Downcast, perhaps, by the pitiless punishment meted out to their bowlers – the home side's total was 309 – the Surrey batsmen were overwhelmed, managing no more than 78. Ulyett, with his fast, bumping deliveries, bowled unchanged throughout the innings, returning an analysis of 20–9–30–7. This, as it turned out, was the best bowling performance in one innings of his whole career.

"Happy Jack" wintered abroad for the second time in 1878–79, when Lord Harris took his team to tour the Antipodes. This was the occasion when the captain and manager signed up ten other amateurs, none of whom could really claim to be a top-notch performer with the ball and, in accordance with the well established tradition that the gentlemen should concern themselves with the run-getting while professionals got on with the bowling, Lord Harris engaged the services of Tom Emmett and George Ulyett. Nobody could criticize the selection of Emmett; though primarily a bowler, he possessed sufficient ability in the other departments of the game to justify his place in the team. Doubtless also, Lord Harris was fully conscious of the fact that Tom's famous sense of humour would never prevent him from placing the interests of the team before his own and, as related elsewhere, this was Tom's most successful tour down under. The wisdom of choosing Ulyett to share the brunt of the bowling was much more debatable. True enough, his record with the ball in the summer of

1878 had been far from negligible, and possibly this exerted some influence over the England skipper when he finalized his team-list. Whatever the thought processes may have been at that time, the fact remains that by now Ulyett had come to regard himself as a batsman who could perform adequately with the ball rather than the other way round. There was also the matter of temperament. Though far from being a sycophant, Emmett had the knack of getting on well with his captain, based on a system of liking and mutual respect. The same could hardly be said of Ulyett, whose northern independence of mind almost smacked at times of insubordination as far as Lord Harris was concerned, and this somewhat ill-assorted pair failed to hit it off during the tour, though they enjoyed better relations in later years.

As Emmett's bowling partner in the minor matches, Ulyett made a valuable contribution, capturing his wickets at less than 10 runs apiece. In the five first-class matches, the first of which was a Test, his performance with the ball was very much below par – only eleven dismissals at an average of 33.36, with a best analysis of four for 13, redeemed by one glittering exploit. It was an entirely different story when it came to his batting, at least as far as the statistics went. Ulyett was triumphant, heading the list with an aggregate of 306, a highest score of 71, and an average of 34.00. It was evident that, as usual, he cast caution to the winds and played largely for his own enjoyment, and it may be imagined that his attitude and performance were topics for discussion in the hotels frequented by the amateurs. In his account of the tour in "Green Lillywhite (1880)," Mr C.A. Absolom makes a pungent comment when describing the first encounter with New South Wales at Sydney, on January 24, 25, 27, and 28, 1879. The English Eleven reached 248 in their first innings, the most successful batsmen being Mr F. Penn (56), Ulyett (51), and the captain (50). Of this Absolom wrote rather tartly that "The scoring on behalf of the Englishmen was very level, Mr PENN'S innings being perhaps the best, and ULYETT'S the worst." He did, however, pay tribute to the Yorkshireman's 71 against Victoria at Melbourne, on February 21, 22, 24, and 25, declaring that the innings was "a very fine one." Praise came also from Lord Harris ("a particularly fine innings").

On the whole, nevertheless, his lordship made no secret of his disapproval of "Happy Jack's" conception of batting, either during the tour or years later, and probably felt in his autocratic way that the Yorkshireman should have been more amenable to discipline in following his captain's instructions. Whereas Emmett was of the greatest use to the team, Lord Harris recollected in a rather curmudgeonly manner that "Ulyett was something of a failure, missing catches and playing some childish innings." Perhaps the peer was subconsciously a little miffed by the memory that Ulyett beat him by a shortish head in the first-class batting averages. At any rate, the jovial professional's insubordination reached its height in the second contest against New South Wales at Sydney, on February 7, 8, and 10, 1879. This was the third first-class match of the tour, and as the first two had ended in defeats, the English skipper was more than anxious to register a victory. He began well by winning the toss, and the opening pair, Messrs A.N. Hornby and A.P. Lucas, put on 125 before they were separated, and in came Ulyett at first wicket down. Not long afterwards, he was joined by Lord Harris at number four, and this pair took the total from 132 to 217, when Ulyett was caught just short of the boundary after playing what his lordship described as "a hard hitting but most extraordinarily lucky innings" – in other words, a typical Ulyett performance.

"Happy Jack" retained a vivid recollection of this and other incidents connected with this particular match. Spofforth was bowling at his deadliest, but Ulyett refused to play it safe ("Ah 'ad a 'itting fit on!"), much to the dismay of his partner, who nagged him with a perpetual harangue between overs ("George, do play steady; we want to win this match"). The Yorkshireman's reply to one of these exhortations took the shape of two 4s and a 3 in the next over. Eventually, after being urged yet again to "play steady," the errant professional remarked, "Boot, my lord, Ah feel rather like 'itting 'em." Lord Harris gave up and snapped, "All right, damn you, go on." He went on, scoring at the rate of a run a minute, and when he was dismissed off one more lofted drive and set off towards the dressing-room, his partner was unable to resist the temptation to utter a final rebuke, saying rather pettishly, "Didn't I tell you you would get out?" Ulyett insisted on having the last word, which doubtless did little to endear him to his skipper. Defiant to the end, he retorted, "Yes, my lord, boot Ah've poot 55 down on t'book and 'ave 'ad a rare good time." There could scarcely have been a more revealing illustration of Ulyett's somewhat self-centred philosophy. As far as he was concerned, come what may, batting was nothing more or less than a form of self-indulgence, with the pleasure of the individual taking precedence over the good of the side. On some occasions, it paid dividends; on others, it did not.

Ulyett's dazzling display of pyrotechnics at Sydney was staged during the infamous Riot Match, when spectators and some of the home side objected to an umpire's decision adverse to their cause, and play was interrupted by an invasion of the pitch by many members of the crowd. The details of this unfortunate affair have been narrated elsewhere, but there were two incidents worthy of note for the complete role played by Ulyett in the proceedings. On the second day, while the English team were waiting – in vain, as it turned out – for the restart of play, Tom Emmett took the opportunity to slip off and change his sweaty socks, and after a while Lord Harris noticed he was missing and asked where he was. This was a heaven-sent chance for "Happy Jack" to perform one of his notorious leg-pulls. Assuming a perfectly straight face and a grave demeanour, he informed the captain that Tom had been so terrified by the crowd that he was last seen tearing away from the ground like a madman, and that a cab had been sent after him to fetch him back! As far as I can recall, Lord Harris did not record his reaction to this somewhat ill-timed jest.

The other incident concerned the events of the final day, when play was resumed with New South Wales having scored 18 runs for the loss of one wicket in their second innings. They were bundled out for 49 by Emmett and Ulyett operating on a damaged pitch. While Emmett was the more destructive (5–21), this was the occasion when "Happy Jack" marked his best bowling performance of the tour in first-class matches, accounting for four of the opposition for only 13 runs. His feat was far more startlingly spectacular that it looks on paper at first. Achieving the hat-trick and one to spare, he took two wickets with the last two balls of one over and two more with the first two deliveries of the next! Such a splendid exploit doubtless redeemed him in the eyes of Lord Harris, if only for the time being.

The weather throughout much of the summer of 1879 was depressingly damp and dreary, and it was hardly surprising that Ulyett's successes with the bat compared less favourably with those of the previous season. His aggregate fell to 868 runs, his average to 22.84, with a highest score of 98 ("a most admirable innings"), but this was sufficient to place him tenth in the national batting averages. He was not called upon to do much bowling and was credited with only sixteen wickets at 15.68 apiece. Nevertheless, against Lancashire at Bramall Lane, on August 11, 12, and 13, he recorded one of his best bowling performances in the visitors' first innings, capturing seven wickets at the low cost of only 32 runs and, it may be added, all of his victims were clean bowled.

"Happy Jack" was able to participate in the festivities of Christmas 1879 at home, but he had not been leading a life of contemplative seclusion and idleness ever since the end of the English season. In the early autumn, he was a member of that party of professionals from Nottinghamshire and Yorkshire engaged by Richard Daft to undertake a short tour of Canada and the USA. Since all the matches were played against "odds," it is possible that Ulyett did not bother himself too much about the cricketing side of the proceedings. His record with the bat was almost disappointing – seventh out of twelve in the table of averages at not much more than 15 runs per innings, and a highest score of 44 – and his most memorable exploit of the tour was probably the practical joke he played upon one of his Yorkshire team-mates during a sight-seeing visit to Niagara Falls. This was the occasion when, not long after catching sight of a snake, Tom Emmett took off his boots and socks to bathe his feet in the cooling waters.

It was Ulyett who stuffed one of the discarded socks with worms, so that when the unfortunate Emmett's bare foot came in contact with the slimy mess, he was convinced that it was the dreaded snake. Uproarious laughter followed, of course, but all my sympathies are with Tom, and I don't think he ever really got his own back on his persecutor. Come to think of it, I cannot offhand recall any particular occasion when "Happy Jack" was ever the victim of a practical joke himself. The very sight of those broad shoulders and brawny arms would have been enough to deter any lesser man from taking such a liberty. And events in the not too distant future would prove that it was extremely unwise to tangle with George Ulyett on any pretext whatsoever.

Like his unfortunate victim at Niagara Falls, Ulyett held a brief, almost non-existent engagement as a member of the ground staff at Lord's. His name appears at the end of the list of ground bowlers for 1880 with the qualification, "for such matches as he is able to play." In the event, he turned out in only one first-class match for MCC during the season, taking part in the fixture with the University team at Cambridge, on May 13, 14, and 15. His name vanished from the roll from 1881 onwards, although he did in fact assist MCC once more in the contest against Kent at Canterbury, on August 6, 7, and 8, 1885.

Although Ulyett was back among the century-makers in 1880, with that excellent innings of 141 against Surrey mentioned previously, and averaged nearly two runs more per innings, his aggregate (929) was still well short of four figures. This comparative lack of success arose from a loss of form in the middle of the season and his besetting sin of impatience, which more than once cost him his wicket just when he seemed to be set for a long score. Nevertheless, he was generally regarded as the best professional batsman in England at that time, with the exception of William Barnes, of Nottinghamshire and MCC. Such a belief in Ulyett's undoubted talents was amply justified, and even more so in 1881, considering that his Nottinghamshire rival experienced a temporary decline in his run-getting powers. The Yorkshireman totalled 1,243 runs at 32.71 per innings, the best he had achieved so far. His reward was the fourth place in the national batting averages – the highest he ever attained throughout his whole career. The three above him in the list were all amateurs and, with Billy Barnes nowhere near in contention, there could be no proviso to the claim that he was the premier professional batsman in the country. His success was all the more remarkable, since in the encounter with Kent at Maidstone, on July 21 and 22, he strained his side so severely while bowling that he was missing from the Yorkshire ranks for around three weeks. Perhaps he was out of practice, having captured only ten wickets at 17.30 each up to the time he was incapacitated, and wisely, no doubt, he did no more bowling in first-class cricket for the remainder of the season. Many a dashing innings he played throughout that summer, with nine half-centuries to swell his aggregate. His best and only three-figure score came in the match between Yorkshire and Surrey at Huddersfield, on June 2 and 3, when, playing "with great freedom," he made 112 ("a grand innings"). Nine boundaries flowed from his bat, and he dominated a partnership which advanced Yorkshire's total from 27 to 161.

The siren songs of sunny climes lured Ulyett away from the damp chills and bitter winds of northern England in the winter months of 1881–82, and though he went from one triumph to another for much of the time, he came perilously close to self-destruction in a situation brought on by his own folly and lack of judgement. Lillywhite, Shaw, and Shrewsbury, the promoters of the tour, had organized an exceedingly ambitious itinerary. The principal destinations were Australia and New Zealand, but instead of following the more usual route, the party – minus Shrewsbury, who was ailing at the time – travelled across the North American continent, playing five "odds" matches as they made their way from east to west. Granted that the opposition was none of the best, but "Happy Jack," it could be confidently claimed, had another "rare good time," with a batting average of just under seventy. His most magnificent exploit occurred in the final contest of this leg of the tour against Twenty-two of San Francisco, on October 20 and 21, 1881, when he smashed the ball to all points of the compass for an unbeaten innings of 167.

The bowling resources of the English team were particularly strong, and although Ulyett was put on from time to time, he was able to concentrate most of his attention on his batting. In all matches, he passed 1,400 runs, and in the seven first-class contests he achieved easily the highest aggregate (549), averaging 39.21 and heading Shrewsbury in the table by one run, Arthur, however, being assisted by two not-out innings. In the four Test Matches, Ulyett's record was outstanding – 438 runs at an average of 54.75. He began with a splendid 87 in the first innings of the opening contest of the rubber at Melbourne, starting on December 31, 1881. In the second innings of the next encounter at Sydney, on February 17, 18, 20, and 21, 1882, he shared an opening stand of 122 with R.G. Barlow – the first hundred partnership for the first wicket in Test cricket. The stand was broken when "Happy Jack" was leg before wicket to G.E. Palmer, terminating "a capital, but somewhat lucky innings" of 67 – yet another typical Ulyett performance. Modest scores of 0 and 23 in the next contest were followed by his finest achievement as a batsman in international matches. In the final Test at Melbourne, on March 10, 11, 13, and 14, he massacred the Australian bowling in both innings, particularly Spofforth's (1–92 and 0–36). Exercising much more self-restraint than usual, which was just as well, since the second top score was Tom Emmett's 27, and giving only one or maybe two possible chances, he remained at the crease in the first innings until the sixth wicket fell, having scored 149 out of a total of 239. The match eventually petered out into a draw, but not before he had twisted the blade in the Australians' wounds "by scoring 64 in brilliant style in his second innings." Ulyett's exploit was a first in more ways than one. No English batsman had hitherto plundered Spofforth's bowling with such a degree of impunity, nor had the Yorkshireman so far reached 149 in a first-class match. Yet there was more redounding to his fame. This was the first Test hundred made by an English batsman in Australia and, in addition, all the runs were scored on the first day – a record which was not surpassed until R.W. Barber amassed 185 at Sydney, on January 7, 1966.

It is unfortunate to have to relate that, as well as winning so much glory, Ulyett tarnished his laurels by becoming involved in an unsavoury incident, which brought no credit to him and still less to the name of English cricket. One of his team-mates on the tours to Australia in 1876–77 and North America in 1879 was Nottinghamshire's John Selby, who seems to have chosen Ulyett for his chum during the visit down under in 1881–82. In addition to being a professional cricketer, the diminutive Selby was also an accomplished professional sprinter, and it appears that during his first trip to Australia he earned a supplement to his cricketing wages by arranging to take part in numerous foot races for wagers. According to Alfred Shaw, a fellow tourist, Selby managed to win most of these contests – "when it was necessary he should succeed." To this statement in his memoirs Shaw appends an ominous rider, saying, "It was in Selby's nature to dearly love 'a plant,' as the sporting term goes." If this judgement be accepted at its face value, it suggests that there was at least something not wholly admirable in Selby's character. It might also be conjectured that Selby, the senior of the pair by over two years, could have exercised a baleful influence over Ulyett and have been primarily responsible for leading his junior astray. By behaviour indiscreet almost to the verge of crass stupidity, they unleashed a series of events, the news of which spread from Australia all the way back to the old country, producing a spate of correspondence in the national and sporting press. An additional black mark against the pair of alleged miscreants was the disruption they caused to the harmonious relations within the ranks of the English team.

A preliminary affair, immediately preceding what might be called the main event, took place during the course of a minor match played at Cootamundra, on December 14, 1881. As related elsewhere, John Selby and his Nottinghamshire team-mate Will Scotton came to blows over what was seemingly a private matter, with the latter emerging as the victor. Then, Ulyett, against whom Scotton did not stand a chance, intervened

John Selby

W. E. Midwinter

with his fists. When asked later to explain his version of this brawl, Ulyett essayed to make light of the whole matter, describing it as "boxing for skill," and when the two antagonists began to lose their tempers and start slugging wildly at each other, he claimed that he put a stop to it, saying, "Now, if you doan't drop it, Ah'll taak you both, and 'jowl' your 'eads together." The prospect of having one's head "jowled" by George Ulyett is, to say the least, rather daunting, since in size and physique he was one of the most powerful men in the team.

The fracas at Cootamundra was probably extraneous to the various machinations of the next match, an ill-starred contest against Victoria at Melbourne, on December 16, 17, 19, and 20, 1881. The home side totalled 251, and having skittled out the Englishmen for 146, attempted to force a victory when the visitors were compelled to follow on. A sterling knock of 80 not out from Arthur Shrewsbury enabled Shaw's team to reach 198, leaving Victoria the apparently simple task of scoring 94 to win. This target proved to be beyond them. Caught on a rain-sodden pitch that might have been tailor-made for Ted Peate, who captured four wickets in his first two overs and ended up with figures of 31–17–30–6, the Victorians were restricted to a total of 75.

While the match was in progress, it was reported that more than one member of the English team was observed being wined if not dined by some shady representatives of the local betting ring, and a rumour quickly reached Shaw's ears that two of his players – easily identified as Selby and Ulyett – had allegedly been offered some sort of bribe to ensure that Victoria would win the contest and thereby line the pockets of the bookmakers. The bearer of these tidings was W.E. Midwinter, another of Shaw's players. Born in England but a resident of Australia, Midwinter spent several years earning his living as a professional cricketer by commuting between the two countries. During the course of his career, in those days when international qualifications were treated in a more relaxed manner, he established a unique record – one unlikely ever to be broken – by playing for Australia against England and, on this tour of 1881–82, England against Australia. You cannot help feeling some sympathy for Billy Midwinter with his divided loyalties, especially as the opposition in the current match was his own state of Victoria. The two alleged recipients of the bribes eventually became aware that Midwinter, whose assistance they had tried unsuccessfully to enlist in their plotting, had "grassed" on them, and they determined to be avenged. Although Midwinter, the tallest member of the team, possessed a splendid physique, he was evidently not particularly skilled at fist-fighting, and he was subjected to a severe "jowling" by Ulyett, possibly assisted in the nefarious deed by Selby.

Having been alerted to the dangers lying ahead in the contest with

Victoria, Shaw kept a wary eye on the activities of the two culprits. There were certainly some scraps of circumstantial evidence, which could have been interpreted as an indication that Ulyett and Selby were not giving of their best to the English cause. The former was dismissed clean bowled by G.E. Palmer in both innings for only 2 and 4, and when Victoria went in for a second time he missed a catch and gave away runs with an overthrow. Selby did a little better with the bat, scoring 6 and 23, and he assisted in getting rid of H.F. Boyle, the Victorian captain, who was threatening to knock off the required runs. Five catches were held in Victoria's second innings – three by Shrewsbury, one by Shaw, and one by Selby. It is inconceivable that two of the promoters of the tour would have been anything but anxious to win the struggle, so clearly it was Selby whom Shaw had in mind when he wrote that "a batsman was out by the ball going up inside the fieldsman's arm and sticking there – not, I have reason to think, with the catcher's intentional aid." One can well imagine that the blood pressure of the betting fraternity rose several degrees at the sight of Selby's ludicrous attempt to miss the catch.

The English team split up on the way home, with Selby and Ulyett going on ahead, presumably with the intention of presenting *their* version of the sorry business first, and soon the storm of what became known as "The Cricket Scandal" broke over the heads of the innocent and others not perhaps so innocent. Letters landed on the desks of the editors of various journals from persons prominent, such as Lord Harris, and some of lesser eminence in the world of cricket. His lordship asserted that he had no reason whatever for supposing Selby, whom he did not know all that well, "other than an honourable cricketer." As for Ulyett, with whom he had had a much closer acquaintance dating back to the days of the 1878–79 tour, Harris declared, "I would willingly stake my honour on his" – which, all things considered, was magnanimous rather than prudent. In addition, his lordship called for an affidavit to be sworn to and signed by those concerned in order to clear their names.

Meanwhile the promoters, fearing no doubt for their own good name, particularly in the matter of being able to organize future tours, rallied to the defence. James Lillywhite, junior, who stood as one of the umpires in the match against Victoria, averred that he had seen no evidence that any member of the team had ever at any time not played to win. As for the allegations of attempts to throw the match, "this evil report must have been circulated by the party offering the bribe in a moment of chagrin at losing his money" – a curious declaration implying that bribery was at least attempted by the Melbourne bookies. Later, in accordance with a request from MCC, Alfred Shaw co-signed a statement with John Selby, denying that any member of the team had been offered a bribe to lose any of the matches, adding that they were unaware of the accusation until their return home. In all this welter of declarations and affidavits, self-interest took precedence over the truth, and in his memoirs years later Shaw told a vastly different story. There was, of course, no watertight case to present against the culprits, and with Selby off the hook and interest in "The Cricket Scandal" on the wane, the matter subsided into oblivion.

The crucial match against Victoria occurred early in the tour of 1881–82, and if George Ulyett felt any pangs of conscience at the time, he certainly did not allow them to have an adverse effect upon his form, considering his prolonged success with the bat down under. Back home, however, while the turmoil of "The Cricket Scandal" thundered and rumbled all around him at the beginning of the English season, it is possible that he might have felt uneasy with the development of events, as the letters and demands for affidavits followed each other in quick succession. After participating in two matches, with a highest score of only 46, he evidently decided that it was high time he took steps to clear his name. The opportunity occurred at Lord's, on May 29, 1882, the opening day of Over Thirty v Under Thirty, arranged for the benefit of the MCC Cricketers' Fund. Ulyett was assisting the senior side for the first time, and after their captain (W.G.) had won the toss and elected to bat, he expressed a desire to make a formal statement before the MCC Committee. It was not, of course, possible to assemble the whole body at such short notice, but the secretary managed to collect together four influential members in his private room. Ulyett, accompanied by two of his team-mates for the occasion (Mr A.N. Hornby and Tom Emmett), presumably to act as witnesses as well as giving some moral support, appeared before the ad hoc group and made the following affirmation: "As far as I know neither I nor any of the team know anything about it. It is not true that any offer of money, as far as I am aware, was made to me or anyone else."

With that the committee and the world at large had to be content. How economical, if at all, Ulyett had been with the truth, it is impossible to say, but this deed of self-exculpation worked wonders, as though, like Christian, he had shed a crushing burden from his shoulders. Going in at first wicket down after the early dismissal of his captain, he shared a stand with Mr Hornby which took the total from 19 to 165. Both batsmen, as was their wont, enjoyed some luck, but Ulyett's innings was "superb." His 138, his highest of the season, included thirteen 4s, three of them off successive deliveries. All in all, he had an excellent record in 1882, achieving an aggregate of 1,542 runs (average 27.53), with two centuries. On one vital occasion, however, his lack of patience brought about his own and England's undoing in the contest with Australia at The Oval, on August 28 and 29. Of his performance in making 26 in the first innings it was written: "Ulyett was top scorer, and yet it is of him I must complain, for, when he was well set, he rushed out of his ground in a wild attempt to drive Mr Spofforth." He was, of course, easily stumped, but if this judgement sounds somewhat severe, how much more so was the opinion of T.P. Horan, a member of the Australian team! The latter declared that the impetuous Yorkshireman never played worse cricket: he gave a stumping chance before he had scored, had his stumps grazed several times, and scarcely made a good stroke.

There was a notable revival in Ulyett's bowling powers in 1882, when he accounted for 61 victims at 15.77 apiece. He did rather less bowling in 1883 but still secured 44 wickets, which included a hat-trick against Lancashire at Bramall Lane, on July 16 and 17, when he achieved figures of five for 16, all clean bowled. His batting, however, rose to previously unscaled heights with a career best aggregate of 1,562 runs (average 31.87). This figure included twelve half-centuries, but by some strange quirk of fate his best score was only 84. In the next season, his aggregate dropped by over two hundred runs and his average by two. On the other hand, he made three hundreds, the first being his previously mentioned 134 against the Gentlemen at The Oval. The other two were even more characteristic efforts. Against Middlesex at Bramall Lane, on August 18, 19, and 20, 1884, he "hit with the utmost brilliancy and dash," and his 107 – all scored before luncheon on the third day (!) – included two 6s and thirteen 4s. His most imperial and imperious performance was reserved for his final innings of the Yorkshire programme in the encounter with MCC at Scarborough, on September 8, 9, and 10. Racing to 146 not out, he scored fourteen 4s and, in addition, hoisted three colossal 6s out of the ground.

Unfortunately, "Happy Jack" failed to reach anything like this form in the three Test Matches against Australia, averaging only 12.00 in four innings. On the principle, however, that if you are out of luck with the bat you could always make up for it with the ball, he registered his best ever performance in Test cricket. In the second innings of the contest at Lord's, on July 21, 22, and 23, 1884, his captain of former days, Lord Harris, gave him his chance on a nasty, bumping pitch. The Australians struggled and lost the battle for survival, when Ulyett pitilessly destroyed them by capturing seven wickets for 36 runs. His extraordinary dismissal of G.J. Bonnor has passed into legend. A batsman after Ulyett's own heart, Bonnor seized the opportunity to punish a half-volley by launching into a terrifying straight drive. Ulyett flung up his right hand instinctively, the ball smashed with stinging force into his palm, and his fingers, by reflex action, closed automatically round it. This was one of the most famous caught and bowleds in the history of Test cricket. I don't suppose that the bowler worried much about it later, but viewed in the cold light of day he was courting disaster. If the ball had sped through a couple of inches lower, he would probably

G. E. Palmer

T. P. Horan

have been out of action nursing a broken wrist for the rest of the season.

At Lord's, as far back as July 18, 1877, Ulyett underwent a chastening and, for him, a most unusual experience. Assisting Gloucestershire and Yorkshire against England, he was dismissed for one run in his second innings after failing to trouble the scorers in his first. This single evidently took him some time to acquire, since while he was at the wickets, the other batsman (W.G.) increased his score by 33. Such a disparity in run-getting rarely if ever fell to "Happy Jack's" lot in subsequent years, particularly when playing for Yorkshire in the 1880s. There have been several illustrious pairs of opening batsmen in the Club's history; first in the line came George Ulyett and Louis Hall. They were about the same height, though Hall, less powerfully built and somewhat stoop-shouldered, looked smaller. His dark hair was usually concealed by a tight-fitting cap perched above a pair of jug-handle ears, and on his lower lip, nestling beneath a moustache even heavier than Ulyett's, he often sported a small tuft of hair. They were total opposites in character and outlook: "Happy Jack" noisy, boisterous, cracking jokes, and enjoying his glass of ale; Hall lean, lugubrious, a quiet, serious teetotaller – the first ever to play for Yorkshire, according to Lord Hawke! – and a part-time Methodist lay preacher. A similar sharp contrast prevailed in their approach to batting, with Ulyett cast in the role of the carefree swashbuckler, and Hall as the earnest, plodding journeyman. Rarely can the styles of two batsmen have been so neatly dovetailed in the interests of a team, for Louis was the supreme stonewaller to end all stickers, though two of his contemporaries would have been eminently qualified to contest his claim. Many a time and oft, the Yorkshire innings began with a long stand, giving rise to such descriptions as "Ulyett batted in very fine style, hitting all round with great vigour, while Hall played in his usual careful manner." On that particular occasion, the first wicket fell at 107, when Hall departed for only 32. It would be possible, though not entirely profitable, to compile a complete catalogue of similar instances, so let just three more suffice: Ulyett made at different times 29 out of 36, 40 out of 56, and 48 out of 60. Each was a perfect foil for the other, and although Ulyett in full flow was by far the more attractive to watch, who, in the end, is to decide which was of greater value to his County? Hall's average for Yorkshire was 23.52, Ulyett's 24.20.

"Happy Jack" paid his fourth visit down under in 1884–85. In stark contrast to his doings in first-class matches on the previous tour, his performance was a doleful saga of almost unrelieved disappointment. Never a man to do things by halves, he tumbled from the top of the batting table to the bottom with an aggregate of 136 runs in twelve innings and an average of 11.33. His only innings of any merit occurred

Louis Hall

in the Adelaide Test, on December 12, 13, 15, and 16, 1884, when he made "a dashing 68." Going to the wickets six more times in Tests, he could manage no higher score than 10. His exploits with the ball against Australia provided a slightly more satisfying result – fourteen wickets at 21.07 each.

Ulyett's performance in the minor matches was of an entirely different character. Scoring far more runs, he dominated the bowling time after time with overwhelming might. His most outstanding exploit occurred in the game with Twenty-two of Maryborough and District in February 1885. After scoring 53 in the first innings, he exactly doubled this figure by knocking up 106 not out in the second. This splendid deed was acknowledged by the award, donated by a prominent local resident, of 250 shares in a gold mine, which the recipient disposed of by auction.

Away from the cricket field, "Happy Jack" became involved in two characteristic incidents. Faced with the urgent necessity of making a two-mile journey to board their ship at Suez, he joined with Alfred Shaw in hiring a boat and a crew of two Arabs. After they had gone about a mile, the two natives rested on their oars, refusing to go any further, unless they were paid an extra fee. Jove-like in his wrath, Ulyett threatened to put one of them over the side, though I doubt whether the words he used were identical with those attributed to him by Shaw. Betraying a woeful lack of judgement, the boatmen persisted in pursuing their efforts at extortion, until Ulyett seized hold of one of them and hurled him into the water. The journey was completed with the two cricketers manning the oars, one Arab cowering in terror in the boat, and the other swimming frantically in their wake. Every time he tried to climb back aboard, "Happy Jack," employing what Shaw delicately calls "his decorated Yorkshire lingo," told him exactly what he would do to him. It was, if you like, another instance of Ulyett's celebrated "jowling" and a prime example of an eminent Victorian's attitude to devious foreigners. The offending boatmen were not only deprived of their whole fee but given into custody as well.

Of much greater fame in the Ulyett legend was the story of the hero's escape from sharks. It was one of "Happy Jack's" favourites, though, according to Shaw, he adorned the incident "with all the embroidery that he was so well capable of weaving around his oft-told tales." Having partaken of a convivial champagne breakfast, the English cricketers set out on a launch to overtake the ship ferrying them to their next port of call. There was a good deal of larking about, and Ulyett began teasing one of the passengers, a young doctor, saying that the latter needed bleeding. Somewhat improbably, the Yorkshireman produced a lancet ("I always carried one to make people believe I knew something about surgery"!!) and advanced upon his victim. The medic shoved his tormentor away so roughly that Ulyett did a backward somersault into the sea. As he struck out and tried to regain the launch, somebody yelled that a shark was coming, and he pulled out his clasp-knife, opened it, and prepared to defend himself. Fortunately, however, Jaws ignored him, and he was hauled dripping into the boat. The white-faced doctor was full of abject apologies, presenting him with a 'possum rug and promising to give him £100 – which promise, in fact, was never fulfilled. A few of the details supplied by the narrator, such as the lancet, the shark, and the clasp-knife, are a little hard to swallow, and it is possible that he combined elements from two incidents in concocting his story. Some two weeks previously, he had undergone the experience of tumbling over the side into what were certainly shark-infested waters, from which he emerged unscathed. Fate, perhaps, inflicted the two duckings on Ulyett as a sort of punishment for his treatment of the Arab boatmen.

Ulyett reached his 1,000 runs and more in each of the next three English summers, his most successful being 1887, when he scored 1,487 runs with an average of 38.12 (eighth in the national table). His aggregate included four centuries, the most he ever recorded in one season. The best, and in fact the highest of his first-class career, came in the contest against Derbyshire at Bramall Lane, on July 18 and 19, which ended in an enormous victory for Yorkshire. At the end of the opening day, the visitors had finished their first innings, and Ulyett had reached 102 not out, having survived a shooter, which struck the bottom of the off-stump, shook the bail, but failed to knock it to the ground. His eventual contribution to the total of 399 was almost exactly half – 199, including nineteen 4s. There is a story that Joe Hunter, the last man, had been warned to play carefully to allow "Happy Jack" to reach 200 but soon hit up a catch. On being reproached for this lapse, he replied that he couldn't trust his partner and was afraid the latter might get out. This, to me, sounds like an adaptation of the tale of Ted Peate and the untrustworthy "Mester Stood" at The Oval in 1882! In some ways, Ulyett's innings was a rather uncharacteristic performance, since he remained at the wickets for nearly six hours, during which he gave only one chance, and not a single 6 appeared against his name in the book. One of the most remarkable features, however, was the fact that he carried his bat through the completed innings. This was the first and, not surprisingly in view of his technique, the only occasion he did so. Louis Hall, with his much safer and less enterprising system of batting, achieved the feat fifteen times, with only five three-figure scores!

Maybe "Happy Jack's" four hundreds represented some form of celebration for the advent of his benefit. He was allotted the contest against Surrey at Bramall Lane, on July 4, 5, and 6, 1887, and any Yorkshire supporter worth his salt would have considered it a right bad do, seeing that the visitors triumphed by an innings and 15 runs. To start with, things looked fairly bright for Ulyett. Given the task of opening the Yorkshire attack, he pulled off his best bowling performance of the season by taking five wickets for 56 runs. With the bat, however, it was almost a case of the beneficiary registering a "pair!" Clean bowled for a cipher at his first attempt, he survived a stumping chance before opening his account in the second. As though grateful for this fortuitous escape, he "hit finely" to make 41.

In financial terms, the affair was an enormous success, since around 13,000 spectators were present on the first day. During the match between Yorkshire and the Australians at the same ground, on May 21 and 22 of the following year, amid much "hearty and complimentary speech-making," the beneficiary was handed a cheque for £1,000, to which the tourists had contributed £20. In making the presentation, Mr M.J. Ellison, the Club president, observed that this was the best benefit ever given to a Yorkshire player, adding "that it was due to unvarying good conduct and sterling cricket." Few would wish to quarrel with the quality of the cricket, but it must be assumed that Mr Ellison had forgotten about the escapade with the ladder as far back as 1873, to say nothing of the murky details of "The Cricket Scandal."

That match with the tourists also ended in an innings defeat for Yorkshire, with Ulyett making 20 and 24. His form against Australia and various Australian teams around this stage of his career had been disappointing. The English seasons of 1886 and 1888, with the tour of 1887–88 intervening, saw him pitted against the old enemy in different guises on some twenty-five occasions. He acquitted himself not too badly on his final tour down under with an average of 22.33 and a highest score of 72. In the two English summers, he failed to reach the half-century, and over the three sessions the Australian bowlers restricted him to an average of under 18. During this period, he assisted England in six Test Matches – three in 1886, one on the tour, and two in 1888 – with pitiful results, averaging less than seven runs per innings. Worst of all was the rubber of 1888. Omitted from the side for the encounter at Lord's, he returned for the matches at The Oval, on August 13 and 14, and Old Trafford, at the end of the same month. He had one innings in each game, and on both occasions, a victim of C.T.B. Turner, he was unable to increase his aggregate of Test runs. These disasters were but a reflection of his overall performance in 1888. One of the cricket annuals for 1889 asserted that he "was in quite his best form last year," which was not too unreasonable on the basis of his doings for Yorkshire. Such a claim, however, could hardly be justified when his record in all first-class matches is taken into consideration. For the first time since 1880, he failed to reach 1,000 runs in an English summer – failed, moreover, by a wide margin, with an aggregate of only 798 (average 17.34) and a highest score of 56.

In spite of his somewhat modest achievements, Ulyett went forth on his seventh and final trip abroad in the winter of 1888–89. One of the members of Major R. Gardner Warton's team touring South Africa was recalled to England by a domestic bereavement, and a message was sent summoning the Yorkshireman to fill the vacancy. He scored a fine century in one of the minor matches but averaged only 16.00 in the two Tests. There was, however, a distinct similarity to the visit down under in 1884–85: an off-the-field incident made a larger contribution to the expanding Ulyett legend. Shortly before he embarked, a friend presented him with a four-gallon jar of whisky. As he made his way on board the ship, announcing that he was going to join the team in South Africa, two of the officers demanded to know what was in the jar. As usual, "Happy Jack" had a ready answer, saying, "They're breaking all t'baats out there owing to t'great 'eat. This is linseed oil to oil t'baats with." His explanation was accepted. Several days later, when he was standing treat to the officers, he revealed the secret of the "linseed-oil jar." His deception was forgiven instantly for the best of all reasons – the excellent brand of the whisky!

Ulyett was rarely caught on the hop and usually managed to extricate himself without much difficulty from an awkward situation. Once, possibly around 1881, when he was playing for Yorkshire in the away fixture with Cambridge University, he was invited to take breakfast with the Studd brothers. During the meal, while he was eating a chop, somebody passed him a dish of Devonshire cream by mistake. Perhaps Ulyett assumed that this was some strange taste peculiar to the upper classes and, not wishing to offend his hosts, helped himself to a liberal dollop of the cream and polished it off without batting an eyelid. This may also have been the occasion when, together with three of his team-mates, he was photographed wearing academic dress and contriving, for once, to look almost serious and ready to step up to the lectern at a moment's notice. The subject of an extempore lecture would doubtless have been the benefits of an education at a university where, as far as he could see, the undergraduates "get taught to drink beer from morning till night with baccy thrown in, just as school children learn reading and writing."

To the profound dismay of Ulyett's multitude of admirers in Yorkshire, his form with the bat was even worse in 1889, "the failure of the popular Sheffield cricketer forming one of the most regrettable features of the season." Time and again, he was dismissed cheaply, once clean bowled for a "pair" while assisting Louis Hall's team against the side got up by Richard Pilling at Holbeck, Leeds, on September 9 and 10, and at the end of the season his aggregate had dropped to only 546 runs, averaging 13.00 per innings. Such a marked decline in batting powers would have put many another player's place in the Yorkshire team in jeopardy. Thanks to his past reputation and a rejuvenation in his bowling, "Happy Jack" was able to survive his prolonged run of ill-luck with the bat. He captured 47 wickets at 17.65 apiece, and in the Roses Match at Huddersfield, on July 18 and 19 – a victory to the visitors by the slender margin of only 3 – he atoned for low scores by registering the best match performance of his career, taking twelve wickets for 102 runs (7–50 and 5–52).

With a more than welcome resurgence in the strength of his batting in 1890, Ulyett and his fans could have breathed a sigh of relief at the end of the season. Once more he was able to claim a place among the batsmen with four-figure aggregates, scoring 1,093 runs at an average of 20.62, and for the first time since 1887 he made a century, marking 107 against Gloucestershire at Bristol, on May 12, 13, and 14. The season was noteworthy also for his final appearance in Test Matches. Selected to assist England against Australia in the first encounter at Lord's, on July 21, 22, and 23, "he played fine cricket" in making 74, the top score of the match. As related elsewhere, the Yorkshire captain refused to release him to take part in the contest at The Oval, on August 11 and 12, while no Yorkshireman was chosen for the final match at Old Trafford, towards the end of the month, which was rained off without a ball being bowled.

Ulyett's last score in Test Matches was the highest he made in England, where, like his contemporary Billy Barnes, he was not particularly successful as a batsman. Judging by the results, both of them seemed far happier playing in Australian conditions. All told, Ulyett appeared in twenty-five Tests, scoring 949 runs at an average of 24.33, and capturing fifty wickets at 20.40 each. It would be far from easy to decide which of the two rendered greater service to England. Ulyett probably just had the edge on batting alone, but Barnes carried off the palm as an all-rounder.

The Yorkshire Eleven for a good proportion of Ulyett's career usually contained several members of what might be called the comic fraternity, not least "Happy Jack" himself. The type of humour was not all of a kind: Tom Emmett and Ted Peate, particularly the former, were famous for their quips and witticisms, whereas Ulyett's comedy was based on his acting abilities and his pronounced bent for leg-pulling. He was especially adept at assuming a character or a role requiring a display of extreme gravity or posing as an individual whose air of unassailable authority and self-confidence was so convincing that his victims rarely saw through the deception. Once, while strolling with Tom Emmett through the streets of a town, his eye fell upon a party of school teachers out for the day on a guided tour. Tickled by the all-pervading atmosphere of solemnity and spotting a vacant place in the ranks, he joined the procession and was so successful at passing himself off as a genuine member of the group that when he suddenly returned to Emmett's side, this apparent desertion by one of their number caused a flutter of consternation among the teachers.

Sometimes "Happy Jack" enlisted the ready assistance of Ted Peate in his pranks, as on the occasion when a new cricketer appeared on a Yorkshire ground for the first time and decided to get some pre-match practice before facing the dreaded Yorkshire bowling. Plenty of persons in everyday clothes were only too ready to oblige him. To start with, he got on quite well, until another bowler (slow left-arm) joined in the proceedings and succeeded in knocking down his wicket several times. Then up came another bowler (fast right-arm) to try his luck, with equally discouraging results. The new cricketer was in the depths of despair. If this was what mere spectators could do, he would have no hope of withstanding the bowling of Peate, Ulyett, and their team-mates. Filled with alarm and trepidation, he made his way into the dressing-room, where he was astonished to see the slow left and fast right-arm bowlers changing into cricketing garb for the match. They were, of course, Peate and Ulyett.

On another occasion, while walking about in Whitehall one evening, the same pair practised a much more audacious deception. Observing an array of carriages in the vicinity of Downing Street, they saw a crowd of guests in evening dress vanishing through the doorway of number 10. Discovering that Mr Gladstone was holding an official reception, the two Tykes decided to gate-crash the event. Instantly assuming the part of a stone-deaf man, Ulyett swept past the protesting door-keepers and, with Peate acting the part of his minder, the two intruders made their way into the throng of guests. Only one of the latter, an amateur cricketer, recognized them but kept quiet about it, and not long afterwards the two gate-crashers made their departure without giving themselves away.

"Happy Jack" never seems to have had any qualms about departing from the literal truth and indulging in implausible flights of fantasy purely for the purpose of creating laughter. Take, for example, his snake story, which would not have been out of place in Baron Munchausen's reminiscences. Once, in a minor match in Australia, the English team had been warned to tread carefully in the lush outfield for fear of venomous snakes lurking in the long grass. After play had been going on for some time without a single reptile putting in an appearance, "Happy Jack" was sent to do a stint of fielding in the deep and soon found himself chasing after the ball, which came to a stop on the edge of a hole in the ground. Just as he was about to pick it up, a snake suddenly popped its head out of the hole and gulped it down! Personally, I am prepared to accept that there may have been some of the creatures crawling about in the field. When it comes to the detail of the ball-swallowing snake, however, I would have to react in the same way as the first Duke of Wellington, when a stranger accosted him with the words, "Mr Jones, I believe." "If you believe that," retorted the Duke, "you'll believe anything!"

Again, if we are to trust his version of events, an up-country match in Australia was the setting for the most outrageous and completely successful leg-pull ever perpetrated by "Happy Jack." The incident, as he presented it, provided him with the script for another of his favourite stories, conceivably narrated with great gusto to many an appreciative audience over the pots of ale on a joyous evening. It is only fair to warn the reader in advance that some of the details apparently varied slightly with the re-telling of the tale, but the essence remained the same. According to Ulyett, he was doing a spell of bowling, and after one of his deliveries was struck away, the batsmen set off for a run. You have to imagine at this point, incidentally, that they were not exactly the surest or swiftest of run-stealers. The ball, intercepted by one of the fielders, was returned promptly to the bowler, who immediately whipped off the bails at his end. Then, observing that neither dithering batsman was in his ground, Ulyett dashed down the pitch and succeeded in putting down the other wicket as well. (This, perhaps, was the version retailed after the fourth or fifth pint of ale, whereas the less complicated one gives a caught and bowled followed by a run out. Whatever the details, the eventual outcome was identical). Ulyett appealed to the umpire, a rather inexperienced local man, who was in a quandary trying to decide which of the two should be given out. As umpire and batsmen were discussing this knotty problem, the bowler intervened in the debate. There could, he said, be no possible doubt in the matter, *both* of them were obviously out. The official was dubious about this assertion, reminding the claimant that two men could not be dismissed off the same delivery, whereupon Ulyett rose magnificently to the occasion. Assuming his most solemn and magisterial manner, he replied, "Ah, laads, but when t'same man poots both wickets down, you see, things are different!" Bowing to the apparently more knowledgeable judgement pronounced by a cricketer of "Happy Jack's" experience and reputation, the trio accepted this novel interpretation of the Laws of Cricket and turned a deaf ear to the repeated assurances from the rest of the English team that it was all a joke. The umpire resumed his position, the two batsmen went out, two new ones came in, and then they all got on with the match!

In what was destined to be his final season as one of England's leading batsmen, Ulyett occupied the thirteenth position in the batting table for 1891. Achieving an aggregate of 1,068 runs at an average of 24.83, he scored two centuries, and both gave ample evidence that he still retained much of his old batting powers. In a stay of two and a-half hours in Yorkshire's second innings at Taunton, on July 23, 24, and 25, he made "an exceedingly brilliant 118" off the Somerset bowling, notching fourteen 4s and dispatching the ball clear out of the ground for two enormous 6s. His other hundred (109), which took him about ten minutes longer, came in the fixture with Sussex at Hove, on August 17 and 18, and it included a dozen boundaries. With Bobby Peel he shared "a splendid stand" of 180 and, according to one of the cricket annuals, "So brilliantly did this pair hit that at one time 73 were made in thirty-five minutes."

On more than one occasion during his cricketing days, Ulyett was a target for the attentions of the gentlemen of the press. His experience of dealing with importunate journalists stretched at least as far back as the visit to Australia in 1876–77. Throughout the early part of the tour, the English team grew weary of the constant badgering by hordes of newspapermen. The exception was Ulyett. As far as he was concerned, the perpetual demands for interviews provided a heaven-sent opportunity for indulging in leg-pulling and displaying his histrionic talents. Nominated by the rest of the team to fulfil the role of spokesman for the whole party, and assuming an air of wide-eyed innocence and excessive affability, he dispensed a steady stream of irrelevant information and disinformation for the benefit of his eager listeners. Some of the copy published in the papers took on an appearance of such improbability that eventually the reporters became suspicious, bringing an end to "Happy Jack's" outrageous press conferences.

Towards the end of his first-class career, Ulyett had a famous encounter with a reporter intent upon a more personal interview. Like his team-mate Bobby Peel, he fought shy of this type of eyeball-to-eyeball confrontation, but he was far more skilful in avoiding the ordeal. When the reporter knocked on the door of the Yorkshire dressing-room and announced the purpose of his visit, the prospective interviewee was elsewhere, and a message was sent to him. The door was flung open a few minutes later, and in strode "Happy Jack," evidently the recipient of some news that both dismayed and delighted him. Clutching a scrap of paper in one hand, he exclaimed, "It's too baad, laads. There'll 'ave to be a change soomwhere!" "What's t'matter, Jack?" asked one of the team. "Why, read this telegram. T'wife 'as 'ad twins." The reporter would hardly have risen far in his profession today. Presented with the ideal opportunity for a human interest story, he utterly failed to exploit it. Refraining even from asking any of those hackneyed, inane questions (e.g., "And how did you *feel*, when you heard the news, Jack?"), he decided that it would be a tactless intrusion to pursue the matter any further at such a time fraught with emotions and abandoned the interview. A brief announcement was published in the paper the next day, congratulating the father on the supposed happy event. There were evidently other journalists clamouring for an interview with "Happy Jack" around this time, since it has been alleged that Mrs Ulyett gave birth to those twins on more than one occasion during the summer.

Sad to say, the season of 1892 demonstrated that the veteran Yorkshireman's ability to dominate the bowling was on the wane. Only rarely was he given the task of opening the batting, and "Except for one good performance against Middlesex at Lord's, Ulyett was not up to his old standard." Restored to his former position at the top of the order in the second innings at headquarters, on June 18, he guided Yorkshire to a victory by four wickets, playing "an exceptionally fine innings of 111," which included fourteen boundaries. This was his only hundred of the season as well as being the final one of his first-class career. In other matches, he failed to reproduce this form, topping the half-century but once. His aggregate fell alarmingly low to only 615 runs, and his average slumped to 14.64.

It is questionable whether Ulyett was worth his place in the Yorkshire side on performance alone in 1893, his last season in first-class cricket. Nevertheless, the Committee probably acted wisely in retaining his services. Several members of the County team at that time were fairly young and inexperienced, and the presence of one or two old-stagers would add some ballast to the Eleven. It is difficult to imagine the jovial, fun-loving Ulyett as a sort of *éminence grise*, yet that was the role he assumed, often captaining the side in the absence of Lord Hawke, with Yorkshire eventually winning the County Championship. Regarded now as a batsman who could knock up a few useful runs rather than one capable of taking the bowling apart, he dropped down the order, settling finally at number eight or nine. Although his average showed the slightest of improvements (15.37), he scored only 446 runs. His best effort (73) occurred in the fixture with Somerset at Taunton, on June 15, 16, and 17. On one or two other occasions, he experienced some success in putting the bat forcibly against the ball, but these were the dying embers of his former greatness. Yet, to the end, he was still capable of attempting a heroic, do-or-die gesture and perishing in the typically grand Ulyett manner. Against Lancashire at Old Trafford, on August 7 and 8 – his last Roses Match – he went down with all guns blazing. When Yorkshire needed only six runs to win, Johnny Briggs sent down an innocent-looking teaser, and "Happy Jack" made a gallant effort to wrap up the match with one more mighty sixer. Far and away went the ball, but not, unfortunately, quite far enough. Lurking in ambush on the long-on boundary stood Albert Ward, a Yorkshireman in exile, who held on to the catch. The veteran made his exit from first-class cricket in the match between Yorkshire and Kent at Bramall Lane, on August 21, 22, and 23, 1893, scoring 9 in his only innings.

Although he turned out in at least one minor match during the next few years, Ulyett spent much of his time acting as mine host at *The Vine Hotel*, in Brunswick Road, Sheffield, where he was once inveigled into giving a prolonged interview to a journalist. Accepting the imposture in good part, he opened a bottle of champagne and warmed to his task of spinning his yarns – thus, happily, preserving them for the benefit of posterity. Even though, in retirement, he retained much of his robust appearance, his health and strength began to deteriorate. It is possible that he may have chafed a little at the role of being a mere spectator, but his interest in Yorkshire cricket was unabated, and this attempt to maintain his links with the glorious days of the past was to prove his undoing. In raw and unpromising weather, when he was already suffering from the effects of a heavy cold, he insisted on going along to Bramall Lane to watch the match between Yorkshire and Kent, beginning on June 13, 1898. Inevitably, he caught another chill, which rapidly developed into an acute attack of pneumonia. In his debilitated state, Ulyett lacked the strength to put up any resistance against a disease often fatal in those days, and he passed away on the evening of Saturday, June 18, in his forty-seventh year.

George Ulyett's record in first-class cricket compares favourably with those of most of his contemporaries. In all matches, he attained an aggregate of 20,823 runs at an average of 23.44, marking a thousand runs in a season ten times and scoring eighteen hundreds, held 368 catches, and captured 653 wickets (including two hat-tricks) at 20.14 each. For Yorkshire alone, he rendered yeoman service with 14,351 runs (average 24.20), 460 wickets (average 17.88) and 238 catches. Never a man for precise statistics, Ulyett pretended to be unimpressed by his achievements, insisting that he wasn't any good as a bowler and never did much at batting and fielding. With such an excellent record as his, however, who is going to treat seriously his tongue-in-cheek claim that Yorkshire played him for twenty years solely for his skill at whistling and his good behaviour?

NOTE.– The details of "The Cricket Scandal" have been adapted from my article, "Bribery and Corruption," *The Journal of the Cricket Society*, IX, 4 (Spring 1980), 9–15.

W.H. SCOTTON
"Patience on a Monument"

OF the private lives and motivation of many of the famous nineteenth-century professional cricketers little profound knowledge has survived. In keeping with the accepted proprieties of the age, the majority of them tended to practise a becoming form of reticence when speaking of themselves and their contemporaries, apart from comparatively harmless anecdotes, occasional guarded hints, or a brief and secret revelation entrusted to the pages of a private diary. On the face of it, many of them were simple, uncomplicated types, who played their cricket, earned their wages, drank their ale to celebrate their triumphs or drown their sorrows, and got on with their lives, taking the rough with the smooth. A striking exception to the norm was Will Scotton, of Nottinghamshire and England fame. There were occasions when he would take a sympathetic friend or acquaintance into his confidence over personal problems. It must not be imagined, however, that, apart from one late, dramatic gesture, he ever made a deliberate attempt to give *universal* publicity to the innermost secrets of his heart, nor was he capable of explaining to the world exactly what made him tick. Far from it, for he was a modest, quiet man for much of his life, but nevertheless it is possible to delve into the events of his career and come up with some conclusions that make him more of a three-dimensional individual than many of his fellow cricketers. A psychiatrist of a later age would probably admit that it would be time ill-spent to linger over some of the latter. Not so Will Scotton, the details of whose life would have swelled the leaves of a modern "shrink's" case-book.

Born at Nottingham, on January 15, 1856, William Henry Scotton received his education at the People's College in the city, where one of his school-mates was Arthur Shrewsbury, with whom he remained closely acquainted throughout much of the rest of his life. Arthur was his junior by nearly three months, and it is highly probable that their association exercised no small influence on the development and evolution of Will's character. An athletic figure in manhood, Scotton weighed a little over eleven stones and was above medium height, reaching only two inches below six feet. He possessed a pleasant singing voice, attained some skill

94

as a footballer, playing at times for Notts County, and was a dab hand with a gun, excelling particularly at pigeon-shooting, but his true talents as a sportsman were displayed on the cricket field. There was cricket in his family, for his cousin, George Howitt, achieved fame as a fast, left-handed bowler with Nottinghamshire and Middlesex, whose tearaway action and speed off the pitch inflicted many a bruise on opposing batsmen. Scotton, too, bowled fastish, left-arm, but he was nowhere near so good as Howitt. At the most, a no more than adequate practice rather than a match bowler, he failed to make any mark in that department of the game: indeed, he was rarely put on in important contests, and throughout his first-class career he took only eight wickets at an average of 51.25. With the bat, however, he far surpassed Howitt – they were, incidentally, both complete left-handers – and he was a most reliable and speedy fielder in the deep, cutting off many runs and holding 122 catches all told. He was not seen to much advantage close to the wicket. The specialist fielder at point for Nottinghamshire was his old friend Arthur Shrewsbury, and when the latter was absent for a whole season, the duties were assigned for a time to Scotton, "but he showed no special ability for the post, and altogether lacked Shrewsbury's brilliancy and certainty" – a wounding observation that can have done little to strengthening Will's morale.

Scotton began playing serious cricket as a teenager, and in 1873 he obtained a professional engagement with the South Derbyshire Club. In the same year, he appeared in two trial matches at Trent Bridge, and although he achieved little out of the ordinary, his potential as a future prospect of distinct promise did not go unrecognized, and he was selected to play for Sixteen Colts of England against Twelve of MCC at Lord's, on May 11 and 12, 1874. As an "odds" match, this did not rate the status of first-class, but nevertheless it gave the youngster a golden opportunity to demonstrate his skill with the bat. Although he was out of luck on his second visit to the wickets, he made 19 – the only double figure – in the first innings. This was a praiseworthy achievement, considering that he had to cope with the wiles of Alfred Shaw and the expresses of Fred Morley.

The same season saw the beginning of Scotton's association with Lord's. Engaged as a member of the ground staff, he retained his appointment throughout the following year. In 1876, however, he transferred his allegiance by crossing the Thames to take up a similar post with the Surrey Club at The Oval. This move gave rise to some speculation that he might have formed the intention of establishing a qualification to play for Surrey. Any such plan was, in the event, nipped in the bud when he relinquished his appointment at The Oval at the end of the season. Though brief, this sojourn south of the river provided him with an opportunity to distinguish himself in an unusual manner. In North *v* South (Thomas Humphrey's

W. H. Scotton

Benefit) at The Oval, on July 20, 21, and 22, 1876, one man on each side
was prostrated by the excessive heat and was unable to continue. "Their
fielding substitute," said *Wisden*, "was the Notts man, Scotton (engaged on
The Oval), who fielded in such dashing brilliant form as to elicit repeated
bursts of applause, *and* (it was stated) a more tangible compliment from
the Surrey Club." After being employed briefly at Oxford University in
1879 and 1880, he signed up again with MCC in 1881 and retained his post
at headquarters until the middle of 1893.

The contest between Nottinghamshire and Derbyshire at Trent Bridge,
on May 17, 18, and 19, 1875, marked an important event in the history
of the home club, not so much for the comfortable victory as for the
debut in first-class cricket of two batsmen destined to occupy a prominent
position in the doings of the County. One was Will Scotton, the other
Arthur Shrewsbury. The former, given the unenviable task of opening the
innings, did little to advance his prospects, being dismissed for 6 and 8.
Shrewsbury, who succeeded his old school chum at the crease, was slightly
more successful with scores of 17 and 10. Scotton, significantly, was not
given another chance to redeem himself that season, whereas his junior
held down a regular place in the side. It may be surmised that the apparent
neglect of the slightly older youth might have had an adverse effect on
his character. The seeds of an inferiority complex may have already been
nestling in the soil as far as Scotton was concerned, and the experience of
1875 caused them to germinate and reach upwards towards the surface of
the ground. Henceforth, a certain ambivalence would reign in Scotton's
attitude towards Shrewsbury: a curious amalgam of admiration and envy
would be accompanied by an almost pathetic attempt to insist perpetually
on his seniority by birth, even by a few paltry weeks.

While Shrewsbury was continuing his triumphal progress towards the
top of the list of leading professional batsmen, scoring a century in 1876
and another the following year, his impressionable school-mate suffered
a term of almost uninterrupted banishment to the wilderness. A solitary
county match in each of those two seasons with an aggregate of one run
and two ducks could have only bruised his feelings and increased his
sense of inferiority. Showing commendable patience, the authorities at
Trent Bridge gave him a slightly more extended trial in 1878 by engaging
him for five matches. An average of 11.50 was nothing to write home
about, but at least he did distinguish himself on one occasion. At Old
Trafford, on July 18 and 19, Lancashire overwhelmed Nottinghamshire
by ten wickets, thanks principally to the bowling of Mr A.G. Steel, who
captured thirteen wickets for only 72 runs. One of the cricket annuals
indulged in some trenchant criticism of the visitors' efforts, while at
the same time bestowing a word of praise where it was due: "Scotton,
a left-handed batsman . . . showed good cricket for his second score of

40, but otherwise the Nottingham batting could hardly be classed above mediocrity." During the course of this match, Will Scotton would have had the opportunity to observe the art of batting as practised by the Lancashire opener, R.G. Barlow. Renowned already for his employment of "barn-door" tactics, which that year had produced the third instance of carrying his bat through a completed innings, Dick Barlow was achieving recognition as the very model of a modern stonewaller. Perhaps the sight of the Lancastrian's technique made a fleeting impression on Scotton, which sank without apparent trace into his subconscious, only to re-emerge at some time in the future.

Like some rare and exotic plant, Will Scotton was slow to mature, but in 1879 he made "An astonishing leap to the front." Playing in thirteen matches, all but one of them for his County, he attained an aggregate of 409 runs at an average of 25.56, more than double the figure of the previous season. In scaling these heights, which secured to him the sixth position in the national averages, he far outstripped the efforts of Arthur Shrewsbury, a feat which might have given a welcome fillip to his morale. The steadiness of his defence came in for some commendation, but it may surprise some readers to learn that, at this stage of his career, he was considered to be an attractive batsman, a punishing hitter quick to go on the attack, and a fast scorer. His highest figure was marked in the match against Middlesex at Trent Bridge, on August 11, 12, and 13. Going to the wickets low down in the order at number eight, he treated the crowd to "Some vigorous hitting," and at the close of the Nottinghamshire innings he was undefeated with 84, the top score of his side. On the same ground a fortnight later, with Kent providing the opposition, he surpassed his team-mates once more. Promoted to number four, he "hit away with such rapidity that for a long time he acquired runs at the rate of one per minute." Snapped up eventually at point, he played an "excellent innings of 77," which included an off drive for 5 and nine 4s. Between these two contests he had varying fortunes, ranging from 51 and 45 (again in advance of his team-mates) in the away match with Lancashire to a "pair" against Gloucestershire at Cheltenham. Apart from this unwelcome lapse, he would have had every reason to look back with pride on his first successful season.

At the beginning of the season of 1880, all the appearances suggested that Will Scotton was set to carry on exactly where he had left off in the previous year. He showed up well while assisting an Eleven of England against Richard Daft's American Team at Lord's, on May 17 and 18, compiling 41 not out on a fiery and at times dangerous wicket. In the return fixture a fortnight later at The Oval, he made the top score of 52, chancing his arm and attacking the bowling "with great freedom." Not long afterwards, against Lancashire at Old Trafford, on June 17, 18,

Arthur Shrewsbury

and 19, he marked his highest figure of the season, smiting eight 4s in his "very well-hit 63." In this match, as usual, Dick Barlow opened the Lancashire innings with Mr A.N. Hornby and gave another painstaking exhibition of stonewalling, being 0 not out when his partner was dismissed with 38 runs in the score-book. Throughout the remainder of the season, the principal characteristics of Scotton's batting were a lack of consistency coupled with a failure to capitalize on his efforts in the first innings. He went to the wickets a second time in eleven of the seventeen matches in which he participated, and on ten of these occasions he failed to reach double figures. His only other half-century came in the fixture with Gloucestershire at Trent Bridge, on the last three days of July, when he played an "admirable innings" of 53. Against the same county in 1879, it will be remembered that he had suffered the mortification of securing a "pair." The bowler dismissing him in both innings was Billy Midwinter, but the Anglo-Australian all-rounder was not permitted to have things all his own way this time. Scotton chose a perfect method of exacting vengeance by lofting one of his deliveries on to the pavilion balcony, with the ball travelling a distance of 97 yards!

Scotton made his debut for the Players against the Gentlemen in 1880, scoring 0 and 4 at both The Oval and Lord's, and his final appearance on the Surrey ground in 1886. He never held down a regular place in the side, assisting the professionals on only seven occasions. This need come as no surprise, seeing that his record in the series was feeble in the extreme – only 70 runs at the very poor average of 5.83. Four times he failed to trouble the scorers, and only at Scarborough, on September 3, 4, and 5, 1885, did he show the remotest semblance of form, scoring 4 not out (at number 6) and 26, his solitary double figure in the series.

Neither Will Scotton nor the rest of the Nottinghamshire team had the happiest of times in the summer of 1881, when seven of the players were at loggerheads with the authorities at Trent Bridge. Master-minded by Alfred Shaw and Arthur Shrewsbury, the group (including Scotton) laid down certain conditions as a basis for agreeing to turn out for the County. One of the bones of contention between the two warring parties was the refusal of the Committee to offer terms of engagement for the whole season to Scotton and his team-mate, Wilfred Flowers. It was to be all or nothing asserted the so-called malcontents, and when the authorities would not accede to their demands, the seven – magnificent or the contrary, according to your point of view – went on strike. Some of them, including Scotton, eventually made their peace with the Committee and consented to resume their places in the side before the end of the summer. As far as Will was concerned, this meant a serious curtailment of his appearances in first-class matches in 1881, though, having signed on again as a member of the MCC ground staff, he was happily not on the bread-line. Nor was this his only source of income, since he had been the landlord of *The Boat Inn* at Beeston since the late 1870s.

With playing in only seven matches that summer, Scotton's aggregate naturally declined, his total being 231 runs, but his average increased to 19.25, and he passed an important mile-stone by notching his maiden century in first-class cricket in the match between MCC and England at Lord's, on July 4 and 5. Going in at first wicket down in the MCC second innings, he exhibited some "vigorous batting" (twelve 4s) and had made exactly 100 runs when he was clean bowled. As though devoted to an exactitude in the matter of figures, he made precisely 50 (the top score of the match) when playing for Alfred Shaw's Eleven against Lord Sheffield's Team at Sheffield Park, on August 25, 26, and 27.

The winter of 1881–82 provided a vista of new fields of endeavour for Will Scotton. Taking part in the tour promoted by his two team-mates, Alfred Shaw and Arthur Shrewsbury, in association with their partner James Lillywhite, junior, he visited the USA, Australia, and New Zealand. The entire programme contained a very large proportion of minor contests against "odds," but seven of those played in Australia were of first-class status, including four Test Matches. Scotton did little to enhance his reputation in the affairs against "odds" with an average barely in excess of 12 and a highest score of no more than 40, but his record was much more satisfactory in the first-class contests. He was not accorded much of an opportunity to play a long innings, since his usual position in the batting order was number seven (and twice, eight) with only a modicum of expertise in the tail that followed him. Yet he performed with sufficient skill to attain an aggregate of 228 runs at 20.72 per innings, which secured for him a place in the middle of the table of batting averages. At Melbourne, on December 31, 1881, and January 2, 3, and 4, 1882, he made his Test debut, scoring 21 before being unfortunately run out in the first innings, while in the second, playing with a little more prudence than was his wont, he notched an undefeated 50 – his highest figure of the tour – which made a material contribution towards denying the Australians a chance of victory. His performance in the international contests was, in fact, the best part of his record: coming in the top half of the table, he totalled 158 runs at an average of 26.33, which was regarded at the time as "excellent form."

Scotton's first tour abroad was marred by one disgraceful occurrence in connection with the match between Victoria and the English team at Melbourne, on December 16, 17, 19, and 20, 1881. The details of this episode, which gave rise to allegations that two of the tourists accepted bribes from one or more of the local bookmakers to throw the match, are narrated elsewhere, but what part, if any, played by Scotton seems to have been on the periphery of the unsavoury business. It appeared at first, on not very strong evidence, that he might possibly have been approached to share in the acceptance of the bribes, to which he answered with an indignant refusal. What is more certain is the fact that, shortly before going on to Melbourne, he became involved in two bouts of fisticuffs during the course of an "odds" match at Cootamundra. As mentioned elsewhere, his first opponent was John Selby, his Nottinghamshire team-mate, and with the advantages of height, weight, and reach on his side, Scotton emerged as the victor in this contest. This result, however, was a mixed blessing for him and soon turned to disaster, since he then found himself confronted by George Ulyett, determined to defend the honour of Selby, his chum for the nonce – though "honour" is perhaps not the word to spring most readily to mind in this particular context. The powerful Ulyett was rather more than Scotton could handle, and the latter was pummelled into submission. The cause of this unseemly brawling was later reported as "a private family quarrel" and more specifically as "marital jealousy." These reasons, with the implication that matters were going awry in Scotton's domestic life, are of importance when taken in connection with future developments in the years to come, and also in contributing some explanation towards an understanding of the changes that took place in his demeanour.

When reviewing the cricket season of 1882 in England, one of the annuals observed that "Scotton's batting was a considerable improvement on any previous form," while another labelled him as one of the "good useful hitters." On figures alone, his record would seem to belie these claims – an aggregate of 532 runs at an average of 17.73, and a highest score of 52. Nevertheless, he played some very useful innings in county matches, but his sole half-century of the season was taken off the redoubtable Nottinghamshire bowling at Lord's, on June 15 and 16, when he made one of the MCC team. On another occasion, he rendered excellent service to his employers at headquarters towards the end of the second week in August with a "splendid not out innings of 115," but since the opponents were Hertfordshire, the match did not count as first-class.

The season of 1883 marked a distinct turning-point in Will Scotton's career. He played in no more than eleven matches, and his overall performance was, to put it as kindly as possible, undistinguished and palpably below par. Perhaps he had other things on his mind, because he never really seemed to get going and could manage no more than a tally of 179 runs at the depressingly low average of 11.93 and a highest score of merely 25. In the hazardous realm of might-have-beens, it would be possible to conjecture that a return of something approaching his old attractive style of batting would have produced some improvement in his record, but an unkind stroke of ill-fortune denied him the opportunity to make amends in the final weeks of the season. Nottinghamshire were playing against Gloucestershire at Trent Bridge, on August 2, 3, and 4.

Having won the toss, W.G. Grace elected to bat and went in first with his brother E.M. Alfred Shaw, the Nottinghamshire captain, set his field, sending Scotton to his usual position in the deep, and opened the bowling. Maybe the Champion had a sudden rush of blood to his head or more likely misjudged the pitch of one of Alfred's crafty deliveries. In attempting to get off the mark, he made an imprudent stroke, lofting the ball far away into the long field straight in the direction of Will Scotton. The latter, to his credit, held on to the stinging catch but at the cost of badly injuring one of his hands in the process. A substitute replaced him in the field, but when the home side had their first and only innings, he took his turn with the bat, going in at number nine and struggling to make four runs (caught and bowled W.G. Grace!). Did Alfred Shaw insist that the sufferer should go to the wickets, or was it the latter's own choice? Whatever the answer might be, it was a strange decision, seeing that two of Scotton's team-mates made three-figure scores, and Nottinghamshire went on to an easy victory by an innings and 36 runs. Will, in his condition, could scarcely be expected to add much of a contribution to the total. So serious was the injury that he played no more for his County in 1883. Some six weeks later, at the very end of the season, he had recovered sufficiently to turn out for MCC against Nottinghamshire (!) at Trent Bridge, but a sure touch still eluded him, and he had to be content with modest scores of 12 and 18.

It is fair to assume that the winter months of 1883–84 were of a momentous consequence for Will Scotton, producing a change in his fundamental outlook on the course of events, though it is unlikely that injury and indifferent health were the sole reasons for the metamorphosis. Character and personal circumstances probably also played their part. If it may be accepted that an individual's physiognomy will reveal some evidence of his soul, then we need only study a portrait of Scotton made about this time to see part of the answer to the problem. The features appear delicate and devoid of any stamp of authority, the eyes a shade apprehensive, and the lack of moral strength is imperfectly concealed by the handsome, sweeping moustache with the points waxed in a not altogether successful attempt to create an impression that its owner was masterful by nature. It looks like the face of a man struggling and failing to appear tough and uncompromising, and knowing at the same time that he has failed. Mention has already been made of his relationship with his school-mate Arthur Shrewsbury, with the suggestion that the latter might have caused him to suffer from an inferiority complex. Many were the occasions in the next few years when these two were associated as the opening pair for Nottinghamshire, and one of the leading sporting journalists of the day always believed that "Scotton counted it an honour to go in with Shrewsbury." At the same time, however, as though to salve his pride, the left-hander always clung to the fact of his earlier birth, and he made a pathetic attempt to assert his seniority by always speaking of "I and Arthur" – a phrase which became a standing joke with the gentlemen of the Press.

Lonely, sensitive, diffident, easily wounded by the pin-pricks of everyday life, Will Scotton was also beginning to develop an unwholesome fear of making mistakes, which would eventually become accentuated out of all proportions. In more modern times, he would have been an obvious candidate for the ministrations of an expert psychiatrist. Perhaps, too, at this period of his life, he might have experienced a certain absence of harmony on the home front and would have derived some benefit from the advice of a marriage guidance counsellor. Little information of so private a nature has, not unnaturally, survived the passage of time, but as we have already seen, there was a grain of evidence to indicate that all may have not been well with Scotton's domestic life, witness the affair of the fist-fight with John Selby at Cootamundra, Australia, on the tour of 1881–82, sparked off by "marital jealousy." Whether it was Selby or Scotton who was at fault, we do not know, but either way would argue for the existence of the not most pleasant and peaceful of atmospheres in the Scotton household.

Another factor to stimulate the change which was about to take place in Scotton's methods on the cricket field may have been the realization that his career appeared to be ebbing away. The free-scoring strokes and the run-a-minute tempo were fraught with danger. Far better to play it safe and avoid the blame for making mistakes. A road to salvation and more lasting success had already been signposted by two of his contemporaries, Dick Barlow of Lancashire and Louis Hall of Yorkshire. This pair of luminaries, both opening batsmen, had given an ample demonstration of the virtues of a cast-iron defence and the ability to maintain a prolonged occupation of the crease while other batsmen attended to the business of run-getting. The sight of them in action, playing maiden after maiden and taking runs only when it was safe to do so, often offered only a minimum of pleasure to a crowd of restive spectators, but they made an immeasurable contribution to the success of the teams they represented. Their technique was one to appeal to Scotton in the present evolution of his mentality. In espousing their cause, he would concentrate on taking few risks and reduce the chances of committing errors, as befitted his newly developed temperament. And so the duo of stonewallers became a trio, all intent on their self-imposed task of barring the way and blunting the cutting edge of the opposition's attack. By some Will Scotton came to be regarded as the "arch-fiend" of the three. Ideally suited by physique for this style of batting, he developed a well-nigh impregnable defence, making full use of his long reach to kill the bowling with an impeccably straight bat. Mere occupation of the crease would eventually become an end in itself, and though he played some long innings of immense value to his side, they were wearisome to the spectators, by whom he was rarely treated as a popular idol. Like Tom Walker of earlier Hambledon fame, he would have been eminently qualified to earn the nickname of "Old Everlasting."

As soon as Will Scotton took guard and began dealing with his opponents' attack at Trent Bridge, Lord's, and elsewhere during the summer of 1884, it was apparent to each and every knowledgeable onlooker that he had "radically altered his former method of play." Gone were the days of flashy inconsistency and the lofted drive: from now onwards, the principal characteristics that stamped his batting were "great powers of defence, and an inexhaustible amount of patience." Incontrovertible evidence of the efficacy of his new technique was registered in only his second appearance of the season when assisting his County against Middlesex at Lord's, on May 26, 27, and 28. Opening the innings with Shrewsbury who made 70, Scotton went for only a single in the first innings, but when Arthur was quickly dismissed for a cipher in the second, his partner assumed the responsibility of guiding Nottinghamshire to a victory by six wickets. Undefeated when the winning run was scored, he had been systematically eroding the confidence of seven bowlers for a period of three and a-half hours, making 104, with one 5 and six 4s, and giving only the barest possible chance. His impregnable defence "was one of the very best features of the match," according to one of the cricket annuals, while another asserted without qualification that this was "one of the best innings he has ever played."

He hit the headlines again at Huddersfield, on July 3, 4, and 5, when he turned out for an Eleven of England against the Australians and was dubbed "the hero of the match." The England Eleven won the toss and took first innings, with Scotton going in at number two. Far from losing his nerve at the early dismissal of his partner, he settled down to give a prolonged and supremely convincing demonstration that the pace and guile of Spofforth, Palmer, Boyle, and others held no terrors for him. Still unconquered when stumps were drawn at the end of the first day, he continued in the same vein the next morning, until finally his superbly organized defence was breached – total 397 for 6. He marked eleven 4s in "his magnificent innings of 134 . . . scored without the semblance of a chance," took part in three partnerships of over 100 runs, and valiantly defied the full might of the bowling for six hours! Although this was the highest score he ever achieved in first-class cricket, it was not his most famous performance with the bat, and more than once thereafter he was the source of grievous discomfort and frustration to the Australians.

In county matches, too, he had ample opportunities to display his newly developed powers of defence. It was the considered opinion of one of the annuals that "Scotton batted best for the victorious side" in the contest against Gloucestershire at Gloucester, on July 14, 15, and 16. Top scorer with 39 in the first innings, he then went on to give an object lesson in the art of survival on a pitch rendered extremely hazardous by rain, making 15 not out in about two hours. Against Yorkshire at Trent Bridge, immediately afterwards, he consumed two hours and a-quarter before being dismissed "for a most patient and excellent 33," while at the end of the month, in the return fixture with Gloucestershire, he spent the same length of time in painstakingly compiling 19!

England and Australia were engaged in three Test Matches in the summer of 1884. The first, at Old Trafford, on July 10, 11, and 12, was unfinished, while the second, played at Lord's later in the same month, ended in a conclusive victory for the home side. Generally speaking, any adverse criticism of the different selection committees was rather muted, "though many would have liked to have seen Scotton included." A.P. Lucas, one of the leading amateur batsmen of the day, had been chosen for the first two encounters, but he was not available for the final contest at The Oval, on August 11, 12, and 13. Admirers of the merits of the in-form left-hander would be amply repaid for their support, since it turned out that Lucas's place "was most worthily filled by Scotton."

A remarkable, even extraordinary match in a variety of ways was this final meeting at the famous Surrey ground. Australia won the toss and, revelling in perfect batting conditions, seemed to be giving every indication that they might have a good chance of repeating the famous victory at the same venue in 1882. They held possession of the crease throughout the whole of the first day, and at close of play their total had reached 363 for the loss of only two wickets. Latish on the second day, they were finally put out for 551, the highest total in one innings in Test Matches so far. Numbers two, three, and four all scored centuries, the best by W.L. Murdoch, the Australian captain, whose 211 was the first double century since the series began in 1877. In this innings, for the first time in Test cricket, all eleven members of the fielding side were given a turn with the ball, including Scotton (eighth on, 5–1–20–0) and, last of all and to the huge delight of the crowd, Shrewsbury (3–2–2–0). Neither, it may be added, was ever called upon again to exercise this unfamiliar function in international contests (in Arthur's case, never in any other first-class match). Tenth in the list of bowlers was the Hon Alfred Lyttelton, England's wicket-keeper, making his final appearance in Test Matches. He had two spells, trying his luck with lobs, and at his second attempt he garnered the last four wickets, ending up as the most successful England bowler with an analysis of 12–5–19–4, the best ever of his career. On the first occasion, he handed his gloves to W.W. Read, the

Surrey amateur, while his deputy on the second was W.G. I have advisedly written "gloves," since it has been suggested that he did not bother to take off his pads while dispensing his lobs, a habit also attributed to George Pinder, the regular Yorkshire wicket-keeper of the previous decade.

There were also some noteworthy features about the next innings. Will Scotton accompanied W.G. to the wickets to open England's reply to the gargantuan total and witnessed the daunting sight of the dismissal of the Champion and Billy Barnes, both gone for 19 each. At close of play, the score stood at 70 for 2, with one more day's play to come. Things did not go well for England, when play was resumed. Arthur Shrewsbury, not out 6 overnight, added only four runs to his tally before giving a catch to the wicket-keeper, and while Scotton maintained his "exemplary defence," the middle and lower middle of the order came and went with depressing regularity, until eight wickets were down for only 181 runs. Enter W.W. Read, the Hon Alfred's first deputy behind the stumps. The timely appearance of Walter Read put an entirely different complexion on the sorry state of affairs. Furious, it has been alleged, at the indignity of being relegated to number ten, a most unaccustomed position in the order for him, he was determined to work off the venom of his spleen at the expense of the Australian bowling.

Will Scotton had gone out to the wickets on this third and last morning of the contest with 21 runs against his name, and when his latest partner joined him his score had crept up to 53. In the circumstances, Read could scarcely have had a better ally than the Nottinghamshire left-hander. While the latter kept up his end and patiently accumulated 31 more runs, his partner gave a dazzling display of run-getting, racing rapidly to his hundred. The stand was worth the precious addition of 151 runs to the England total, when Scotton finally succumbed to a catch off Giffen's bowling and departed for 90. Not long afterwards, Walter Read was clean bowled for 117. His stay at the wickets had been comparatively short, only two and a-quarter hours, and no less than eighty of his runs came from boundaries. With a deficit of 205 runs facing them, England were, of course, compelled to follow their innings, and they had lost two wickets in scoring 85, when the proceedings came to an end. On paper, the visitors' total of 551 could not fail to look anything but impressive, but in fact they made a tactical error in remaining so long at the wickets and not scoring quickly enough, leaving insufficient time to bowl England out twice. It has been calculated that, even allowing for the leisurely tempo maintained by Scotton, the home side scored their runs at a faster rate than the Australians.

There can rarely have been a greater contrast to be seen in the batting styles of England's heroes. From the point of view of the spectators, Walter Read's dashing performance was by far the more attractive of the two, and nothing should be allowed to detract from the splendour of his aggressive batting nor his service to England's cause. Yet, in the end, it was Will Scotton who deserved the principal honours. While admitting that the Surrey amateur's methods were more pleasing to the eye, one of the cricket annuals observed that "Scotton deserved even greater credit. By his unwearied patience and stubborn defence he fairly saved the game." Similar views on the left-hander's achievement were also expressed elsewhere. Burdened by even greater stress than on the occasion of his earlier exploit against the same opponents at Huddersfield, he gave a marvellous exhibition of mental and physical stamina. He sustained this stupendous feat of intense concentration for a period of five hours and three-quarters without wavering, and throughout this prolonged and selfless vigil he never gave the ghost of a chance. Though not often regarded as a match-winner in spite of the fact that he was sometimes featured in this role, he was at this stage of his career a superb match-saver.

Immediately after this contest with the tourists, the hero of The Oval carried on where he had left off in Nottinghamshire's easy victory over Middlesex at Trent Bridge. The visitors won the toss and, electing to bat first, achieved a useful total of 211, the best contribution being a splendid innings of 80 from Mr I.D. Walker, the Middlesex captain. The established partnership of Shrewsbury and Scotton began the home side's reply, but the former did not last long. On the next day, the left-handed opener settled down to another heart-breaking display almost devoid of boundaries – only three here as opposed to nine at The Oval. Three more wickets fell, and then he became associated with William Gunn in a partnership calculated to grind the Middlesex will to win into a fine-grained powder. Scotton defended his sticks for three hours and three-quarters in making 66 ("a very fine defensive innings"), while Gunn spent almost five hours in amassing 138, though he did manage to strike sixteen 4s. So, you might say, another yawn-making innings by Will Scotton, and what was there so special about that? This match, in fact, contained an unusual and somewhat rare incident. During the course of the stone-waller's dead-bat defiance, Mr I.D. Walker was bowling, probably slow, under-arm lobs, which would have made many another batsman water at the mouth with glee. One particular delivery was played sedately back towards the bowler, and as Donny Walker stooped to stop the ball his cap fell off, and he made an instinctive grab for it. In an extraordinary piece of bad luck, cap and ball arrived in Donny's hand at the same time. This was tantamount to stopping the ball with his head-dress, and on the spur of the moment Scotton demanded that five runs should be given to him for the hit. In accordance with the strict letter of the law, the umpire to whom the appeal had been addressed allowed the claim, and the batsman received his five runs. The umpire's decision was a source of annoyance for the Middlesex team, especially the bowler, since it was patently obvious that the contact between cap and ball had been purely accidental, and that Donny Walker had not deliberately stopped the ball with something other than a part of his person. A more imaginative official might have allowed his mind to go beyond the then Law 41 under which the bowler was penalized, and have considered the question of "fair or unfair play" to which Law 43 referred. It has been said that this bizarre incident "threw a damper over the game," and what with that, the interminable innings of Scotton and Gunn, and the misfortune of having to cope with the bowling of Alfred Shaw and Wilfred Flowers on a worn wicket, the visitors more or less gave up the ghost.

The weather throughout the season of 1884 produced pitches usually more favourable for run-getting rather than wicket-taking and, in the old . phrase, Scotton was one of the batsmen who made hay while the sun shone. At the end of the summer, he would have had every justification in feeling a heart-warming glow of pleasure when he surveyed the extent of his achievements. A perfect vindication of his recently developed technique of batting is reflected in his record – an aggregate of 897 runs at 34.50 per innings and the fourth position in the national batting averages. His morale and confidence in his abilities might well have been boosted by the thought that W.G. Grace came fifth in the table, while his old friend and "rival" Arthur Shrewsbury occupied the twelfth place. The Australians would doubtless have derived little pleasure from the sight of Will Scotton taking guard and calmly reaching out with his forward defensive stroke as one delivery succeeded another. Five times he appeared against them, averaging 42 runs each innings. The cricket annuals, in reviewing his progress, were unstinting in their praise, commending him for his consistency and the absence of false strokes in his play. One asserted that "his defence during this year has been excelled by no other batsman in England," while another claimed that "on public form [he] was really the best professional batsman of the year." There was at this stage no overtly adverse criticism of the somewhat pedestrian tempo in his rate of scoring. When you compare him with his two contemporaries who practised the art of stonewalling, it may be surmised that Scotton was a source of even greater frustration to opponents. Dick Barlow and Louis Hall were both right-handers, but with Scotton being left-handed he provided an additional cause of exasperation with the perpetual necessity of re-arranging the field. It now remained to be seen whether he would be able to continue maintaining those long periods of intense concentration, and whether his role of match-saving would degenerate into stonewalling as a mere mannerism for its own sake.

Will Scotton spent the winter of 1884–85 at the Antipodes once more as a member of the team chosen for the second tour promoted by Shaw, Shrewsbury, and Lillywhite. George Ulyett was one of the party, but John Selby was not selected, and there is no indication that Scotton was ever called upon to put up his fists this time. The programme was a heavy one with a plethora of "odds" matches, but it also included eight first-class contests, of which five were Tests. When compared with his record of the previous tour in 1881–82, his performance showed a partial reversal, with a distinct improvement in the "odds" affairs and a slight decline in those rated first-class. In the latter, he scored 224 runs, four short of his aggregate of 1881–82, but his average was lower, working out at 17.23. His best achievement, the only really outstanding one, occurred early in the tour in the first Test Match at Adelaide, on December 12, 13, 15, and 16, 1884, when he opened the innings with Arthur Shrewsbury, the captain of the side. The latter failed to score, but his partner put on another of those displays which made him a holy terror in the eyes of the Australians in 1884 and for some years to come, until his name would be automatically cited by them as a symbol of remorseless stonewalling. After the dismissal of Shrewsbury, he shared a stand of 96 with George Ulyett, to which the latter contributed 68. The Yorkshireman's successor at the crease was Billy Barnes, whose methods were somewhat closer to Ulyett's than Scotton's. An even more prolific partnership ensued, in which "both men played finely, each in his own style," and the total was advanced from 107 to 282, at which point Scotton, doubtless to the delight of all Australians, was stumped. He gave a couple of chances in his "most patient and invaluable innings of 82," and he spent six hours at the wickets in compiling his runs, while Barnes went on to notch 134 at a quicker rate of scoring. England won this match by eight wickets, and though the left-hander was soon out in the second innings, he had made a considerable contribution to the victory. This, incidentally, was the highest score he ever made in Test Matches in Australia.

There were indications in some of the "odds" matches that stonewalling was evolving into an end in itself. In one of them he "compiled 62 with customary care," while in another, played on a concrete pitch covered with two layers of cocoa-matting, he totted up 60 in a sojourn of nearly five hours. The inhabitants of Moss Vale would have had more reason than many of their fellow countrymen to recall the visit of the English team, who took on the local Twenty-two on January 21 and 22, 1885. Among the more remarkable features of this minor contest were the dismissal of the home side for 14 in their first innings and some excellent bowling and batting by some of the Englishmen. Of equal or even more fame – though "notoriety" would be a rather more appropriate term than "fame" in this instance – was one of the most extraordinary exhibitions of self-indulgent stonewalling ever recorded. Shrewsbury and Scotton opened the innings, and when the former was bowled for 20 with the total at 34, play was adjourned for luncheon. Ulyett took Shrewsbury's place after the interval and played a brilliant innings of 56. During this stand, Scotton advanced his score by four singles. Barnes came and went for 23, then Bates and Scotton became associated and were still at the wickets at close of play. If I had said that they saw the time out, this would seem to suggest that the rate of scoring was no more than sedate. Whereas this would most certainly apply to Scotton, it would have been a gross calumny on Bates, whose proportion of the stand of 124 on the first day was 101! The left-handed opener was the last man to be dismissed, when he skied the ball and was caught by the grateful wicket-keeper. In his emulation of a garden snail, Scotton had surpassed himself. Out of the first 124 runs scored, his share amounted to only 25. When stumps were drawn, the total stood at 248, to which he had contributed no more than 44 runs in a period of four and a-quarter hours. Having survived four chances, he finally ran out of luck and departed for 123 – his highest figure of the tour in all matches – after playing the "goose game" for eight and a-quarter hours! Nobody, I think, would wish to disagree with *Wisden's* comment that Scotton's "play had been of the most tedious description."

I have seen no suggestion that the good people of Moss Vale felt any urge to acknowledge Will Scotton's performance, even on the grounds of staying power, but perhaps they had all sunk into a hypnotic trance at the sight of that eternal pendulum movement of his bat, or were pondering over the possibility of having acquired a new permanent resident in their community. It was a different story at Gympie, in Queensland, about a fortnight later, when it was announced that the batsman making the highest score would be handsomely rewarded for his achievement. At the end of the match, resulting in a victory for the visitors by eight wickets, the prize belonged indisputably to the Marauder of Moss Vale, who made 41 in the first innings and, for that matter, 15 not out in the second. His batting on this occasion was in reality a testimony to his skill in coping with adverse conditions. The match began on a Saturday, and when stumps were drawn Twenty-two of Gympie had been dismissed for 74, and the tourists had lost six wickets in struggling to 103. Scotton, however, who went in at first wicket down, was still there after plodding his way to an undefeated 17, though in this instance the word "plodding" is a little unfair. Throughout the whole of the first day, the batsmen on both sides had laboured under the difficulties of playing on a turf wicket "of a very rough description." There were evidently complaints about this monstrosity of a pitch, since when Scotton and J.M. Read resumed their innings on the Monday, they had the advantage of batting on the truer surface of a matting wicket, which had been laid down that morning. The promised prize for the highest score was 250 shares in a gold mine. As these would have been of little use back in the old country, the winner disposed of them by auction, pocketing "a useful sum by the transaction."

It may be remembered that Will Scotton was very fond of shooting, and on several occasions during the tour he managed to get out into the country and have some sport with a gun. He had a particularly enjoyable time at Benalla, Victoria, at the end of December 1884, where an "odds" match took place. First of all he spotted a bear (koala?), stalked it and succeeded in killing it. He then turned his attention to the birdlife around him and began blazing away rather indiscriminately at the flocks of parrots fluttering about. It must be assumed that he was no ornithologist, since he grew tired of this quarry and switched his aim to the laughing jackasses (kookaburras) and had already brought down one or two before he was hastily reminded that their habit of killing snakes and other pests on cultivated land made them prohibited game. If it reached the ears of the residents of Benalla, the sound of Scotton's prolonged fusillade would have hardly raised an eyebrow. Since the town was situated well within the territory through which the late, lamented Ned Kelly and his gang of bushrangers used to roam but a few years back, the noise of firearms being discharged there was no doubt a common occurrence.

Back in England in the summer of 1885, Will Scotton took some time to settle down, suffering perhaps from a certain malaise and staleness after so many months of almost uninterrupted cricket and two long sea voyages. His increasing phobia of making mistakes was possibly reflected in his performance in the encounter with Surrey at Trent Bridge, on May 25, 26, and 27, when the home side were struggling to avoid defeat in their second innings. He shared a stand with Wilfred Flowers, and, significantly, they "showed untiring patience, never attempting to score unless they saw an absolute certainty." Immediately afterwards, against MCC at Lord's, he registered two of those time-consuming innings which were becoming his trademark, taking a whole hour to score 10 in his first innings and eighty minutes to reach 12 in his second. It may be remarked here that "untiring patience," with slight variations, becomes a veritable leitmotif in the descriptions of some of his performances. For Nottinghamshire against England at Trent Bridge, on June 11, 12, and 13, he spent ninety minutes in compiling "a steady 28," before departing to a catch in the slips. You might have been justified in hazarding a guess that the promoters and selectors for this contest were either practising a form of mental cruelty on the spectators or blatantly pandering to all devotees of the art of stonewalling. Included in the England side at numbers two and three were that pair of limpet-like batsmen, Louis Hall and Dick Barlow. The former, dismissed for 0 and 1, was permitted little opportunity to take root at the crease, but Scotton's effort was put in the shade by Barlow, who in his first innings dawdled along to 31 in well over two hours!

There were other occasions when Scotton was praised for his dogged tenacity, the word "admirable" being the favourite epithet. Against Yorkshire at Bramall Lane, on June 29, 30, and July 1, he "showed admirable defence" in making 33 in a stay of two hours and a-quarter. This performance, however, took on the appearance of something close to fast scoring, when Louis Hall provided Yorkshire's Roland for Nottinghamshire's Oliver. After seeing the first twenty-five overs go by without opening his account, Hall toiled for three hours and a-quarter in making 39! In the return fixture at Trent Bridge a fortnight later, Scotton's second knock lasted only ten minutes short of three hours, and "his innings of 49 was in every way an admirable one." He marked his highest figure of the season in the home match against Derbyshire, beginning on the last day of August, when he defended his wicket for three hours and a-quarter, scoring 64 ("a really admirable innings").

Scotton's record at the end of the summer showed a distinct decline from the high standards of 1884, and his batting average was almost halved, sliding down to 18.05. There was one performance deserving of memory, however, which crystallized the best or worst of what might be termed vintage Scotton, according to your individual point of view. Nottinghamshire crushed Gloucestershire in one innings at Trent Bridge, on July 23, 24, and 25. Top scorers for the home side were the two opening batsmen, Arthur Shrewsbury who scored a century, and Will Scotton. "The cricket was decidedly slow," since Arthur was no firecracker either, and there were several long successions of maiden overs. It took about four hours fifty minutes for the visitors to achieve their first success, when Scotton was finally dismissed when the total had edged up to 159. To this figure he had contributed only 46, and "At one time he was batting for an hour without making a run!"

The season of 1886, by contrast, saw Will Scotton at his most prolific. With an aggregate of 979 runs – the highest he ever attained – and an average of 26.45, he came twentieth in the batting table. It should not be imagined, however, that his obsession with impregnable defence was ever relieved by any exhibition of attractive scoring strokes, apart from one exception. Criticism of his mind-numbing slowness and apparent lack of even the slightest desire to push the score along was voiced on more than one occasion. Assisting his County against the Australians in the second week of July, he was top scorer with 45 in the second innings, but this was spread out over three hours thirty-five minutes, and "The cricket was of the slowest description . . . tame and slow." In the contest against Yorkshire at Bramall Lane, on August 9, 10, and 11, a somnolent partnership with Shrewsbury for the first wicket realized no more than 48 runs in an hour and forty minutes, while a stand with an unusually timid Billy Barnes yielded 46 in an hour and a-half. Scotton was eventually dismissed for 32 after defying the Yorkshire attack for three hours ten minutes, a performance described bluntly in *Wisden* as "tedious in the extreme." Yet it should not be forgotten that he made the top score of the match on a pitch ruined by rain.

In all fairness to Will Scotton, he was not the sole culprit in the Nottinghamshire side, since there were others, such as Arthur Shrewsbury and William Gunn, who rarely accelerated into the fast lane. What might be condemned in one set of circumstances during a county match might be deemed praiseworthy in another context. Take, for example, his performance in the second Test against Australia at Lord's, on July 19, 20, and 21. He remained at the wickets for about two hours, during which he scored no more than 19 runs, but his defence was regarded as being "among the best features of the match." On at least two other occasions during the summer, he achieved a kind of glory, which far out-weighed any of the criticism aimed at him. His most heroic performance, ostensibly, was recorded in the fixture with Surrey at Trent Bridge, on June 14, 15, and 16. Rain on the first day restricted the visitors' total to 172 but, ominously, they had lost only two wickets, and on the next they succeeded in adding 110 more runs. The old firm of Scotton and Shrewsbury made a more than adequate reply, and at close of play there were 101 runs in the book for the loss of Arthur's wicket, while his partner had just passed his half-century. Dire disaster stared Nottinghamshire in the face on the morrow when, with one exception, numbers three to ten failed to reach double figures. The ninth wicket fell at 180, and then something approaching a miracle happened. Will Scotton, completely unperturbed, was still there, batting in his customary fashion, when Mordecai Sherwin, the stalwart wicket-keeper of generous proportions, came out to keep him company. Mordecai, with a career best of 37, was never regarded as much of a batsman, but in this time of crisis he contributed 25 to a stand of 43, and between them the pair saved the follow on. The match, naturally, was unfinished. Scotton's "unwearying patience" was prolonged for a period of six hours and a quarter, during which he gave only two hard chances at the wicket. He scored 110, with seven 4s, and for the first time in his career he carried his bat through a completed innings. For once, he was the favourite of the Trent Bridge crowd, and a collection was made amounting to a little over £13. Two-thirds of this sum was presented to the centurion, and the remainder went to Sherwin.

At The Oval, on August 12, 13, and 14, the England batting was opened by W.G. and Will Scotton for the third time that season. In the two previous Tests, their association had not been very fruitful, since although the left-hander had reached double figures in all three innings (21, 20, and 19) his partner's aggregate was only 30, with a highest score of 18. The Champion was due to take his revenge. Both batsmen concentrated on survival at the beginning, but when the slowness of the wicket vanished W.G. started to dominate the proceedings and punish the Australian bowling. Scotton, who in his previous match had just played that innings against Yorkshire which *Wisden* considered so tedious, carried on with the same tactics. With the Champion racing into top form, Will settled for keeping up his wicket

William Gunn

Mordecai Sherwin

and batting "with extraordinary patience even for him." The two partners, admirably complementing each other for the occasion, put on 170 runs in three hours and three-quarters, at which point Scotton was bowled. By this time, W.G. had passed three figures, while his partner had made 34. It makes you tremble to think what would have been the Australians' state of mind, especially as "at one period the famous Notts left-hander was in an hour and seven minutes without making a single run!" His performance found no favour with one of the contributors to *Punch*. In a parody of the piece by Tennyson, beginning "Break, break, break, On thy cold grey stones, O Sea!" the comic poet opened his version with the couplet "Block, block, block, At the foot of thy wicket, O Scotton!" and went on to compare him unfavourably with W.G. (who made 170) and Walter Read (94). Yet there was a certain stark splendour and admirable abnegation in Scotton's contribution to the highest first-wicket stand hitherto recorded in Test Matches. He had, so to speak, out-Scottoned Scotton, but he had played "an innings of immense value to his side," and England, with three successive victories, inflicted a whitewash on their opponents.

The same partnership with W.G. inflicted yet another period of misery upon the Australians at the Scarborough Festival, on September 2, 3, and 4. Opening the batting for Lord Londesborough's Eleven, they fell not far short of equalling their stand at The Oval, putting on 159. The Champion, with 92, was the first to leave, and when Scotton was dismissed he had made 71 ("as good an innings as he played last season"). Although he displayed his usual impregnable defence, he succumbed to the Festival spirit in a fashion almost reckless for him by striking ten boundaries – more than half his score – and "he hit with far more than ordinary freedom." The scoring rate during this first-wicket partnership was about one run a minute.

Will Scotton's historic innings and partnership with W.G. Grace at The Oval in 1886 marked the end of his service for England in home Test Matches, and, sadly, the following winter saw the end of his career in international contests. One of his principal contributions to the tour of Australia in 1886–87, promoted once again by Lillywhite, Shaw, and Shrewsbury, was his talent for singing, not only on the voyage out and back but on dry land as well. A member of the choir for church services on Sundays, he also took part in various festivities, such as charity concerts, and more than once he joined some of his team-mates in blacking up their faces and presenting "a nigger-minstrel performance." Social activities also included card-playing, and on one occasion he came out as the winner of a whist drive. On the cricket field, unfortunately, he proved far less versatile, and his efforts realized little in the way of success, either in "odds" contests or first-class matches. He began the tour in his customary role of opening batsman, usually with Shrewsbury, but his performance was so indifferent that he was dropped down the order. Confined to four innings of single figures in the two Tests, he showed little improvement in the remaining first-class fixtures, failing to reach a half-century, and his wretched average of 11.29 placed him firmly at the bottom of the table, trailing behind even Mordecai Sherwin! Nor was his record in the minor affairs much better – an average just one run higher. Only once, towards the conclusion of the programme, was there a glimpse of something special. Restored to his former position of opening batsman in the drawn match with Fifteen of East Melbourne Club, on March 11, 12, and 14, 1887, he made 71. *Wisden*, in a brief report, paid tribute to the fine batting of George Lohmann (100) and Scotton, adding rather sternly, "the latter of whom had by no means sustained his reputation during the previous part of the tour."

There was, however, one memorable incident in Will Scotton's last visit down under. Arrangements to get up a third Test Match fell through, and substituted in its place at Melbourne, on March 17, 18, 19, and 21, 1887, was an encounter between Smokers and Non-smokers. As a demonstration of their superior fitness, the latter compiled the enormous total of 803, the highest hitherto attained in a first-class match. In other circumstances, the Smokers' score of 356 would have been considered eminently respectable, but of course they were obliged to follow their innings, and the game headed towards an inevitable draw. The honour of receiving the final delivery of the last over fell to Will Scotton, who had scored 18. Tapping the ball gently in the direction of point, he ran quickly after it and seized hold of it as a prized souvenir of such an historic match. The same idea had occurred to those members of the fielding side close to the wicket, one of them, perhaps, Arthur Shrewsbury, who usually stood at point, and who had made 236 for the Non-smokers – at that time his highest score in first-class cricket. In their frustration they appealed to the umpire. Since the latter had not called "over," the ball was deemed to be still in play, and Will Scotton achieved the unique distinction of becoming the first, and as far as I can discover, the only English batsman to be dismissed "handled the ball" in a first-class match in Australia. The umpire's decision did nothing to destroy the victim's satisfaction in securing and retaining possession of his trophy (where is it now, I wonder?). All the same, it was hard luck on Arthur at the time, but we need not waste much sympathy on him, seeing that he made 267 against Middlesex the following August.

There was an unfortunate *contretemps* in the aftermath of this tour. Shrewsbury was in Australia again next winter, and he had undertaken to try and retrieve a debt of £40 from a firm which, Scotton claimed, was still outstanding to him for the sale of bats during 1886–87. Shrewsbury made enquiries and was convinced by the firm that the money had already been remitted to England, implying that Scotton was guilty of sharp practice. Whatever the rights and wrongs of the case, Shrewsbury felt aggrieved and took it upon himself to address a caustic word of complaint to Alfred Shaw, his business partner, which did little towards prolonging that friendship with Scotton dating from their schooldays.

With the disappointments of his final tour down under behind him, Scotton had the opportunity to rehabilitate himself and stake his claim as one of the leading professional batsmen in England in 1887. There was some improvement on his form of the previous winter, but not, unfortunately, enough to retrieve the situation. His aggregate of 349, which included two half-centuries, yielded an average of only 19.38. There was, however, one characteristic performance redounding to his credit. At Old Trafford, on August 18, 19, and 20, Lancashire defeated Nottinghamshire by ten wickets. Without Will Scotton, this humiliation would have been far worse. Batting first on a soft, drying pitch, the visitors were dismissed for 92 in only two hours fifty minutes. Their chief destroyer was Dick Barlow, who registered one of the best bowling performances of his career (8–26) as a sort of starter to another stonewalling effort from *him*. Scotton opened the innings with Shrewsbury on the nightmarish wicket. So great were the disadvantages under which he laboured that "even he was frequently beaten by the bowling." In the face of such adversity, however, he courageously exhibited "all his well known patience." When the final wicket fell, Scotton, the top scorer with 35, was still there unconquered, carrying his bat through a completed innings for the second time in his career.

Although the season of 1887 might have suggested that he was making a partial recovery from that last, disastrous tour of Australia, future events were to demonstrate that Scotton was now probably insufficiently equipped both mentally and physically to withstand the strain of perpetual concentration at the crease and the pressure of personal matters. It is possible also that, in a perverse kind of way, he missed the reassuring presence of his partner Shrewsbury, for Arthur, detained down under on business matters, took no part in first-class cricket in the English summer of 1888. The Australians were on tour in the old country, but Scotton's overall performance was so lamentable that the question of a recall to the Test team could scarcely have arisen, and W.G. had to settle for new opening partners. Although his final aggregate increased to 459 runs, Scotton's average slumped dramatically to only 14.80. In a record blemished by too many mediocre innings there was the occasional flash of staunch defiance to relieve the darkness of the gathering gloom. In the first innings against Middlesex at Lord's, on June 7, 8, and 9, he was the ninth man to go after a dogged resistance lasting four and a-quarter hours, making the top score of 67 "by patient and characteristic batting." Against Yorkshire at Trent Bridge, in the first week of July, his 26 was the best figure in the second innings. One report described much of this game as being "tedious and devoid of interest." Scotton, however, was not the sole offender, since Louis Hall for the visitors devoted a whole hour of his first innings exclusively to obdurate defence. In the return at Bramall

Lane, on July 23 and 24, Nottinghamshire succumbed ignominiously to the Yorkshire bowling twice. Skittled out for 24 at the first attempt, they reached 58 at the second, and Will Scotton carried his bat through the whole innings for the top score of 17.

Before the Australians went to Lord's for the first Test, they were engaged in several matches in the Midlands, the last of which came off at Stoke-on-Trent, on July 12 and 13. Opposing the tourists was a rather motley collection of cricketers, taking the somewhat ambiguous title of An Eleven of England. The captain of this Eleven was Mr A.H. Heath, an old Oxford Blue and currently skipper of the Staffordshire Club. He had experienced some difficulties in finalizing his side, and although it contained one or two good names, not one of the party could have laid claim to a place in the best team that England could muster in 1888. Mr Heath's problems were compounded by the weather. The ground was almost waterlogged on the first day, but in order not to disappoint the crowd a start was made at 3.00 p.m. Winning the toss and batting first, the Australians had the best of the conditions, since none of the bowlers could get a proper footing on the saturated turf. Their innings closed at 242 the next day, but a hot sun operated to their advantage when their opponents went in. C.T.B. Turner ("The Terror"), the natural successor to F.R. Spofforth ("The Demon") as Australia's principal strike bowler, was "simply unplayable" on the treacherous surface. The frail resistance of the unhappy Eleven crumpled before his onslaught, and their first innings, which lasted only seventy minutes, realized 28 runs. Marking the best performance of his career, "The Terror" took nine wickets for 15 runs, the tenth being run out, but one possible victim eluded his predatory hand. Number two for the Eleven was Will Scotton, who fell short of a double-figure score by one run but succeeded in carrying out his bat. Two more hours sufficed in securing an overwhelming victory for the visitors. The Eleven's total in the second innings amounted to 79, and "Scotton again played better than anyone else." A stint of intense grafting prolonged for about eighty-five minutes yielded 20 precious runs, the top score of his side. In isolation, and as a matter of statistics pure and simple, his performance has the appearance of little out of the ordinary, but in reality his battle against Turner and the vagaries of the pitch assumes the character of a remarkable deed of derring-do.

There was little cause for rejoicing in the season of 1889. Will Scotton's feet were on the slippery slope, and he proved incapable of achieving much to halt that fatal descent leading remorselessly into obscurity. His average (14.32) was only slightly lower than the figure of the previous summer, but his aggregate declined by 101 runs to 358. Shrewsbury missed a few matches through injury, but only twice was Scotton his partner in opening the Nottinghamshire innings. From time to time in the earlier part of the season, the stonewaller appeared at the top of the order, but ere long he was removed from that all-important position and relegated to number six. On one occasion, however, in the contest against Yorkshire at Bramall Lane, on July 22, 23, and 24, when Arthur was absent, he went to the wickets first with his captain, Mr J.A. Dixon, and marked a sterling performance with 51 at his first attempt, followed by easily the top score of 50 in the second innings. This reversion to the form of his earlier years was like a tiny island surrounded by a grey, barren sea. Although he was never dismissed without scoring, he only managed to get into double figures a dozen times, one less than scores in the bracket of 1 to 9.

Misfortune, bleak and unrelenting, trod even closer on his heels in 1890. He was accorded the task of opening the innings only once with Shrewsbury – with a minimum of success. Sent in last in the first match of the season, he moved up and down the order, ranging from number four to number nine. With the aid of four not outs, his average rose by nearly two runs per innings, but the standard of his batting had deteriorated to a dismal level almost beyond recall, while his staying powers had dwindled to a pitiful extent. It would be kinder to pass over the details of much of his performance, apart from two exceptions. Against Sussex at Hove, on June 9, 10, and 11, he made a worthy contribution of 50 not out – his best of the season – towards Nottinghamshire's easy victory. In the previous fixture at Gravesend, on June 5, 6, and 7, Kent just managed to hold out for a draw with one wicket to fall, in a match marred by the slow rate of scoring adopted by some of the batsmen on both sides. As might be expected, the principal exponent of these delaying tactics was Will Scotton, who on this occasion sank to his personal nadir by coming so close to a state of eternal immobility in his second innings that he spent two hours all but five minutes in scoring 6 not out! A merciful declaration brought an end to the tenacious tedium of Scotton and his partner, much to the relief of spectators and cricketers alike. He turned out for his County in the next few matches, culminating in the contest against Yorkshire at Trent Bridge, on August 7, 8, and 9, in which he scored 20 and 1. By now, however, with nothing to offset the poor quality of his batting, he had become *persona non grata* in the eyes of the Nottinghamshire Committee, and he was omitted from the side for the remainder of the season.

The Trent Bridge authorities had, in fact, resolved to dispense with his services for good and all, a decision destined to have far-reaching consequences for Will Scotton. He made his final appearance in first-class cricket in the fixture between Cambridge University and MCC at Cambridge, on May 21, 22, and 23, 1891. Batting at number four in the visitors' first innings, he failed to score, somewhat surprisingly dismissed by a stumping. His first-class record, beginning in 1875 and ending in 1891, including three tours to Australia, was spread over 237 matches, during which he scored 6,527 runs at an average of 18.97. This aggregate included four centuries,

C. T. B. Turner

the most outstanding being his chanceless 134 against the Australians at Huddersfield in 1884. Notwithstanding the failures of his final tour in 1886–87, his performance in Test Matches was appreciably better. In fifteen games, eleven of them in Australia, he marked 510 runs at an average of 22.17, his highest score being that famous 90 at The Oval in 1884. He was undoubtedly at his best in the four contests on his home soil, scoring 184 runs at 36.80 per innings – double the average he attained in the three tours of Australia.

In 1891, when Will Scotton was only thirty-five, it became obvious that he would never be recalled to the Nottinghamshire team. This was a bitter blow to his pride, and from the grievous wound inflicted there was no recovery. From now onwards, he became a prey to fits of black depression. After that final appearance for MCC at Cambridge, he played in only a few minor matches, but he still held his appointment on the ground staff at Lord's. During the season, he was accustomed to living as a lodger at 91, St John's Wood Terrace, where his landlady was Mrs Ellen Lansdown, the wife of a station-inspector on the Metropolitan Railway.

The season of 1893 found Scotton in worse straits than ever. The lasting trauma created by his permanent omission from his county side was augmented by another factor: he had recently been divorced from his wife. Over this matter there is some mystery, for it was declared later that he was single and had never been married, but perhaps this was an attempt to cover up the apparent shame arising out of divorce in those days.

So, in the spring and early summer of 1893, Will Scotton was residing at his lodgings in the vicinity of Lord's. His mental condition by now had become pitiable in the extreme, and he was probably suffering from something akin to a nervous breakdown. Minor mishaps loomed large in his life, assuming gigantic proportions and threatening to crush his soul. Never the strongest-minded of men, he gave way easily to adversity, and there had been occasions in the past when he had been found weeping over his bad luck at the wicket and his loss of form. This over-sensitive side of his nature now began to exercise a dominating influence over him, and he gave way to tears at the slightest provocation. In this time of stress, he took to drinking on the sly, and the effects of liquor upon this hitherto abstemious man were observed by his landlady and his friend, George Francis Hearne. The latter, who was the pavilion clerk at Lord's and also an occasional professional cricketer, had known Scotton for some eighteen years and had been with him for part of the tour of Australia in 1884–85. Now, assuming the privilege conferred by a friendship of such long standing, Hearne wrote a letter to the unhappy man, urging him to pull himself together. This failed in its intentions and, coming as it did from a minor MCC official, probably served only to exacerbate Scotton's persecution complex and contribute to a recently developed and unwarranted obsession that he was going to be dismissed from his post at Lord's.

Meanwhile, Scotton's morbid dread of making mistakes was nourished by events occurring in the last week of June and the first few days of July. Late in June, he went to Mitcham to stand as umpire in a minor match, but on his arrival he found that one of the teams was short of a man, and he was prevailed upon to take the absentee's place. Also participating in this game was the rising Surrey fast bowler, Tom Richardson, and during the course of play Scotton damaged one of Richardson's fingers. This injury was severe enough to prevent Tom from appearing on the cricket field for a fortnight or so, presumably with a loss of wages, and the burden of his responsibility for this lay heavily upon the hyper-sensitive Scotton. In the same week or thereabouts, he fulfilled a two-day engagement at Sandhurst. Shortly afterwards, on Tuesday, July 4, he went to Clifton for another stint of umpiring duties, and he returned to his lodgings on the Thursday afternoon in a state of acute distress over a decision he had made in giving a batsman out, and which he subsequently believed to have been wrong.

The exact course of all Scotton's movements during this period is difficult to trace. One day, he visited a well known photographer in Cheapside to have his picture taken in cricketing costume and said that he would like "to have four dozen copies to distribute among his relatives and friends." On the surface, this desire to provide a memento of himself seems innocent enough, but hindsight suggests that there may have been a more sinister motive. The subject, it appears, expressed satisfaction on seeing a proof of the photograph, which was sent to him at St John's Wood Terrace, on Saturday, July 8.

On the morning of Friday, July 7, Scotton had his breakfast and left his lodgings at about ten o'clock, telling Mrs Lansdown that he was going to Lord's. Either this was a deliberate deception or else he changed his mind, for he did not go to his place of work. Perhaps this was the day of his visit to the photographer in Cheapside. Returning to St John's Wood Terrace during the afternoon, he remained there for the rest of the day, apart from going out for about half-an-hour in the evening. According to James Chandler, a cricket-bat handlemaker, who also lived at Mrs Lansdown's house, it was clear that Scotton had spent some of the time seeking oblivion in drink.

Chandler had been acquainted with Scotton for several years and, like the landlady and G.F. Hearne, he had noticed his fellow lodger's increasingly strange behaviour. In his loneliness and affliction on that Friday evening, Scotton evidently felt the need to communicate with somebody, so he wandered into Chandler's room and sat down on the couch for several minutes. He talked in an aimless, incoherent fashion and was obviously intoxicated, but suddenly, leaping to his feet, he went over to the open window, insisting that he could hear his brother John's voice outside in the street. It was, of course, an irrational delusion, for John Scotton, a licensed victualler at Nottingham, was nowhere near St John's Wood Terrace at that time. The wretched man then collapsed and wept bitter tears for about ten minutes, sobbing that he wanted to spend the night on Chandler's couch. In the end, however, he returned to his own room and retired to bed at about eleven o'clock – much to the relief of James Chandler, no doubt.

On the Saturday morning, Mrs Lansdown went to the back parlour, which Scotton occupied as a bedroom, but her lodger told her he intended to stay in bed all day. She noticed that he seemed quieter and more depressed than ever, but at times he talked in a rambling and inconsequential manner, maintaining that he was being unfairly treated by both his employers and colleagues at Lord's. He reverted also to another notion he had recently conceived, that people were coming after him – the tragic belief of a partly insane man who knows he is going insane and dreads being taken away to a place of restraint.

The landlady left him, and he slept during the afternoon to awake seemingly better and refreshed by his rest, and he "made a good tea." Later, between eleven o'clock and midnight, Mrs Lansdown and her daughter took a fish supper to the back parlour. Her lodger appeared to be in better spirits and ate his meal with relish, saying that he would have the remaining portion of his fish for breakfast. He chatted pleasantly, declaring his belief that "he could enjoy a good night's rest," and Mrs Lansdown noticed that this was the first time she had seen Scotton smile for three days.

Around 7.30 a.m. on Sunday, July 9, the landlady got up to prepare breakfast for her lodgers. An hour later, as was her custom, she carried a tray to the back parlour. Receiving no answer to her knock, she opened the door and entered . . . The room was a ghastly shambles, and the terrified woman screamed for Chandler to come to her aid. The bed was in wild disorder, and on the floor lay the body of Scotton, clad in a blood-soaked nightshirt, an open razor clenched in his left hand with which he had severed his jugular vein. Urgent messages were sent, summoning the police and Dr Robert James Carter, who lived in St John's Wood Terrace. Arriving on the horrible scene shortly before nine o'clock, the physician pronounced that life was extinct. He gave his opinion later that Scotton had been dead for several hours, but this may not have been accurate. According to one report, the body was still warm when Dr Carter came on the scene, and the landlady, while preparing her lodgers' breakfast, had "heard a peculiar choking noise in the deceased's room, but took no notice of it."

On the next day, Monday, July 10, an inquest was held at the Marylebone Coroner's Court. Among those called as witnesses were John Scotton (the dead man's brother), Mrs Lansdown, Chandler, the doctor, a police inspector, and G.F. Hearne. After hearing their evidence, the jury deliberated briefly before returning a formal verdict "that the deceased died of his own act while of unsound mind."

(Those who like to see all loose ends tied up may wish to spare a moment's thought for Mr R.W. Thomas, "that well-known sporting photographer" with the studio in Cheapside. Mr Thomas was left with, probably, an unpaid bill and certainly with four dozen copies of a portrait of Scotton on his hands. He announced his predicament in the pages of one of the sporting newspapers with a wide circulation, urging "those desirous of securing copies" to communicate with him as soon as possible. I don't know how many potential customers responded to this invitation, but one can imagine that if a copy were to be offered for sale in an auction of cricketana today, it would probably attract some promising bids).

The funeral took place at the General Cemetery, Nottingham, on the afternoon of Wednesday, July 12. Although not many persons knew of the time and place of interment, there were some "choice floral tributes," and a small gathering of friends and relatives "assembled at the graveside." These included the deceased's son, Master Harold Scotton, and his brother and sister-in-law. Present also was a Mr J. Selby, destined to die of a paralytic stroke but six months later. What were his thoughts at this time? Did he perhaps recall with regret that fight at Cootamundra in 1881? The heavens themselves seemed also to mourn the passing of William Henry Scotton, for when "the last rites for the burial of the dead were being performed a heavy storm broke over the cemetery."

While the jury at the inquest were reaching their verdict on Monday, July 10, an important sporting event was taking place not far away. It was the first day of the annual match between the Gentlemen and the Players at Lord's. Five members of the Nottinghamshire team appeared for the Players, and the side included three more Nottinghamshire men who had joined other counties. Top scorer for the professionals in their second innings, with a well played 88, was Arthur Shrewsbury. Fate ordained that the latter should tread along the same *via dolorosa* as his erstwhile partner, Will Scotton. Tormented by the belief that he was suffering from an incurable disease, Shrewsbury bought a five-chambered revolver and shot himself a week later on Tuesday, May 19, 1903.

NOTE.– Some of the aspects of Scotton's personality and the circumstances of his suicide and the aftermath have been adapted from my article, "Scotton's End," *The Journal of the Cricket Society*, X, 1 (Autumn 1980), 27–30.

WILLIE BATES
"The Dashing Young Yorkshireman"

I HAD my one and only encounter with William Ederick Bates on Friday, August 14, 1931. After a lapse of some thirty years, County Championship cricket had made a welcome return to Scarborough. It was evidently a popular move, since the attendance on Wednesday, August 12, the first day, was only slightly below 8,000 – imagine, nearly *eight thousand spectators* at a county match! Three Yorkshiremen in exile, including two who had played for their native county (W.E. Bates and J.T. Bell), were assisting Glamorgan, the visiting team. For those small boys, of whom I was one, the occasion provided a blissful opportunity to add to our collection of cricketers' autographs. Yorkshire made 378, and their opponents, condemned to the martyrdom of facing Bill Bowes and Hedley Verity on a pitch ruined by rain, were comprehensively defeated by an innings and 120 runs. It was, of course, a matter of pride that we boys should obtain *all* the signatures of *both* teams, and when the match was over I was still one name short on the Glamorgan page in my book. The missing man was W.E. Bates, and rumour said that he was in the bar at the rear of the pavilion. Rumour was correct, I found. There, consoling himself with a pint, stood my quarry. He was on his own, and the opportunity was too good to be missed. In his days as a Yorkshire professional some twenty years previously, W.E.B. had been such a snappy dresser that his team-mates called him "The Marquis." On this occasion at Scarborough, he was still presenting a certain appearance of sartorial splendour. After all those years, I can still see him in my mind's eye. He was dressed in the height of fashion for a sporting gentleman who had just played, or was just about to play, a round of golf. On his head he had a large flat cap with the peak slightly tilted over one eye, and he was clad in a jacket and ample plus-fours of a gingerish hue. It was definitely taboo in those days for small boys to go into bars, so I tiptoed over the threshold, taking care not to attract the attention of the barman. Arriving in front of W.E.B., I made my request as politely and quietly as I could. Patiently he set down his glass, took my book and pencil, and added his signature to the appropriate page. Our conversation was somewhat one-sided, since he said never a word, and as I thanked him his fingers were already closing round

126

Willie Bates   *Courtesy Roger Mann*

his glass. Thanks to his kindness and forbearance – nobody, after all, really likes to be disturbed in the course of enjoying a quiet pint – my quest was complete. Not until many years later did I discover that W.E. Bates was the famous son of an even more famous father.

William Ederick's celebrated parent was born at Lascelles Hall, on November 19, 1855. His first and only forename was sometimes set down formally as William, although he was in fact christened Willie. By neither was he commonly known, for the world at large plumped for a more alliterative version and always called him Billy Bates. As regards the location of his birthplace, he was extremely fortunate. A miniature settlement in its palmy days, Lascelles Hall was virtually a suburb of Huddersfield. It consisted then of little more than a country gentleman's residence and a cluster of cottages largely inhabited by hand-loom weavers and their families. A close-knit community, many of its members were fast-bound by the ties of inter-marriage, so that almost everybody seemed to be related to somebody in varying degrees. Some were pure native Hallians; others had moved into the village and been absorbed by the original dwellers. Weaving was their acknowledged trade, but cricket was their occupation. The men practised in the afternoon, returning home to complete their stint at the loom by candle-light. No less keen were the youngsters, such as Billy Bates. Often lacking regular equipment, they improvised with crewelled yarn balls, while for bats they filched the detachable legs from the stools on which their fathers sat at the looms.

In the 1860s and 1870s, Lascelles Hall was regarded as one of the leading nurseries of Yorkshire cricket, and the local club was of such a high standard that it had no qualms about taking on opponents of first-class or near first-class status. At one time or another, some twenty of its members turned out for the County, and when Yorkshire played against Gloucestershire at Clifton, on August 13, 14, and 15, 1874, no less than six of the visiting team hailed from the Lascelles Hall district. The same number assisted Yorkshire against Derbyshire at Derby, on August 20, 21, and 22, 1877.

The presence in the Yorkshire Eleven of so many players from one small locality inevitably caused some heart-burning in other parts of the County, nowhere more so, perhaps, than in Sheffield, the origin and home of other famous cricketers. At the time when Lascelles Hall was coming into prominence and for many years afterwards, Sheffield was the dominating force in the organization and administration of Yorkshire cricket. Proud of their supremacy, the authorities at Bramall Lane looked askance at any challenge to their commanding position, and it is possible that more than one Hallian (e.g., David Eastwood, Henry Lockwood) failed to establish himself permanently in the side because of a feeling that too many Lascelles Hall men were playing for Yorkshire!

Such an attitude proved to be no barrier to any Hallian who chose to earn his wages by playing cricket somewhere in the summer and picking up his weaving in the winter. So rich were the cricketing resources of the district that many of its sons had no difficulty in obtaining engagements with other clubs, among them Billy Bates. Following a glowing recommendation from the secretary of Lascelles Hall CC, he was offered and accepted the post of professional in the Rochdale district. Similar appointments in the north came his way during the next year or so, but whenever he was available he turned out for his own club, of which he became a regular member in 1873 or thereabouts. It was some measure of his promise and prowess that, according to one report, he was engaged as the professional at Lascelles Hall in 1877, a momentous year for Billy Bates.

A lithe, comely figure, five feet ten inches tall and weighing between eleven and twelve stones, Bates was a man brimming over with energy and enthusiasm. He wore his hair short, with the then fashionable centre parting, and a neat, well groomed moustache of quite moderate proportions adorned his upper lip. The attention he gave to personal neatness was not confined merely to the hair growing on his head and face. On the cricket field, his spruce turn-out was a model for all young, aspiring players to emulate. When it came to plain clothes – though "plain," in one sense, is scarcely appropriate here – he almost certainly set an example to William Ederick. So fastidious and gorgeous was the apparel of Billy Bates that his Yorkshire team-mates called him "The Duke" – hence his son's nickname, "The Marquis." The father was not one of the comedians in the Yorkshire side, which, perhaps, was just as well, since there were several of one sort or another around in the 1880s. Equable of temperament, with a frank and generous disposition, he was the personification of good-natured tolerance towards his fellow men, without, however, going to such extremes as to allow others to impose upon him. There was nothing boisterous about his demeanour, and his sense of humour was quiet and underplayed. It was most usually expressed during the course of a match, when it was his custom to deliver a racy commentary on the progress of the play. His remarks on these occasions, though pungent at times, were devoid of any malice. Cheerful, enthusiastic, and endowed with those all-round talents after which many hanker in vain, he enjoyed a far-reaching popularity by no means confined to the shores of the British Isles.

With the backing of his fellow Lascelles Hallians, Billy Bates submitted to the authorities at Bramall Lane an application for a trial in the colts matches early in the season of 1877. The credentials of those endorsing his request were of the highest, since his sponsors were old John Thewlis and Ephraim Lockwood, John's nephew, two of the brightest stars of the Lascelles Hall galaxy. Old John, now approaching fifty, had retired from the first-class scene in 1875, but Ephraim was currently the best batsman in the Yorkshire team as well as being the captain. Bates showed such striking promise in the trial games that he was marked down for promotion to a higher sphere, and his rapid advance to the realm of first-class cricket was ensured by the most favourable of circumstances. Five regular members of the County side – T. Armitage, A. Greenwood, T. Emmett, A. Hill, and G. Ulyett – on tour of Australia and New Zealand in the winter of 1876–77, were not available for the first match of Yorkshire's programme, against Middlesex at Lord's, on June 4, 5, and 6. This particular fixture was under the aegis of Lord Londesborough, and the selection and management of the team was vested in Roger Iddison, the nobleman's agent for all matters appertaining to cricket at that time. Roger, one of the shrewdest brains in the game, a stalwart member and captain of the Eleven but a few years previously, drafted several youngsters into the side, among them Billy Bates, making his first-class debut at the headquarters of cricket. In spite of their weakened state, the visitors were able to overcome the absence of the five returning tourists, achieving a victory by 35 runs. Bates did nothing particularly spectacular, scoring 3 and 12 and capturing five wickets for 94 runs. He was not called upon for the next two fixtures, and in all he turned out in seven matches for Yorkshire with only modest results – a batting average of 12.70 and eight wickets at 25.87 apiece. The next season, however, would establish him as one of the rising stars of the younger generation.

Billy Bates developed into an excellent all-rounder, one of the finest of his age. As a batsman, at his peak, he was without any exaggeration brilliant. His style was graceful, correct, and the extreme opposite of comatose. Lord Hawke had no hesitation in recording his belief that Yorkshire never had a more attractive bat than Billy, adding, "until Hobbs came, I think he was the most engaging of all professional run-getters." Even allowing for a by no means modest amount of county pride, his lordship's opinion must carry considerable weight, when you think of the host of batsmen he had the opportunity to observe throughout his long association with Yorkshire cricket. "Hitting with great freedom everywhere" and similar words of praise proliferate in descriptions of Bates's batting. Shouldering arms to let a ball go by outside the off-stump was anathema to him. Always eager to go on the attack, he sought to set about the bowling from the first delivery he received, a technique which inevitably caused him on occasions to lose his wicket prematurely, and one of the cricket annuals mingled reproof with praise, saying, ". . . will sometimes throw his innings away for a slog, being a splendid hitter." He employed all the strokes, even the then unorthodox pull, but the most majestic was his on drive off a ball pitching on or near the leg-stump. Even when he played the forward defence, there was such power in putting the bat against the ball that the stroke was transformed from a block into a straight drive. When well set on a good fast wicket, he was in his element, sometimes scoring at the rate of a run a minute or even faster. Should your side be trying to beat the clock, then Billy Bates was your man. If only a time machine could enable us to re-capture him in full flow! You would, of course, probably see a couple of catches go to ground, but the sheer joy of watching him perform makes you, for once, envious of your ancestors. "His big scores," recollected W.G., "were all made in a free, dashing style," and you can hardly wonder at the perspicacious female fan who bestowed upon him the nickname of "The Dashing Young Yorkshireman."

When Bates was completing his application form for a trial with Yorkshire in 1877, he wrote the single word "bat" under the heading entitled "Your Special Proficiency," and made no mention of his skills with the ball. This was curious, to say the least, since in the early part of his career he achieved greater fame as a bowler rather than as a batsman. Although he was capable of sending down a quickish, unexpected yorker, his normal pace varied from slow to medium, achieving the difficult combination of accuracy of pitch with an extensive amount of break from the off. He was a genius at finding a spot to suit his delivery, and this faculty, together with the work he got on the ball, made him almost unplayable on a pitch that suited him. In such conditions, many an unwary batsman was trapped into giving a catch by the ball popping up very quickly and very high. After a few seasons, he began to lose some of his accuracy and spin, but in his heyday he was a formidable adversary. W.G. Grace, whose wicket he captured seventeen times, was sometimes ill at ease when facing him, while W.L. Murdoch, the Australian captain and one of the best batsmen of the 1880s, fell victim to Bates's wiles on ten occasions. Although usually intent on the immediate job in hand of conquering his opponents, Billy was known, according to legend, to be not entirely averse to introducing a little levity into the proceedings. This usually took the shape of deliberately bowling a tempting half-volley purely for the wicked pleasure of seeing a startled Tom Emmett at mid-off making a hasty jump in the air when the ball was struck straight at him with the speed of a rocket going into orbit.

The same enthusiasm Bates gave to his batting and bowling was reflected in his performance in the field. Nobody could ever have accused him of slackness or a lack of effort in trying to cut off the ball and keep down the runs, and he was always ready to take any position required of him without demur. Yet for all this selfless dedication, it was fielding that represented the chink in this all-rounder's armour. "As a field," said a reporter in a leading cricket magazine, "he is uncertain, and not the safest of catches." This judgement was published around the middle of Bates's first-class career, but similar remarks occur elsewhere at other times, and it was the general opinion that this unfortunate failing prevented him from gaining the very highest honour of all. At times he would pull off a blinding catch, but he had the unlucky habit of missing the easy ones. This fatal flaw in his performance had its good side, making him remarkably tolerant of butter-fingered team-mates, who deprived him of a victim. On such occasions, he seldom lost his temper, and once, when as many as five chances off his bowling were muffed in the space of about fifteen minutes, his only reaction later was a dry comment that he had seen better fielding in his time.

This exceptional forbearance, coupled with the knowledge of his own failings in this respect, was illustrated in one of Yorkshire's matches in the 1880s. Bates was doing a stint of bowling, and one of his twisters lobbed up gently off the bat in the direction of the veteran Ephraim Lockwood at point. For such a stroke, it was normally a foregone conclusion, and the batsman took the first step on his sad journey back to the pavilion. To the amazement of all concerned, however, the ball slipped through Ephraim's capacious hands and dropped on the grass. Apart from an audible sigh of relief from the lucky batsman, not a sound was heard. During this brief but pregnant pause in the proceedings, various members of the fielding side reacted in different ways. The hapless Ephraim hung his head and fixed his eyes on his clumsy, outsize feet. Tom Emmett gazed up at the heavens, doffed his cap, and thoughtfully scratched his head. An ominous snort emanated from Ted Peate's flared nostrils, while Lord Hawke thrust his hands into his trouser pockets and became absorbed in a study of the grass between his boots. The tension was unbearable, and if anybody should have felt aggrieved it was the unfortunate bowler, but Billy Bates swiftly assumed the role of peacemaker. He hastened over to Lockwood's side, patted him on the back, and said, "Never mind, Ephraim, Ah've doon t'same thing mesen." The incident was an excellent example of Billy's good nature, and also of a kind of commendable solidarity, with one Lascelles Hallian consoling another at a time of adversity.

Bates held down a regular place in the Yorkshire side in 1878 and never relinquished it until his retirement from first-class cricket. There was some improvement in his batting with an aggregate of 389 runs (average 14.40), but there was an inconsistency about his performance throughout the season. His most outstanding exploit occurred in the contest against Nottinghamshire at Bramall Lane, on June 24, 25, and 26. Going in at number eight in Yorkshire's only innings, he notched his maiden first-class century ("a praiseworthy innings"), marking 102 with eleven boundaries, and giving only one hard chance. For good measure, he emphasized his all-round prowess by capturing seven wickets for 75 runs.

It was, in fact, Bates's bowling which caught the eye in 1878. At the end of the season, he occupied the thirteenth position in the national bowling table with 99 wickets – pity about the missing one – at the excellent average of 11.68. Five or more victims in one innings succumbed to his off spin on eight occasions, the best performance – indeed, one of the best of his whole career – occurring in the Roses Match at Huddersfield, on August 8, 9, and 10. Since rain wiped out play on the final day, he was allotted only one tilt at the Lancastrians. Opening the attack in partnership with his captain, Tom Emmett, Billy registered the remarkable analysis of 30.1–13–45–8. His best match performance came off in the encounter with Gloucestershire at Bramall Lane, on July 29, 30, and 31 (Tom Emmett's Benefit), when he captured eleven wickets for 106 runs. In the visitors' first innings, he was not so successful by some standards, conceding 68 runs for only four wickets, though all of them were clean bowled. Unchanged with George Ulyett in the second innings, he proved much more deadly, taking seven for 38 (three clean bowled). There were some illustrious names among his victims – Messrs W.R. Gilbert and G.F. Grace twice, W.G. and Billy Midwinter once. A fortnight after the meeting with Gloucestershire, he had another outstanding match, when Yorkshire went south to Hove and inflicted an overwhelming defeat by 226 runs on Sussex. Billy, it is true, did not accomplish much with the bat (4 and 16), but he was spectacularly triumphant with the ball. The home side had a miserable time when it came to their turn to go in. Lasting not much more than an hour, their first innings totalled 35, with a highest individual score of 7, coming, oddly enough, from the number eleven. At their second attempt, the veteran James Lillywhite, junior, marked 12, which was exactly half of the Sussex total. This humiliation inflicted on the Sussex men was wrought largely by Billy Bates and Tom Emmett, who bowled without relief throughout the match, the former taking nine wickets for 34 runs (7–19 and 2–15) and the latter ten for 21 (3–12 and 7–9). At the end of the season, high hopes were entertained in some quarters that Bates was "the coming Alfred Shaw." These hopes were to be only partially and not permanently realized.

The following season saw an improvement in Bates's aggregate, which increased to 462 runs, and his average, which rose to 17.11, and again he found a place among the century makers. In the match against Lancashire at Bramall Lane, on August 11, 12, and 13, 1879, he atoned for his failure with the ball (not a single wicket) by making the top score. It was Bates at his best as a batsman. Going in at number five, he hit up 118, "a grand innings," in which he gave not a single chance. As a bowler throughout the season, he was in the van, and although his tally of victims fell to 87, he disposed of them at the astonishing rate of only 10.14 runs apiece, coming ninth in the national bowling averages, the highest position he ever achieved. Seven times he obtained five or more wickets in an innings, including the best ever performance of his first-class career. The contest between Surrey and Yorkshire at The Oval, scheduled for August 25, 26, and 27, was ruined by incessant torrents of rain, and play was only possible on the first day. Winning the toss, Yorkshire batted first and battled their way to a total of 92, to which Bates contributed 21. Four of his team-mates succumbed to the fast left-arm deliveries of an old acquaintance – Emanuel Blamires, who had made his debut for Yorkshire in the same match as Billy in 1877 and had subsequently moved on to sign up with the southern county. The date of debut was not the only common bond between "Nimrod" Blamires and Billy Bates: they were both expert players of the northern game of Knur and Spell. When Surrey went to the wickets, they fared even worse than their opponents in the atrocious conditions and were summarily dismissed for 59. Bowling unchanged with a new partner, Edmund Peate, Bates "proved almost unplayable," marking the astonishing return of 34.3–20–21–8!

"The Dashing Young Yorkshireman's" other memorable exploit with the ball in 1879 occurred in the contest between North and South at The Oval, on July 17 and 18, got up for the benefit of the veteran Surrey and England slow bowler, James Southerton. A.G. Steel, the amateur all-rounder, had been originally selected to assist the North but was unable to come, and Bates was called up to replace him. An easy victory by nine wickets for the northerners in only two days was the outcome of the affair. The responsibility for this result rested largely with two of the three bowlers employed by the North – the fast left-hander Fred Morley, Bates, and Alfred Shaw. Curiously enough, the last-named, of whom Bates in modern parlance was supposed to be a sort of clone, bowled to little effect, claiming only one wicket at a cost of 35 runs. Morley, conceding 80 runs, disposed of nine of the opposition, but the young Yorkshireman was the star of the northern attack. You might have said that Billy was moved by the desire to put on a very special performance in honour of the beneficiary, Jimmy Southerton, a fellow member of the off-breakers' guild. In a sustained stint of devious trundling, he was rewarded with match figures of ten wickets for only 43 runs (5–18 and 5–25), lifting the prized scalp of W.G. in the second innings with a catch off his own bowling. In an attempt to acquire further contributions to Southerton's benefit fund, a scratch game was got up to fill the third day, but it was curtailed by rain. The North knocked up 218, and when time was called the South had lost four wickets. One of these was a run out, the other three fell to the ten-wicket man.

Shortly after the end of the 1879 season, Bates set forth on his first visit overseas as a member of the team led by Richard Daft on a brief tour of Canada and the USA. As mentioned elsewhere, all the matches were played against "odds," in which Bates performed quite well with both bat and ball.

In 1880, Billy's tally of wickets increased slightly to 90, but his trundling, with an average of 15.44, was more expensive by over five runs each. Nevertheless, he had his days of triumph, with five or more wickets in an innings on six occasions and ten or more in a match twice. His best performances came off in the two fixtures with Nottinghamshire. At Trent Bridge, on June 28 and 29, he bowled unchanged with Ted Peate. Both were "in splendid form," but amidst tense excitement the home side scrambled home by two wickets. The dominating role fell to Bates, who captured eleven wickets for 67 runs (6–34 and 5–33). Yorkshire had their revenge later in the season, when they won by five wickets at Bramall Lane, on August 9, 10, and 11, and he returned match figures of ten for 68. His performance in Nottinghamshire's second innings (34–20–29–6) was regarded as his finest of the season.

With the bat, however, Bates had a rather disappointing season, for although he attained his highest aggregate so far (695), he went to the wickets far more times and, with no not outs to assist him, his average declined to 15.79. Still, there were some moments of dazzling splendour embedded in a succession of mediocre scores. At The Oval, on July 1, 2, and 3, he made an inauspicious debut in the series Gentlemen v Players, taking no more than two wickets and scoring only two runs, marking at his first attempt what an enterprising journalist once referred to as "a cockseye." In the equivalent fixture at Lord's immediately afterwards, it looked as though his run of ill-luck was continuing unabated – only two wickets in the match and a single in the first innings. The second, however, showed up Bates in all his glory. With the somewhat unexpected assistance of the wicket-keeper, Richard Pilling (career average 9.85), he dominated an eighth-wicket stand, which increased the total from 141 to 223. At that point, having earlier survived a hard chance, he was caught by the amateurs' skipper. His "splendid innings" of 87 included eight 4s and five 3s. Some weeks later, on August 12, 13, and 14, he atoned for his earlier failure at The Oval by trouncing the Surrey bowling. The match had been designated as a benefit for James Street, the former Surrey fast man. Such occasions seemed to bring out the best in Billy Bates, and this contest was no exception. In his only innings, he "hit tremendously hard," making a rapid 57, and although he failed to smite a sixer, his scoring strokes included four 5s!

From the standpoint of all-round performance, 1881 was one of the most successful seasons of Billy Bates's whole career. Scoring 941 runs at 20.91 per innings, his highest aggregate and average so far, he played some excellent knocks, including two particularly noteworthy exploits. In North v South at The Oval, on July 14, 15, and 16, got up for the benefit of Henry Jupp, the famous Surrey and England batsman, he shared a prolific stand with John Selby, during which "a rare turn at leather-hunting ensued."

Was there, I wonder, much sympathy extended to Mr J. Robertson, the Middlesex fast bowler, who ended up with two northern wickets and conceded 148 runs? Bates punished him without mercy, notching three 4s in one (four-ball) over, and at one stage Mr Robertson delivered four overs for the addition of 30 runs to the total. Top scorer for the North, the Yorkshireman had stroked his way to "an admirable and very freely hit 93," when he had the misfortune to put his leg in the line of a straight one. Even better was a magnificent performance only one week later. In Yorkshire's second innings against Kent, on July 22, he took full advantage of the "limited dimensions" of the ground at Mote Park, Maidstone. Promoted to open the batting in place of George Ulyett (absent with a sprained side), he gave a dashing display of "splendid cricket," rattling up 108 out of 148 scored while he was at the wickets, and giving only one chance when he had reached 76. All his runs, of which only ten came in singles, were made before the luncheon interval, and his hits included eighteen 4s (exactly two-thirds of his score) and one 6.

As a bowler, Bates performed wonders, with a three-figure tally of wickets in a season for the first and only time in his career. Coming twentieth in the national bowling table for 1881, he disposed of 121 batsmen at an average of 16.28. His haul of five or more wickets in an innings amounted to nine, his highest ever, and the number of his victims in a match reached double figures twice. The best return in one innings occurred quite late in the summer, when he captured seven for 45 while assisting Alfred Shaw's Eleven against Lord Sheffield's Eleven at Sheffield Park, on August 25, 26, and 27, adding one more wicket in the second innings. Ted Peate, his regular bowling partner for Yorkshire, who was opposed to him in this match, went one better by taking nine wickets, including Billy's in the first innings. Nottinghamshire at Trent Bridge, on June 27 and 28, proved vulnerable once more to the Yorkshire pair of slow men, who did all the work for their side in the whole match. On a wet pitch, their bowling was "very destructive," particularly Bates's, whose figures were eleven wickets for only 47 runs (5–30 and 6–17). Against Middlesex at Huddersfield, on August 18, 19, and 20, he was the County's most successful bowler once again, but was a little more expensive, conceding 108 runs in exchange for ten wickets (4–52 and 6–56).

In view of his undoubted success over the whole season, it is a little unkind, perhaps, to find fault with Bates, but the fact remains that he suffered at times from inconsistency with both bat and ball, especially the latter. On the one hand, you could point to his excellent trundling for the Players against the Gentlemen at The Oval, on July 1 and 2 (6–50 in the second innings), and at Hove, on August 8, 9, and 10 (5–73 and 3–16). These eight wickets together with scores of 50 and 23 were in keeping with the Bates tradition, for this was yet another benefit match! On the other hand, however, an unhelpful pitch or occasional indisposition – for he was not always blessed with the best of health – could produce an adverse effect upon his performance. Or, sometimes, he lost line and length and became very ordinary. Against I Zingari in the final match of the Scarborough Festival, on September 5, 6, and 7, he was pitted against some of the most powerful amateur batsmen in the country, and "Bates's bowling was very expensive, his three wickets costing just 100 runs."

There was one other aspect of Bates's all-round performance in 1881: he held 33 catches, the greatest number in one season throughout his whole career.

The summer of 1881 was noteworthy in yet another way, since it witnessed Billy's marriage to his sweetheart, Sarah Elizabeth Medley. According to Ted Peate, the happy event ought to have taken place after the season was over, when the husband could have given his "oondivided attention" to his new state of bliss. In fact, during the following winter, Billy went on his first major tour abroad as a member of the team got up and managed by Lillywhite, Shaw, and Shrewsbury. His form was a bit in and out in the minor matches on the American leg of the journey, but he knocked up a fine 63 in New York. At the beginning of the voyage starting at San Francisco, he became the recipient of a mark of royal favour. Kalakaua, King of the Sandwich Islands, together with his retinue, was a passenger on the same ship, returning to his realm after an extended world tour. During his brief stop-off in England, he had been taken to see some cricket at The Oval, where he had been introduced to a few of the English team, and he was evidently delighted to renew the acquaintance ("we were quite old pals," said Ted Peate). Although he tried in vain to persuade the ship's captain to delay the voyage for a day at the Islands in order to see the Englishmen play a game, Kalakaua was probably not too well versed in the intricacies of cricket. He was, however, fond of the company of the cricketers and delighted in their singing. His favourite air was "The Bonny Yorkshire Lass," as sung by Billy Bates, and every morning he would send for Billy and his friends to attend him in his cabin for some musical entertainment. Once, by way of variety, His Majesty endeavoured to cajole Tom Emmett into giving a performance. Old Tom, who had no voice, was much too shy to make a spectacle of himself and offered a ready excuse, saying, "Ah beg your Majesty's pardon, boot Ah make it a roole never to sing out of England." In the face of this disappointment, the king perhaps consoled himself by calling for yet another rendering of "The Bonny Yorkshire Lass," and Billy duly obliged.

Bates acquitted himself well in the minor matches of the tour and was one of the most successful members of the team in the first-class contests. He scored 349 runs at an average of 29.08, coming fourth in the table, and achieved the best bowling average, taking thirty wickets at 17.33 each. His best all-round performance occurred in the return match with Victoria at Melbourne, on February 24, 25, and 27, 1882. Going in with the total at 60, he survived a stumping chance when he had made only 20. His dismissal came with the score at 173 after a slashing innings of 84 – his best of the tour. When Victoria went to the wickets again, he accounted for five of his opponents, conceding merely 17 runs.

At Melbourne, on December 31, 1881, and subsequent days in the new year, Billy Bates made his debut in Test cricket and "played splendidly" in his inaugural innings, making 58, followed up by a useful 47 in the second. He also took four wickets, oddly enough with the same analysis in each innings (2–43). Single figures with the bat in the second and third matches were counter-balanced by 23 and 52 not out in the final contest at Melbourne, on March 10, 11, 13, and 14, 1882. An aggregate of 192 and an average of 27.42 placed him third in the table, and he topped the bowling with sixteen wickets at 20.87 each. His success, however, is not to be measured in terms of statistics alone. Because of his spirited style of play and his good-natured enthusiasm, he became exceedingly popular with the cricketing public in Australia, and in the next few years it is believed that requests were made for the inclusion of the Yorkshireman's name in the team list. Like Morris Leyland, Bates was always ready to go on a tour, and out of seven consecutive winters in the 1880s he spent five of them down under.

It is possible that the extensive amount of travelling as well as the number of matches in which he participated might have had a temporarily adverse effect on Bates's constitution, for he was out of sorts at times in the summer of 1882. Notwithstanding this handicap, he still managed to pull off some excellent performances, particularly with the bat. For the first time in his career he achieved a four-figure aggregate – 1,011 runs, average 20.22. He played several vigorous, hard-hitting innings of merit, with his fair share of luck, but his most brilliant exploit undoubtedly occurred in the contest between Over Thirty and Under Thirty at Lord's, at the end of May. This was the match in which Mr A.N. Hornby (91) and George Ulyett (138) indulged in some heavy scoring for the seniors in the first innings and still ended up on the losing side. The success of the juniors was attributable in no small measure to the partnership of Bates and Peate – not so much in bowling, though Peate claimed ten wickets for 159 runs, but in batting, for which the slow left-hander was scarcely the most obvious of candidates. Bates, at number six, began his innings at the start of play on the second day, when Under Thirty had made 136 for the loss of four wickets. The fifth dismissal came after only eight runs had been added, and so mediocre was the support he received at the other end from numbers seven to ten that the ninth wicket fell at 238 – still behind the seniors' total. Ted Peate now joined Billy and was by no means a sleeping partner in the stand that ensued, which advanced the total to 359 and was only terminated when Peate was unluckily stumped by a ball rebounding from the keeper's pads on to the wicket. Good fortune was on Billy's side at least three times: badly missed at mid-off when he was only 28, he also gave a couple of chances in the slips later on, which was, perhaps, only to be expected of somebody hitting out "with great freedom." In spite of these blemishes, "it was certainly a grand innings." Piling on the runs at the rate of fractionally under one a minute, he took out his bat for an unbeaten 144, all obtained before the luncheon interval. This was the highest score of his career, and his hits consisted of seventeen 4s, eleven 3s, fourteen 2s, and no more than fifteen singles!

Immediately after his triumph at Lord's, Bates stood out as the Man of the Match in the contest between Yorkshire and Derbyshire at Huddersfield, on June 1 and 2, with a splendid all-round performance, scoring 54 in his first innings and capturing nine wickets for 63 runs (3–32 and 6–31). Overall, however, there was a slight suggestion that the lethal quality of his bowling was beginning to lose some of its edge. His tally of wickets fell to 82, captured at an average of 18.51 each. Five or more victims in an innings succumbed to his spin on only four occasions, and not once did he dispose of ten batsmen in a match. This comparative decline was a little surprising, since the conditions prevailing in 1882 tended to favour slow bowling (Ted Peate took 214 wickets). Nevertheless, Bates was able to enjoy the satisfaction of getting rid of W.G. three times in the two contests between the Gentlemen and the Players, dismissing the Champion for low scores twice at The Oval, on June 29, 30, and July 1, and in the first innings at Lord's straight afterwards.

Bates went off abroad again in the winter of 1882–83 as a member of the Hon Ivo Bligh's side touring Australia with the intention of regaining the recently invented Ashes. A photograph of the team shows Billy maintaining his dashing, "ducal" image. Neatly moustached like a cavalry officer, spruce in spotless whites and a large, broad-brimmed sunhat, he is clutching a ball and gazing confidently at the camera. Performing well in the minor contests, he also enjoyed much success in the first-class matches, scoring 271 runs at an average of 27.10 (fourth in the table) and capturing twenty-four wickets at 17.81 apiece (third). He did even better in the four Tests, coming third with the bat (28.66) and top with the ball (nineteen wickets, average 15.05). His bowling figures were boosted by one extraordinary performance in the Second Test at Melbourne, on January 19, 20, and 22, 1883.

Before the match ever started, plans were laid to thwart W.L. Murdoch's well known good fortune in winning the toss. The Governor of Tasmania presented the England skipper with a special lucky coin, which did the trick, and the visitors took first innings on a fine, fast wicket. So powerful

A. C. Bannerman

H. H. Massie

were their batting resources that Billy was put down at number nine in the order of going in. Joining Mr W.W. Read after two batsmen had gone for ducks with the total at 199, he survived an extremely hot catch to Giffen, the bowler, and a simpler one to Horan. Completely unrattled by these escapes, for after all missed catches featured regularly in many of Bates's knocks, he was soon attacking the bowling "in his well-known dashing style." The next morning, with Horan atoning for his earlier failure, the Yorkshireman yielded to a catch, having made 55 in "an exceedingly well-played innings."

Not long afterwards, Australia began their reply with H.H. Massie forcing the pace and Alec Bannerman stonewalling. At the luncheon interval, the former had made 26, while the latter, in a flawless display of a total lack of perpetual motion, was still not off the mark. The early England bowlers were out of luck, and on came the changes. With the total at 56, Massie was clean bowled for 43, and Murdoch took his place. The Australian captain, seemingly infected by a bad attack of Bannermanitis, withdrew into his shell, and the rate of scoring slowed down to ten runs in half-an-hour. Yet there was some merit in this excessive caution. Shortly after Massie was dismissed, Bates came on to bowl and instantly found a spot, delivering with deadly, rhythmical accuracy and reducing the Australian pair to helpless impotence. The total inched gingerly up to 72, and then Bates succeeded in getting one past Bannerman's cast-iron defence. Horan, his successor, could manage only three before being magnificently caught and bowled by Billy Barnes off a forcing stroke, and P.S. McDonnell came to the crease.

Normally a fine, attacking batsman, Percy McDonnell was given no chance on this occasion to live up to his reputation. After making three, he suffered the same fate as Bannerman. Number six was George Giffen, the accomplished all-rounder. He lasted no more than one delivery, hoodwinked into presenting a simple return catch to the bowler. Bates was on a hat-trick! Next man in was the gigantic G.J. Bonnor, whose heroic proportions earned him the nickname of "Joombo" from the crowd at Bramall Lane.

A fervent disciple of long-handle tactics, Bonnor had been known to boast with, admittedly, some justification, that he could annihilate the English slow bowlers. There were times, however, much to the dismay of his team-mates, when he abandoned his natural methods and tried to adopt a safer, more orthodox technique. Success did not always crown this departure from the norm. Yet, in the present situation at Melbourne, an educated guess suggested that Bonnor would be extra careful and concentrate all his faculties on preserving his wicket and warding off the hat-trick. As he made his way out to the crease, a hasty plot was hatched to bring about his downfall. The principal conspirators would be Bates and

W. W. Read

Walter Read, the latter volunteering for the task of fielding at silly mid-on. Bates would bowl a fast, shortish ball on the leg-stump, forcing Bonnor to play a slow, forward defensive stroke, and Read would be perfectly positioned to take the catch. The plan worked to perfection. As Bates was approaching the bowling crease, Read crept in closer. Nonplussed by the unusual pace and line of the delivery, Bonnor played forward diffidently, and the ball plopped safely into the expectant hands of silly mid-on. Neither the dumbfounded crowd nor the crestfallen batsman could believe what had happened, but Bates had secured his hat-trick.

The Yorkshireman's triumph was far from over. Australia, put out for 114 (Murdoch 19 not out in two and a-half hours!), with Bates capturing seven wickets for only 28 runs, were compelled to follow their innings. Bonnor was the top scorer with 34, but the home side could manage no more than 153 and lost by an innings and 27 runs. Billy, who had delivered 26.2 overs in the first innings, was on for most of the second. He proved more expensive, conceding 74 runs, but added seven more victims to his tally. His full analysis was 59.2–28–102–14 – the best match figures of his whole career.

Disgruntled at their defeat and smarting under the castigation of the sporting press, the Australian team harboured some dark thoughts, alleging that the spot on the pitch which gave so much assistance to Bates's off breaks had been caused by the spikes or plates in the boots worn by R.G. Barlow bowling at the other end. In support of their argument, they pointed out that the Yorkshireman had been nothing like so successful hitherto. In this they were right nor, for that matter, was he in subsequent matches. As for Dick Barlow's part in the affair, he could well have had something to do with causing the offending spot with his follow-through, since he delivered left-arm and usually over the wicket. The row over Barlow's boots was prolonged into the next Test at Sydney, on January 26, 27, 29, and 30, 1883, and some hard words were exchanged.

In spite of these suggestions that Bates had been provided with an unfair advantage, nothing should be allowed to belittle the magnitude of his marvellous deeds. As a reward for dismissing McDonnell, Giffen, and Bonnor with three consecutive deliveries, "he got a very smart silver tall hat for his pains" – a remarkable trophy, whose whereabouts today are unfortunately unknown. A further reward, in recognition of his all-round performance in the whole match, was a "present" of £31, the proceeds of a collection taken when play was over. A less tangible but more permanent acknowledgement of his merits was an unassailable place in the records of cricket. Billy Bates was the first English bowler to achieve a Test hat-trick, and the first man to score a half-century and take ten or more wickets in a match for England.

As far as batting was concerned, the hero of Melbourne seemed none the worse for his labours down under, and in the English summer of 1883 he achieved his second four-figure aggregate, marking 1,024 runs at an average of 23.27. He did not make a century, but he played several innings remarkable for big hitting, fast scoring, and his own contribution to the total while he was at the wickets. His highest figure of the season came in Yorkshire's match against Kent at Dewsbury, on June 7 and 8. Top scorer "with a brilliantly hit 79, out of 125 runs put on while he was in," he gave a magnificent exhibition of driving, and three times he lofted the ball over the ring of spectators. In Edward Pooley's benefit match, North v South at The Oval, on June 21, 22, and 23, he attacked from the start, knocking up a rapid 35 and plundering two 4s and a 3 off one over from W.R. Gilbert, the amateur slow bowler. So prodigious was the enormous power of one of these hits that the ball smashed into the pavilion rails and rebounded to within five yards or so of the wicket. For the Players against the Gentlemen on the same ground, a week later, he played "a magnificently free and dashing innings of 76, made without a chance," and his last thirty runs took him only eight hits! The top half of the Yorkshire order developed a wobble in the first innings of the encounter with MCC at Scarborough, on August 30, 31, and September 1, but Bates retrieved the situation. Of the 112 runs put on while he was in, he rattled up 75, "a performance for which he was loudly cheered on his retirement." Assisting Tom Emmett's Eleven against R.G. Barlow's Eleven at Holbeck, Leeds, on September 10, 11, and 12, he opened the batting in both innings and staged his most dazzling display of the season, scoring more runs than all his opponents put together! At his first attempt, having profited from a missed catch when he had made 8, he contributed 25 out of the first 26 runs scored – not, in fact, too surprising, seeing that his partner was Louis Hall – and was out leg before for 64. Top scorer in the second innings as well, he was responsible for 79 out of 119 runs from the bat, gave no chance, and smote three enormous 6s right out of the ground. As usual with Billy, a feature of all this run-getting was the low number of singles in each of these innings.

There was, regrettably, a marked falling-off in the standard of his bowling – a tally of 60 victims as opposed to 82 in the previous season. He laboured, no doubt, under the disadvantage of operating in conditions more favourable for batting, both as regards the weather and the gradually increasing smoothness of the pitches. His sixty wickets cost 19.51 runs each, and only once was he able to reproduce his old skills. In the benefit match for H.R.J. Charlwood at Hove, on August 20, 21, and 22, 1883, he routed Sussex with figures of eleven for 112 (5–55 and 6–57).

Bates spent the following winter in England. This, from the domestic point of view, was more than fortunate, since on March 5 his wife presented him with a son and heir, the William Ederick Bates mentioned previously. Without the extra income emanating from a tour overseas, Billy seems to have resumed his original trade: at the registration of the birth the father's occupation is declared not as "professional cricketer" but as "fancy weaver."

Perhaps the increase in his family responsibilities had an adverse effect upon Bates's form in the summer of 1884. His bowling, seemingly lacking any penetration, was nothing short of disastrous – but thirty expensive wickets at a cost of 25.23 apiece! On one solitary occasion, against Sussex at Bramall Lane, on June 12 and 13, he succeeded in recording a meritorious deed, capturing six wickets for 26 runs in the second innings.

As a batsman, he did rather better, achieving an aggregate of exactly 1,000 runs, at an average of 23.80. Contemporary writers asserted that he was "uncertain," and it must be admitted that his overall performance might with some justice be described as somewhat patchy – magnificent one day, mundane the next. Nevertheless, he scored three centuries, more than in any other season, and he was particularly hard on the Cambridge undergraduates. Assisting Mr C.I. Thornton's team at Cambridge, on May 22, 23, and 24, he shared a big partnership in the second innings with A.J. Webbe, the Middlesex amateur, and made a "most brilliantly-played 113," which contained eleven 4s. Thornton's team won, Sunday intervened, and another match began, with Yorkshire as the visiting side – in other words, Bates again! The home team made 114, and by close of play Yorkshire had passed this total, and Bates (80 not out) had easily overtaken Louis Hall (49 not out). There were, in the end, three centuries for the northern county, Bates's 133 being the best. This was his highest score of the season, and his innings was, for him, a little slow, taking nearly three and a-half hours. It was marred by three chances, but it was still considered "a brilliant display of hitting," and it contained sixteen 4s. His third century won the most praise. The encounter between Nottinghamshire and Yorkshire at Trent Bridge, on July 17, 18, and 19, was selected as the benefit match for J.C. Shaw. Once again, on these occasions, Billy Bates pulled out all the stops. In Yorkshire's second innings, he was at the wickets just over two and a-half hours, scoring 116 out of 137 runs, with fifteen 4s. Although he gave a hard chance at 69, his exploit received a lyrical treatment by *Wisden*, in whose account it is described as "an achievement which has certainly never been surpassed by the celebrated Yorkshireman, and which, *all things considered*, has few parallels in the history of the game." Perhaps the writer's judgement was influenced by events on the third and final day. Arthur Shrewsbury spent slightly more than three hours in reaching 61, and his partner Will Scotton about two hours and a-quarter – only twenty minutes or so shorter than Bates – in compiling 33.

Apart from his three centuries, Bates played a few other innings to make the mouth water. In Gentlemen *v* Players at Lord's, on July 7, 8, and 9, he made 45 ("a fine display of clean hitting") and a "dashing 72," sharing stands on both occasions with Ulyett. In the second innings, this pair put on 142 for the fourth wicket, scoring at a rapid rate and at one period hitting 4s in every over. Against Kent at Gravesend, in the middle of August, Bates just failed to reach another century. With no more than one hour left for play at the end of the first day, he opened the innings with Ulyett and dominated an incredible partnership, taking the total to 99 when stumps were drawn! His final score was 97 (stumped), and though he gave a chance or two, his innings was studded with some magnificent drives, including one that went right over the pavilion for 6. As a mark of his inconsistency, however, it might be added that he played forty-two completed innings in 1884, and in no less than twenty-three he made a single-figure score.

"The Dashing Young Yorkshireman" paid his third visit to the Antipodes in the winter of 1884–85. For him, personally, the tour was a great success, as had been his previous outings down under, and he proved to be one of the most valuable members of the team in both contests against "odds" and first-class matches, which for the first time included five Tests. In both types of cricket, he averaged over twenty with the bat, his most outstanding feat in the minor affairs occurring in the fixture with Twenty-two of Moss Vale, on January 21 and 22, 1885, when he raced to a carefree 111. This was the occasion when he had a partnership with Will Scotton, contributing 101 out of 124 on the first day.

In eight first-class matches, he reached an aggregate of 363 and, without the aid of a not-out innings, came third in the batting table (30.25). Equally successful in the Test Matches with 222 runs and the slightly higher average of 31.71, he attained the same position in the order. Used somewhat sparingly in the bowling department and delivering far fewer overs than five of his team-mates, he nevertheless captured fourteen wickets at 14.71 each, with only one man ahead of him in the list. In the Test Matches alone, however, he came top with ten wickets at almost the same cost (14.80). His record in this instance was something of a curiosity. Delivering in six innings, he had no success in four of them, but he bagged five for 31 in Australia's first innings at Adelaide, on December 12, 13, 15, and 16, 1884, and five for only 24 in the second innings at Sydney, on February 20, 21, 23, and 24, 1885. In the same encounter at Sydney, he hit up "a fine and free 31," his most remarkable stroke being "a grand hit to long-on, off Spofforth, clean over the fence for 5."

Came the following summer back home, and Bates carried on more or less where he had left off in Australia. His batting was especially brilliant, and at the end of the season he had amassed 1,161 runs (average 25.23), the highest aggregate he ever achieved. Not a single hundred stood against his name, but he passed the half-century on no less than ten occasions, coming twice within striking distance of a three-figure score. His finest performance, and one of the most famous of his whole career occurred in the Roses Match at Huddersfield, on July 23, 24, and 25, 1885. The venue, of course, was Billy's home ground as far as county matches were concerned, and it is said that several of the Yorkshire supporters had promised him some substantial "presents" if he made a century. Resuming his innings at 19 not out on the second morning, he inflicted a severe strafing on the bowling from the start, notching ten 4s. By the time the hands of the clock were pointing to two, his score was 98, with one ball to come before the luncheon interval. The bowler was Alec Watson, who had been assisting Lancashire with his off breaks for over a decade. Watson, a wily bird, applied a little elementary psychology, reasoning that Bates would attempt a grand gesture, and sent down a wickedly deceptive delivery. With a sudden rush of blood to the head, the batsman charged out of his ground, hopelessly misjudged the length and break, and was clean bowled. Although he had just failed to keep his side of the bargain, Billy still got his "present" – a munificent sum of £14 from a collection made at the ground. On the afternoon of the final day, Yorkshire were faced with the task of getting 148 in just under three hours. Two quick wickets went cheaply, whereupon the local hero, surviving an early chance, played an innings even more piratical than his first. The runs for victory came in slightly less than two hours. In only eighty-five minutes, he scored 82 not out, flogging the bowling to all points of the compass, with eleven 4s and only fourteen singles. Some measure of his all-round value to Yorkshire may be further gauged by his performance with the ball – match figures of seven for 133 (6–85 and 1–48).

Other sterling deeds with the bat included 72 out of 106 for the third wicket at Trent Bridge, on July 13, 14, and 15, though Bates blotted his copybook by missing Shrewsbury twice in the field; a faultless 70 in only seventy-five minutes against Gloucestershire at Gloucester, immediately afterwards; and 84 off the same opponents' bowling at Bradford, at the end of the month. In point of runs scored, these figures were surpassed by a brilliant piece of batting for Alfred Shaw's Australian Team against Louis Hall's Eleven, on September 14, 15, and 16. His 93 was marred by two chances, but he had his revenge for his dismissal at 98 in the Roses Match by hoisting one of Alec Watson's deliveries clean out of the ground for a 6. A most unusual event, however, took place in the contest with Derbyshire at Derby, on August 10, 11, and 12: a stand with Louis Hall put on some 20 runs, of which Billy's share was only 6!

The same season saw a slightly limited revival of his bowling, compared with 1884. His tally of wickets was more than doubled, rising to 78, but they cost him a little over twenty runs apiece. Three times he disposed of five or more batsmen in an innings, and undoubtedly his best performance with the ball occurred in Yorkshire's defeat of Surrey at Bramall Lane, on July 20, 21, and 22, when he returned match figures of eleven for 68 (4–25 and 7–43). All in all, July 1885 was quite a prolific month with bat and ball for Bates.

There was a departure from Bates's normal routine in the following summer. Since making his debut in the series Gentlemen v Players in 1880, he had been a permanent fixture in the professionals' team, but in 1886 he was missing from the sides chosen for the matches at Lord's, on July 12, 13, and 14, and The Oval, in the next three days. No Yorkshireman, in fact, took part in the encounter at headquarters, since the County Eleven were engaged in battle with the Australians at Bramall Lane on the same dates. Apart from one innings played "in the most dashing style" at the end of May, Bates had been beset by a sequence of low scores, but in the contest with the tourists he regained some of his old form with top scores of 57 and 44 ("some really brilliant cricket"). From then onwards, apart from a few lapses, he batted much better, achieving eventually an aggregate of 1,018 runs at an average of 23.67.

In reaching his thousand, he enjoyed considerable assistance from two exuberant and entirely characteristic performances late in the season. In Yorkshire's second innings against Sussex at Hove, on August 23, 24, and 25, he opened the batting with Louis Hall and was primarily responsible for the hurricane rate of scoring. The hundred went up after only eighty minutes, and at close of play the total stood at 182, with both men still in possession, Bates 136 not out (sixteen 4s), Hall 43 not out. The century maker failed to add to his overnight score the next morning, when he lost his wicket at 186, having been at the crease for only two and a-half hours. Yorkshire returned to home territory to spend the next three days playing against Derbyshire at Holbeck, Leeds. Taking first innings, the home side achieved a fairly modest total of 161, and of this number 154 came from the bat. The score card makes very peculiar reading: nine of the team were restricted to single figures, and the Hon M.B. Hawke reached 18. Towering high over this dismal catalogue of failures stood the splendid and undaunted effort of Billy Bates – no less than 106, with twelve 4s! It is only fair to add that his two centuries, as might be expected, were not without fault. The first contained two chances, the second three. In a backhanded way, the second hundred showed the versatility of Billy's stroke play. The first chance was dropped by long-on, when he had made 62; the second, at the fateful figure of 99, was grassed by mid-off; and the third, just before he finally went, eluded the slips. In justice to the batsman and his "brilliant display of hitting," it must be said that all three catches were very difficult.

Bates did rather less bowling in 1886, with a lower tally of wickets (65) but a rather better average (16.60). His best performance in one innings occurred in the match against Lancashire at Dewsbury, at the end of July, when there was so much rain that a draw was inevitable. The visitors, in their only innings, were put out for 53. Opening the attack for Yorkshire was the old partnership of Bates and Peate. The latter, whose days as a Yorkshire player were fast approaching their end, had no success, but Bates captured six wickets for a mere 19 runs. For sheer all-round splendour, however, consider that contest with Derbyshire mentioned above. The Yorkshire victory by 121 runs owed much to the efforts and energy of one man. Billy Bates performed the all-rounder's match double by scoring a hundred or more runs and taking ten or more wickets. His figures were 120 runs (106 and 14) and ten wickets for 75 (5–30 and 5–45) – a magnificently memorable exploit.

A fourth visit down under occupied the following winter, and in all matches, both minor and first-class, Bates had his usual good measure of success. Against Victoria at Melbourne, on March 4, 5, 7, and 8, 1887, with some exceptionally good hitting, he notched 86, his highest first-class score in Australia. In all first-class matches he scored 383 runs (average 21.27) and took twenty-eight wickets at 19.92 each. His best bowling came off in the final contest of the tour between Smokers and Non-smokers at Melbourne, on March 17, 18, 19, and 21. As mentioned elsewhere, the Smokers made 356 in their first innings, but six of their batsmen fell to Bates for only 73 runs. His performance in the two Tests was less impressive. At Sydney, on January 28, 29, and 31, he opened the batting and scored 8 and 24. His bowling was economical rather than penetrating (21–9–19–1 and 17–11–8–0). At the same venue, on February 25, 26, 28, and March 1, he made 8 and a well played 30. Put on in Australia's second innings, he was England's most successful bowler, delivering twenty-six overs, half of which were maidens, and disposing of four of his opponents for 26 runs.

The second contest at Sydney was Billy Bates's final appearance for England, whom he represented fifteen times on four tours to Australia. He never got the nod on home soil, the selectors giving preference to Dick Barlow and Billy Barnes as all-rounders. The usual reason given for his omission from the team in England was his uncertainty at fielding. It has to be admitted also that when the Australians visited England during his career, he enjoyed no outstanding or consistent success when assisting such teams as Yorkshire, the North, and the Players of England, his highest score being 57 and his best bowling six wickets for 41. All the same, you cannot help feeling that, particularly as a spunky batsman, he might have played his part in converting defeat into victory in the Ashes Test at The Oval, in 1882. With bat, ball, or in the field, he could hardly have performed worse than some of those who found favour in the eyes of the selectors.

Bates's Test record, for the time, was a good one – 656 runs at an average of 27.33 and fifty wickets at 16.42 each – and when these statistics are set up in comparison with those of contemporary professional all-rounders, he comes out well. Three in particular come to mind: R.G. Barlow, William Barnes, both mentioned above, and George Ulyett, all of whom assisted England in home and away Tests, and all of whom made more appearances. Dick Barlow scored fewer runs at a lower average and took fewer wickets for a more expensive average. Billy Barnes scored more runs, including a century, but his average works out lower than Bates's though higher than Barlow's; as a bowler, he just edges in front of Bates with fifty-one wickets at 15.54. George Ulyett scored more runs than any of the other three and comes second of the four, but he averages three runs less per innings than Bates; he took exactly the same number of wickets as his fellow Yorkshireman, but they cost him nearly four more runs each. So, were the selectors entirely fair in never giving Bates a single chance to play for England in England?

In reviewing the events of the season of 1887, one of the cricket annuals expressed the opinion that Bates's best days as a bowler lay firmly in the past. Justice was on the side of the annual, for although he twice took five or more wickets in an innings, his total bag was only forty-nine victims, and these wickets were bought at, for those days, huge expense, costing nearly twenty-eight runs each. This was the worst seasonal bowling average of his whole career. His batting, however, was still a potent force to be reckoned with, and he ended the season with an average of 24.90, but he just missed a sixth four-figure aggregate, scoring 996 runs. He had another good outing against Derbyshire at Derby, on June 27, 28, and 29, finding the boundary a dozen times in his score of 103, compiled in only two hours ("a fine illustration of determined hitting"), and to this feat he added eight wickets in the match. This was his only century of the season and, as it turned out, the tenth and last of his career.

Equally spectacular was his performance against Nottinghamshire at Bramall Lane, on August 22, 23, and 24. On the final day, Yorkshire were confronted with the task of making 119 runs in ninety-five minutes. It was the sort of challenge that appealed to Bates, who was promoted to open the batting with George Ulyett. The latter went cheaply, but his partner, determined to fling the bat at everything, "played one of the most remarkable hitting innings that has ever been seen." He had an easy let-off when he had made 30, but nothing daunted he continued to hit out at every delivery, until finally he went to a catch with the total at 91, to which he had contributed 63 *in only fifty-seven minutes!* Sad to say, Billy's noble deed was set at nought. His team-mates failed to follow his superb example, and Yorkshire ran out of time just three short of victory, with two wickets still to fall. The Sheffield "grinders" gave vent to their disappointment and fury with a crowd demonstration, accusing the Nottinghamshire players of deliberate time-wasting, an allegation which, however, found no support with the Yorkshire team.

Gentlemen v Players at The Oval, on July 14, 15, and 16, was the setting for another brilliant display of Bates at his best, with "some of the hardest and fastest hitting of the season." His final figure of 81, the top score of the match, contained twelve 4s and only eleven singles. As often in the past, luck was on his side, since he gave two chances to mid-on. The first of these, very early in his innings, was by a strange coincidence put down by Walter Read, the man who had helped him to secure his hat-trick with a catch at silly mid-on in that famous Test at Melbourne, in 1883.

With the two encounters in 1887, Billy Bates made his final appearance in the series Gentlemen v Players. From 1880 to 1887, he assisted the professionals in sixteen of the eighteen fixtures during the period. Particularly successful with the bat, he came well within the top twenty cricketers from both sides in the nineteenth century, scoring 698 runs at an average of 26.84, with highest scores of 87 and 81, and three other half-centuries. His bowling record was rather less distinguished – thirty-four wickets at 21.11 apiece, with two instances of five or more victims in an innings, his best figure being six for 50 at The Oval, in 1881.

Within certain limits, it could be inferred that Bates in his manhood had led a reasonably happy and contented life, and hitherto his lines had fallen in comparatively easy places. Endowed with rare talents in the game he loved, with the additional income arising from his employment at the loom, domestic security, and the prospect of enjoying a certain amount of modest prosperity for several years to come, he could have been regarded as a man contented with his lot. A drastic change, however, lay in the offing for Billy Bates. Fortune, once a kindly mother bestowing her occasional gifts and favours, was suddenly transformed into a cruel stepmother administering a series of harsh blows that sent the victim reeling to the point of no recovery.

In the winter of 1887–88, Bates set off south for his fifth visit to Australia, as a member of the team captained at first by his county skipper, the Hon M.B. Hawke, and subsequently by Mr G.F. Vernon. This was the occasion when there were two separate teams from England touring down under, leading to a certain amount of chaos and financial embarrassment for the promoters. Bates was destined to play but a small role in the proceedings. He took part in several matches, including three of first-class status, in the opening weeks of the programme. After a contest at Melbourne, on December 10 and 12, Vernon's team had games at Maryborough straight afterwards, and Sale, on December 19 and 20. Bates participated in the first of these fixtures but, being a little off colour, stood out of the side for the second and third and remained at Melbourne, where the other English team (Shrewsbury's) had just finished a match with Victoria.

Since Shrewsbury's men had several free days before their next encounter, they and one or more of the Victorian team were engaged in some net practice on December 21. Also present and joining in the play was Billy Bates, who was sending down a few balls to Jack Blackham, the Australian wicket-keeper. In the adjacent net, W. Newham, the Sussex amateur – another version says it was Walter Read – was loosening up with the bat. Suddenly, just as Bates was in the act of bowling, Newham (or Read) lashed out at a tempting delivery, and the ball smashed with sickening force into Bates's face immediately below the right eye. With the assistance of George Ulyett, the victim was removed to the pavilion and then to an hotel, where he was examined by an oculist, who inserted two stitches in the wound.

In the days succeeding the horrific accident, a slight amount of blurred vision returned to Bates's right eye, but it was impossible to say at that time whether he would ever recover his sight. It was, of course, useless for him to go on with the tour, and he was sent back to England on the ship *Orizaba*, while attempts were being made by Vernon, his skipper, and the Melbourne cricket authorities to raise some funds for him. With his world in ruins and racked with pain, Bates foundered in the depths of the blackest despair, and it was rumoured that he attempted to commit suicide, possibly during the voyage home. Arriving back in England on March 10, 1888, he underwent an examination by an eminent oculist the next day. The news, according to one report, was not encouraging, and it was feared that the damage caused by the injury would be permanent. Bates was packed off home, ordered to take things easily, and to avoid any reading or writing, if possible.

The oculist's prognosis, if reported correctly, proved to be on the pessimistic side. No more than a month later, Bates was able to write a letter acknowledging one of the expressions of sympathy he had received. According to his own statement, he had been able to see about the length of a cricket pitch with his damaged eye at the time of his arrival back in England, but now, after only a few weeks, he assured his correspondent there had been so much improvement that his range of vision extended over a mile! He also added that he was planning to take up cricket again during the coming season.

There might have been a slight element of bravado in all this, as though Bates were trying to cheer himself up in the midst of so much overwhelming adversity. The horror of the injury to his eye was not the only cross he had to bear, and from that time until the closing of his days misfortune in one form or another was never far away. A tragic state of affairs awaited him on his arrival home. Little William Ederick was desperately ill, and Mrs Bates, whose health had been frail for the past two years, was worn out with nursing him.

Richard Daft, writing in the early 1890s, recollected that he had recently played against Bates ("one of the best all-round men I ever knew") in a minor match at Ilkeston and thought that the return of the latter to the scene of his former glories was still a possibility. This optimistic wish was never to be fulfilled. Whatever plans he may have laid while he sat recovering from his accident and coping with his domestic problems, Billy Bates was finished with first-class cricket. There was much to be proud of in his record as one of the leading all-rounders of his time. He scored 10,249 runs at an average of 21.57, with ten centuries, the best being 144 not out in 1882, and he achieved a four-figure aggregate in five consecutive English summers (1882–1886). These bald statistics, unfortunately, give on their own little evidence that we are dealing with one of the most attractive and engaging batsmen of the 1880s, with a rare genius for rapid run-getting and forcing the pace. His tally of wickets amounted to 874, captured at 17.13 apiece. Only once did he claim a hundred wickets in a season, but on fifty-two occasions he took five or more in one innings, and ten times he dismissed ten or more opponents in a match, his finest performance being that in the Melbourne Test in 1883. Of the uncertainty of his fielding there can be not much doubt, but there was a distinctly tigerish quality when it came to his own bowling. Of the 238 catches he held during his first-class career, more than a-fifth of these were caught and bowled!

The exact details of Bates's activities during the next few years are rather obscure. An account in one local newspaper referred to a "disaster in business" after his return from Australia but does not elaborate on this statement. Although his career at the top was over, he did not forsake cricket completely. From time to time, he turned out for Lascelles Hall, and he held professional engagements at Haslingden, in Lancashire (1891), and Leek, Staffordshire (1892). Around this time also, there was the prospect of appointments as a coach in South Africa and at an English public school.

Like some other cricketers of the period, Bates had apparently over-looked the necessity of making adequate financial provision for the future, possibly anticipating that a good benefit would yield a nest-egg for his retirement. Unfortunately, he had not played long enough for Yorkshire to qualify for a regular benefit, but now, in his hours of distress, attempts were made to supply him with an income. A minor match or matches were got up on his behalf, and subscription lists were opened. As a vivid testimony to the beneficiary's world-wide popularity, contributions emanating from as far away as India, South Africa, and Australia were made to the fund. One of the most touching, perhaps, was a small donation from a private soldier stationed in Malta. In these various ways, several hundred pounds were raised and, with Lord Hawke, Mr E.W. Hirst (Lascelles Hall and Yorkshire), and Louis Hall acting as trustees, this sum was invested in Huddersfield Corporation Stock, with the interest to be payable to Bates in his lifetime. He was also for a while in receipt of a small weekly pension (a few shillings) from the Cricketers' Benevolent Fund.

The younger Bates, as we have seen, recovered from his juvenile ailments and in fact lived until 1957, but a few years after his horrifying accident the father suffered yet another cruel and grievous blow. His wife, Sarah Elizabeth Bates, who had been anything but robust over the last few years, sickened and passed away in 1891. William Ederick was given a home with one of his aunts, and the widower went to stay for a while with his mother. Deprived of the influence of the feminine guiding hand which his wife could have provided, and depressed at his exclusion from life at the top, Billy Bates began to go gradually downhill. Though not much over thirty at the time of his injury, he had lost much of his dash. An exemplary character during his days in the Yorkshire Eleven, cheerful and generous to a fault, he became irritable, morose, and fretful of the inactivity forced upon him. He had a large circle of acquaintances, whose intentions were, on the whole, doubtless well meant, but it could scarcely be claimed that their attempts to take him out of himself did him much good. Endeavouring to maintain his old associations, he made a point of attending some of the county matches, but to those who knew him he appeared "only a ghost of his former self." His general health began to deteriorate and, losing the will to keep himself up to the mark, he tended to let things slide. As the 1890s were drawing to a close, he neglected to renew his annual subscription to the Cricketers' Fund and, as the inevitable consequence, his small pension was withdrawn. Thanks to the intervention of his old team-mate Louis Hall, serving on the society's administrative body, the other members of the committee were persuaded to rescind their decision and resume payment of the pension.

Bates was not the only former Yorkshire cricketer to suffer want around this time. Old John Thewlis, that fellow Lascelles Hallian, distant kinsman, and sponsor of Billy in earlier days, was discovered by the writer, A.W. Pullin ("Old Ebor") living in poverty in the Manchester district. "Old Ebor" took steps to publicize the details of Thewlis's plight in one of his famous "Talks," and as a result belated attempts were made to relieve the near septuagenarian's immediate distress. Old John, unfortunately, was not destined to enjoy an easier existence for very long. Having decided to spend the Christmas holiday of 1899 at Lascelles Hall, he arranged to meet some of his friends at *The Tandem Inn*, a place popular with the local cricketers. Perhaps the excitement proved too much for him, since he was suddenly taken ill and removed to the house of some of his relatives, where he died on December 29.

The interment took place shortly afterwards and, given the time of the year, one can well imagine the state of the weather. Among the mourners standing around the grave was Billy Bates, frail in health but determined to pay one last tribute to his old friend. Exposed to the biting wind sweeping across the cemetery, he contracted a severe chill. A fatal inflammation of the lungs developed and, like George Ulyett some eighteen months previously, he was unable to withstand the inroads of the disease, which carried him off late on the afternoon of January 8, 1900.

Bates's sudden and unexpected demise prevented "Old Ebor" from having a "Talk" with him, and the history of Yorkshire and England cricket is the poorer for that. "Old Ebor," however, was moved to pen one of the most poignant tributes ever dedicated to one of the great players, and no sketch of Billy Bates could be appropriately concluded without its quotation. A brief threnody in miniature, it creates an image of the man with a combination of pathos and humanity:

> May the sod rest lightly on poor Bates's grave! He had his failings – who has not? – but he had also trials that fall to the lot of few men. He was a great cricketer, and a most kindly soul.

Robert Peel   *Courtesy Roger Mann*

ROBERT PEEL
"A Rare Plucked One"

EDMUND PEATE, one of the finest slow left-arm bowlers in the history of Yorkshire and England cricket, enjoyed the most successful season of his career in 1882, but the luck ran against him in the contest between the Gentlemen and the Players at The Oval, on June 29 and 30, and July 1. He took only two wickets in the match, and during the Gentlemen's second innings he had the misfortune to sprain his ankle so severely that he was *hors de combat* for almost a fortnight. Absent from the second fixture between the Gentlemen and the Players at Lord's following straight after the encounter at The Oval, he was still on the sidelines for the contest between Yorkshire and Surrey at Bramall Lane, on July 10, 11, and 12. All was not lost, however, since the Committee were in the fortunate position of being able to call upon the services of a left-hander, who had showed distinct promise when assisting Twenty-two Colts of the County against the Yorkshire Eleven at the beginning of the season.

The Colt, on leave from a professional engagement at Oldham, enjoyed a story-book debut in first-class cricket. In all, seven of the Yorkshire team were put on to bowl, delivering slightly more than two hundred overs in the visitors' two innings, and close on half of these were allotted to the newcomer. This immense burden – immense even for a slow left-hander – was rendered more onerous by an injury to Ted Peate's usual partner, Willie Bates. Sprained ankles seem to have been an occupational hazard for Yorkshire slow bowlers at that moment, since by the close of play on the first day Bates had hobbled off the field and took no further part in the match. The new boy, however, rose to the occasion, when greatness was thrust upon him. After having noted the absence of Peate in its match report, one of the cricket annuals went on to observe that "the capital bowling of his substitute, Peel, a colt of great promise, caused his loss to be little felt." The substitute recorded match figures of nine wickets for 129 runs (4–46 and 5–83) – more than ample consolation for a failure with the bat.

Anxious, perhaps, to assert his claim to the premier position in the Yorkshire ranks, Ted Peate returned to the side for the fixture against the Australians at Dewsbury, on July 13, 14, and 15. It was probably

Edmund Peate

too soon, but needs must, since Bates was still nursing *his* sprained ankle, and Peel took the off-breaker's place to lead the attack against the tourists – two slow left-handers opening the bowling! Peate (0–44) was completely outshone by his new partner, who captured six for only 41 runs. This was Peel's best performance in one innings in the season – a noteworthy feat against such illustrious opponents, since the Australian team of 1882 was regarded as one of the most powerful batting sides from down under in the Victorian age. His best match figures were those achieved against Surrey on the occasion of his debut. All told, he turned out in seven matches for Yorkshire, claiming twenty-nine wickets at an average of 12.75. With the bat he did little, apart from a fighting not-out innings of 35 to save the follow on in the away match against Derbyshire at the end of the first week in August. This courageous exploit gave grounds for the belief, later to be amply justified, that he would develop into much more than a bowler pure and simple.

Born at Churwell, Leeds, on February 12, 1857, Bobby Peel was a mature twenty-five years old at the time of his initial appearance in first-class cricket. A short, solid, stocky man, he stood no more than five feet six inches tall and weighed around eleven stones throughout his career. Of Anglo-Saxon type in appearance, he wore his hair quite short and, in his youth, parted on the left side and falling in a soft cowlick over his forehead. In later years, he sometimes adopted the more elaborate style of a centre parting. A neat moustache, of more modest proportions than the luxuriant soup-strainers cultivated by some of his contemporaries, and short, smooth, flat sideburns completed his facial adornment. There was nothing noticeably extrovert about his personality on the cricket field. Constantly absorbed in the progress of the game, dour, unemotional, and quiet of demeanour, he was not given to any excessive display of mirth or high spirits. A different side to his being surfaced in between times. A boon companion with a fund of stories, he possessed a puckish sense of humour and was well known for his tendency to play practical jokes upon his team-mates, in keeping with the ethos of the Victorian age and far from unknown in later times. Of formal education he had little, or at any rate little seems to have rubbed off on him. I have been told that, at the age of twenty-one, he did not sign his name in the orthodox manner on his marriage certificate, but if not capable of this simple action at that time, he certainly possessed the knowledge to perform it at a later date, as will be explained at the end of this sketch. It is pertinent, however, to bear in mind the testimony of Flora Thompson of *Lark Rise to Candleford* fame. When recalling the days of her childhood and teens, which coincided with Bobby's career on the cricket field, this celebrated authoress spoke on one occasion of the attitude adopted by some of her older acquaintances, who had a limited knowledge of reading and writing but were shy about broadcasting the fact to the world at large. "Some who could write their own name quite well," she remembered, "would make a cross as signature to a document out of nervousness or modesty." Perhaps Bobby was feeling nervous on the day of his nuptials.

When reviewing the events of the season of 1882, some of the writers contributing to the various cricket annuals were not averse to bestowing a modicum of commendation for the efforts of the newcomer. Their praise, however, was of necessity somewhat conditional when making prophecies of what the future might hold in store for Bobby. It was, of course, inevitable that comparisons with his famous team-mate should appear in their observations. Although Peel had made a promising beginning, "the extreme similarity of his delivery to that of Peate will, as far as Yorkshire is concerned, militate, at least for the present, a little against his chances." The syntax is rather tortuous, but if you read this judgement twice you can grasp the meaning. Similar views about Bobby's prospects were expressed elsewhere, with the declaration that, "unless his batting should materially improve, he is not likely to secure a permanent position," and the same writer went on to add that it was "rather a misfortune that he was not born in one of the Southern Counties." The mind boggles at the thought of anybody possessing the temperament and personality of Bobby Peel making a long and successful career in the south. His salvation would depend largely upon two possibilities – a material improvement in his batting, as mentioned above, and a decline in the bowling powers of Ted Peate, who reached his apogee in 1882. Bobby bided his time, and as things turned out, both were destined to be realized in the not too distant future, and soon he would be aspiring to a place in the ranks of England's leading all-rounders.

In the following season, Peel held down a regular position in the Yorkshire team and ended with a tally of 51 wickets at an average of 15.80 in all matches, though he failed to secure five in an innings. Nevertheless, one of the cricket annuals maintained that he was "rapidly becoming a dangerous rival to Peate," and whenever the opportunity presented itself, Peel had little difficulty in demonstrating his value as an integral member of the Yorkshire bowling. As a batsman, too, he made considerable progress, almost trebling the average he had achieved in his first season. His top score was 74 in the contest against Gloucestershire at Bradford, on July 30, 31, and August 1. Batting at number eight, and with the somewhat unlikely assistance of Ted Peate, he shared in a partnership of 126 with "some free and determined hitting," which made a sizeable contribution to Yorkshire's ultimate victory by eight wickets. It was, however, just as well that the two left-handers came off with the bat, since on this occasion they accomplished little between them with the ball.

Bobby Peel was a brilliant fielder, always willing to take any position assigned to him, though his chosen place was not in the out-field, since he did not possess a good throwing arm over a long distance. He was seen at his best closer to the wicket on the off side, and one of his contemporaries who knew him well described him in the fashionable idiom of the day as "a clinking cover-point." At times also, he would fill the position of silly mid-off. Wherever he stood, he was keen, active, and quick on his feet.

Although he showed some early promise as a batsman on a few occasions, Peel took some time to develop his powers in that department of the game. On his own confession, he was so absorbed in bowling and fielding in his early days that he gave little attention to batting. Once he had secured a more or less permanent place in the Yorkshire side, the performance of some of his team-mates fired him with a spirit of emulation, and he began to nurture a hunger for run-making. At the height of his career, he had become, in the judgement of W.G. Grace, "the best professional left-hand batsman in England." A powerful hitter to the on as well as the off, and a fast scorer when the conditions and circumstances were favourable, he was also able to adapt his technique to the preservation of his wicket in an emergency. When runs were wanted he made them, but when a crisis was looming over the destiny of his side he had the admirable knack of coming in and devoting himself to dogged resistance. Once, in a match of pre-eminent importance, he occupied the crease for nearly two hours or, in the recollection of one member of the fielding side, three and a-half hours, and his eventual score of 53 included thirty-seven singles and not one solitary boundary! Another of his suffering opponents shook his head as the little Yorkshireman dead-batted yet another delivery. "I hope," he complained, "that you are not going to develop into one of those wretched Scottons, Bobby." The latter, completely unruffled, replied, "Aye, aye, but Ah moost plaay t'game." And play it he did to such an effect that his team achieved a memorable victory.

At the time when his first-class career had just finished, Peel was asked by a knowledgeable journalist to give his views on the vexed and perpetual question of whether a good bowler would be prone to lose his edge if he took to batting as well. Bobby declined to accept this theory as a matter of general principle. Success as an all-rounder was a distinct possibility – there were, after all, several as eminent as he in his own day – always provided that the individual possessed an exceptionally strong constitution. Without this seemingly inexhaustible stamina, a would-be all-rounder was doomed to failure and the inevitable physical breakdown after a few years. Peel's formula for success, however, contained a further qualification. Some special consideration should be shown to any cricketer required by his captain to excel with both bat and ball. A batsman's hands will get jarred by the constant impact of the ball on the blade, and after a long innings the fingers lose their sensitivity and experience a certain numbness. "A bowler to be of any use," opined Bobby, "must be able to feel the ball run from his fingers." As a man who would be called upon to do a great deal of bowling once his side had taken the field, and even open the attack as was frequently his lot, he held the firm belief that an all-rounder should be sent in early in the innings in order to give his fingers time to recover from the effects of batting. As far as Yorkshire at least were concerned, Bobby's wishes were realized: a tail-ender at the beginning of his county career, he steadily rose to claim a position in the middle of the order.

Bobby Peel and Ted Peate both began life as fast left-arm bowlers, and both soon converted themselves to slow, the former being influenced to a certain extent by the latter. Although the results they achieved were similar, there was one notable difference. On becoming one of the slow men, Peate gave the impression of being a survivor from an earlier age, adopting a round-arm action almost on a level with the shoulder. Peel, on the other hand, opted for a higher delivery in keeping with current trends. Bowling off a short run with a beautiful, easy action, he would bring his left arm from behind his back "with the suspicion of a flourish." A master of length and accuracy of pitch, he could turn the ball both ways though more often than not from leg to off. Should an obdurate batsman prove impervious to the wiles of spin and break, Bobby still had more than one shot left in his locker. He was adept at holding back the ball and sending it down with a higher trajectory. As the ultimate reserve, he would resort to a particularly dangerous delivery, quickening his pace to make the ball come with his arm.

Most effective, or at any rate achieving more spectacular successes, on a worn, sticky, or crumbling pitch, he could in fact bowl under any conditions, not merely to keep down the runs but to vanquish the opposition as well. Never flummoxed by a slow wicket, his counter-stroke was to increase his pace and endeavour to convince his opponent that conditions were by no means so favourable for batting after all by making the ball turn more quickly than usual. Few of his contemporaries could match Bobby's voluminous knowledge of the game nor his canny capacity for speedily spotting a batsman's weakness. "He was like a terrier on a rat," said Archie MacLaren, never more so than when luring a batsman an infinitesimal distance further from his crease with every succeeding delivery, until one last forward defensive stroke became a despairing, off-balance stretch spelling disaster for the unfortunate victim. Some of the greatest batsmen of the age placed a high premium on his skills. Andrew Stoddart was a frequent victim in their encounters; Ranji considered him the foremost slow bowler of his time; Gilbert Jessop held the firm belief that Bobby was the most difficult bowler he had ever faced, more so even than the little Yorkshireman's successor, Wilfred Rhodes, for Bobby's flight was more puzzling and deceptive than the great Wilfred's; and W.G. Grace, who surrendered his wicket twenty-nine times to the slow left-hander, found him a mettlesome opponent.

Even more lavish praise emanated from Archie MacLaren, who summed him up as "A rare plucked one." Sacrificing county pride and loyalty to personal preference, Archie went on record with his belief that Peel rather than his second great rival, Lancashire's Johnny Briggs, was "the greatest left-hander of my time." This was no mere whim but a solid opinion based on his experience of playing either on the same side as Bobby or else in opposition to him. Archie had evidently spent a great deal of time in a close and penetrating study of Peel and his technique in action. For the Lancashire amateur there was a certain kind of sophisticated pleasure to be derived from watching the changing expressions on Bobby's face, as the slow man was establishing a complete mastery over an unfortunate batsman and preparing to deliver the *coup de grâce*.

Another view of Peel and his bowling appears in the reminiscences of Lord Hawke, his county captain. Equable of temperament and completely unemotional, or at all events exercising a perfect command over his emotions, Bobby took his punishment from a rampant batsman without complaint and rarely lost his length. By the same token, when success came his way, his demeanour was equally phlegmatic and devoid of any gesture of delight, once his task was accomplished. Ostentatious antics were beyond the pale, as far as Bobby was concerned, for "when at his deadliest and congratulated afterwards," said Lord Hawke, "one could detect no gleam of pleasure in his countenance." Bobby, transported by some enchanted time machine to the cricket fields of the late twentieth century, would have been like the proverbial fish out of water. Not for him the back-slapping jubilation and the mutual smiting of hands that often celebrate the fall of a wicket nowadays. Such braggadocio and posturing were as alien to his nature as they would have been to Arthur Mitchell's ("Th'art makin' a spectacle of thesen!"). Ever the introvert on such occasions, Bobby always preferred to savour his many moments of triumph within the secret places of his heart and preserve the appearance of studied indifference to the outer world.

There was one aspect of Peel's bowling that calls for a brief comment. Archie MacLaren's description of his action in bringing the ball from behind his back "with the suspicion of a flourish" gives rise to a tremor of doubt. I can recall at least two slow or slow-medium left-arm bowlers in not so distant times, who were accustomed to sending down the occasional faster delivery with all the appearance of a blatant throw. This vice is not, of course, confined to the slow left-arm fraternity, and in Peel's own time some objections were raised to the deliveries of two members of the Australian team touring England in 1896 – Ernest Jones (fast right-arm) and T.R. McKibbin (slow-medium off breaks). F.R. Spofforth, the scourge of English batsmen in a previous generation, penned a forthright letter to the editor of *The Sporting Life* on the subject of throwing. While condemning his fellow countryman McKibbin, "The Demon" felt it was only fair to mention an English bowler in the same context, "and although I could name many I am anxious not to injure any one." This pious declaration is immediately contradicted by the next two sentences, which read: "So I will take Bobby Peel, one of England's best bowlers, and one who has no need to resort to throwing. I acknowledge he does not often take to it, still it is well known to cricketers that at times he does 'shy'." As far as is known, Bobby was never called for throwing, nor in his estimation was there ever any question about the fairness of his delivery until the matter was raised towards the end of his career. When reminded some years later of Spofforth's accusation, he remarked that it had not done him the slightest harm, adding, "As a matter of fact, Ah *can't* throw."

Ted Peate, less deadly on the harder wickets of 1883, polished up his skills to cope with somewhat similar conditions in the following season and was once again the principal component of the Yorkshire attack. With Peate's resurgence, Bobby Peel had to content himself with the role of second or third-change bowler on many occasions. Although his tally of wickets fell from 51 to 43, his average was almost unchanged. The opportunity to demonstrate to the Yorkshire captain and committee that he was far more than an adequate replacement for the premier left-hander of England came when Peate was too ill to turn out in the match against Gloucestershire at Bradford, on July 28 and 29, 1884. The strength of the opposition, it must be admitted, was materially weakened by the absence of E.M. and W.G. Grace, who were mourning the death of their famous mother, but this factor should not be allowed to detract from Bobby's excellent all-round performance. Winning the toss, W.G.'s deputy took first innings, and the southern county found themselves confronted by the attack of the veteran Tom Emmett and Bobby Peel. Although three other bowlers were put on, the opening pair were solely responsible for the summary dismissal of Gloucestershire for only 117 runs, with Bobby capturing six wickets for 40, his best analysis in one innings so far. Yorkshire's reply lasted well into the second day, with Peel, at number ten, contributing a meritorious knock of 34 not out to the final total of 301. The visitors could manage only ten more runs than previously at their second attempt and were heavily beaten by an innings and 57 runs, with Peel securing five wickets for 47. This was the first but by no means the last time that he took ten or more wickets in a match. Once again, one of the cricket annuals observed that Peate's "absence was not felt."

When Lillywhite, Shaw, and Shrewsbury were completing the arrangements for their tour to Australia in 1884–85, they encountered more than one difficulty in finalizing the constitution of the team. In the end, the party was made up of thirteen professionals, but in effect only the dangerously low complement of eleven, since Lillywhite and Shaw rarely put on flannels. One of the individuals to benefit from the defection of those originally invited to participate in the tour was Bobby Peel, and after his selection was announced, one journalist expressed the opinion that his performances so far "have hardly been sufficiently brilliant to warrant his inclusion in a representative team of English professionals." Having delivered this pontifical statement, the writer went on to sugar the pill with the proviso that "it is certain that the sturdy little left-hander, who has done such good service to Yorkshire during the last three summers, will not be the least useful member of the thirteen Players who are touring in Australia this winter."

This prophecy proved to be accurate, at least as far as his trundling was concerned, for Bobby loitered near the bottom of the batting averages. The programme consisted of thirty-three matches, of which only eight are rated as first-class, the remaining fixtures being against "odds." In all contests, Bobby amassed an aggregate of 356 wickets, a strike rate of more than ten per match, with an average of 5.70, as near as can be ascertained, since there are slight variations in the statistics reported in different accounts, especially in the minor matches. In the latter, admittedly against rather weak opponents, he was by far the most successful England bowler, accounting for 321 victims at an average of less than five runs apiece. Four times he recorded a match return of over twenty wickets (best 24–62), but his most remarkable feat occurred in the fixture with Twenty-two of Moss Vale on January 21 and 22, 1885. Bowling unchanged in partnership with William Attewell, he was primarily responsible for dismissing the home side for 14! *Wisden* concludes the report of this match by observing that "The batting of the Twenty-two was alone remarkable for its extreme feebleness against the bowling of Peel." On a concrete pitch covered with matting, the little left-hander registered one of the most extraordinary feats of bowling in "odds" matches – no less than eighteen wickets for only 7 runs! On this occasion, as on a few others, he was not put on in the second innings, presumably to delay the conclusion of play or to give other bowlers a chance to try their luck.

As far as Bobby was concerned, this particular match was also memorable for the incident of a best laid scheme that went a-gley. Having laid a bet with a friend that he would score at least four runs when his turn came to bat, a member of the Moss Vale team approached George Ulyett and asked to be introduced to Peel with the idea of persuading the latter to help him win his wager. There was a promise of two bottles of champagne as a reward, whereupon Ulyett suggested firmly that they had better have one of them there and then, "to test it." This was agreed, and the bottle was emptied between them. In order to make sure that everything would go off as planned, the Moss Vale player had a quick word the next morning with Wilfred Flowers, the Nottinghamshire professional, who set his mind at rest by telling him he would be given an easy one to hit. As the would-be hero marched confidently to the crease with his bat over his shoulder, he passed Bobby and said, "Peel – you know?" "Yes; it's all right, sir," answered Bobby, who was by no means averse to the prospect of a second bottle, and his first delivery was a very slow full toss. Swinging his bat wildly, the unfortunate Moss Vale man failed to connect, and the ball landed neatly on the top of the stumps. Striding off the pitch, the infuriated loser yelled at Peel, "You've done with me for ever. No more champagne!" You cannot help admiring the foresight of George Ulyett, when he arranged for half the reward to be settled in advance.

In the eight first-class fixtures of the tour, including five Tests, Bobby was the leading wicket-taker with thirty-five victims, but he proved to be rather more expensive, with an average of 19.22 and last in the table of six bowlers. It is, however, only fair to remember that he delivered far more overs than anybody else. His record in the Test Matches was not remarkably outstanding for those days, although he captured more wickets than any other bowler – twenty-one at 21.47, coming fourth in the table – but at least he had the satisfaction of celebrating his international debut by taking five wickets for 51 runs at Adelaide, on December 12, 13, 15, and 16, 1884. With the bat he did little, occupying the last position with an average of 7.40.

After his overall performance on the tour down under, it was confidently expected that Bobby would establish himself as one of the leading bowlers in England in the summer of 1885. Ted Peate was still in the Yorkshire side and emerged as one of five English bowlers to capture a hundred or more wickets in the season in all matches, but the onset of incipient corpulence was beginning to tell against him. Bobby, however, failed to take advantage of this godsent opportunity to challenge his rival. Recalling his success as a bowler the previous winter in Australia, one of the annuals remarked that he "failed in any way to maintain the reputation he had gained there." Often coming on as second or third change and sometimes not even given a turn with the ball, he claimed only forty-seven costly wickets at an average of 25.08. On one solitary occasion, exploiting the conditions of a slow, rain-soaked pitch at Bramall Lane, on May 25, he achieved an excellent performance by capturing seven wickets for 51 runs in Kent's first innings. Otherwise, he did little to suggest that he was ready to step into Peate's shoes. This unwelcome decline in his bowling was to a certain extent offset by the excellent quality of his fielding and an improvement in his batting. Twice he passed the half-century, making his highest score of the season against Middlesex at Bramall Lane, on August 17, 18, and 19. His battling 71 included "a splendid hit to leg" for five runs, which would probably have delighted some of the senior members of the crowd, who in their youth were wont to applaud such a stroke as the acme of perfection in the art of aggressive batting.

A tragic and all too rapid acceleration in the decline of Ted Peate's erstwhile deadly powers and physical condition was only too apparent in 1886. The days of glory as the first-choice bowler for Yorkshire and England were receding into the past, and in fact Ted was dropped from the side in August, never to return for an inter-county contest. Did the burly figure of Peate exercise a daunting influence over Bobby and inculcate a sense of inferiority in his heart and brain? It is an interesting question for speculation, to which there is no immediate answer, since neither man, as far as I know, ever expressed a recorded opinion on the matter. If Bobby had proved a disappointment in the bowling department in 1885, how much worse was his record in 1886. Even the departure of his rival in the last few weeks of the season had no immediate effect in boosting his morale. To make no bones about it, his bowling in all first-class matches was wretched in the extreme – only fourteen wickets at not far off forty runs each! The inevitable outcome of such a miserable performance taken in isolation could well have been Peel following Peate into obscurity, but happily he was rescued once again by his batting. Increasing his aggregate of runs to 732 and attaining the very respectable average of 20.33, he registered his highest score in first-class cricket, a vigorously struck but "somewhat lucky" 75 against Middlesex at Lord's, on June 7 and 8. Never again, however, would Bobby be in the position of having to rely on his batting as a means for his salvation.

In 1887, a prey to physical infirmities and a mere shadow as regards his bowling, though not, alas, in the matter of his physique, Ted Peate played for Yorkshire only twice in first-class fixtures, neither of them against another county. He returned to the realms of club cricket to perform prodigious feats in the less demanding conditions of one-day matches. Judged on the basis of Bobby's record for the season, the final departure of Peate acted like a tonic on his successor. With this impediment removed from his path, he ruled for a decade without the threat of any competitor aiming to wrest from him the role of Yorkshire's slow left-hander, until he, too, like Peate, lost his place in the County Eleven. As will be seen, however, the same state of affairs did not always obtain in matches outside the County Championship, and, in one way or another, it was Peel's misfortune to find himself continually in contention with another trundler of first-rate ability.

It was in 1887, then, that Bobby Peel finally gave convincing proof of his quality in all departments of the game, witness the 1888 edition of *Wisden*, which observed that "Peel's all-round work for the [Yorkshire] eleven cannot be overpraised." Amassing 835 runs, he increased his average to 25.30, though a three-figure score continued to elude him. Against Lancashire at Old Trafford, on August 25, 26, and 27, he made a "punishing 66," a performance noteworthy for his "clean and well-timed" strokes on the leg side, while at Scarborough, a few days later, he was "seen to great advantage" in hitting up the top score (71) in Yorkshire's return contest against MCC. His most meritorious innings occurred earlier in the season in the encounter with Sussex at Bradford, on June 20, 21, and 22. In his only visit to the crease, he smote twelve boundaries in a "wonderfully well-played innings of 91." All in all, this was a good match for Bobby, since in the visitors' first knock he took five wickets for 65 runs.

With far more opportunities to turn over his arm now that Ted Peate was gone, Bobby experienced a spectacular increase in his role as a bowler. From only fourteen wickets at an average of 38.50 in 1886, he progressed to eighty-five at the much lower cost of 17.31 apiece, a feat which earned him the eleventh position in the national bowling averages. Five times he took five or more wickets in an innings, his best being seven for 72 on a slow pitch against Sussex at Hove, on August 15, 16, and 17. That "all-round work" which drew a word of commendation from *Wisden* was much in evidence in this match as well, since in Yorkshire's first innings "Peel hit brilliantly for 46," while in the second he rendered material assistance in staving off defeat and batted doggedly to secure the draw.

In spite of his improvement with the ball, it could not as yet be claimed that Bobby Peel was dominating the Yorkshire bowling to the same extent as his predecessor had done, and one sure sign of brilliance and consistency was missing from his record in 1887: not once throughout the season did he succeed in claiming ten or more victims in a match. When making a judgment on Yorkshire's doings, one of the annuals asserted that the bowling "did not show any bright particular star . . . There was really nothing very formidable in the Yorkshire attack." Those sentiments were echoed elsewhere, when a contributor to *Wisden* mourned the decline and absence of Ted Peate, "for at present Yorkshire has no one to fill the place which formerly was his." With the blessed gift of hindsight, it is safe to say that the mantle of the once formidable Ted was destined to fall on Bobby's sturdy shoulders and, notwithstanding the strictures of the two cricket annuals, there were some tokens of recognition that he was worthy of encouragement.

The first sign in 1887 that Bobby was becoming a force to be reckoned with came with his selection to assist the Players against the Gentlemen. He made his debut in the series at Lord's, on July 11 and 12, and he also

John Briggs

took part in the Oval fixture straight afterwards. The professionals' bowling resources were especially strong, and Arthur Shrewsbury, the Players'
skipper, used Bobby rather sparingly in both matches. Economical rather
than penetrative would perhaps best describe the Yorkshireman's bowling,
but nevertheless he had the consolation of playing two useful knocks of 25
and 29. At The Oval, the following year, on July 12, 13, and 14, he figured
largely in the rout of the amateurs (by an innings and 39 runs), recording
his best performance with the ball in the series. Opening the attack with
George Lohmann on a pitch badly affected by rain, Bobby struck an early
blow by dismissing W.G. for 3 and finished with figures of six wickets
for only 34 runs. He was not put on in the second innings. In the whole
series, between 1887 and 1897, he appeared in twenty matches, achieving a
satisfactory all-round record. With the bat, he attained an aggregate of 476
runs at an average of 19.83, his highest score being 71 not out at Lord's, on
July 8, 9, and 10, 1895. With the ball, his record was forty-eight wickets at
16.06 each.

As far as Yorkshire cricket was concerned, Bobby may have had things
all his own way from 1887 until his retirement, but once he entered the
sphere of various representative matches, such as the encounters between
the Gentlemen and the Players, he came up against a dangerous competitor
in the shape of the chubby, diminutive Johnny Briggs, whose ebullience
or dismay on the field formed a sharp contrast to Bobby's more dour
demeanour when in action. Johnny, the darling of the Old Trafford
crowd, was a wizard with the ball, and there was a perpetual and
unresolved debate as to whether Briggs or Peel was the greater of these
two slow left-handers. Often, when not involved in county matches, they
played together on the same side, and on other occasions one would appear
to the exclusion of the other. In most of the Gentlemen *v* Players matches
from 1887 to 1891, the names of Briggs and Peel were both to be found in
the professionals' team. If the order of being put on to bowl in the first
innings may be taken as any kind of a guide, then it must be admitted that
Briggs was usually given preference over Peel. The latter might possibly
have considered himself unfortunate to be deprived of the opportunity to
add to his bag of six for 34 in the first innings at The Oval, in 1888, when
the Players' captain – a Yorkshireman, too! – put Briggs on instead of Peel
in the second innings, particularly as Johnny claimed five victims for only
28 runs – victims which could have been Bobby's! The all-round records
of the two in the series make interesting reading, while contributing little
towards the arguments about their respective merits. Peel had the higher
aggregate of runs (476) and the slightly better batting average; Briggs took
more wickets (56), but Bobby's were obtained at a slightly cheaper rate
(16.06 as opposed to 17.60).

A second acknowledgement of Peel's potential took the form of an invitation to visit Australia in the winter of 1887–88 as a member of G.F. Vernon's team, sponsored by the Melbourne Club. This was the tour when the Hon M.B. Hawke (family bereavement) and Willie Bates (eye injury) were compelled to drop out of the side and return to England, but their early departure was not the only problem encountered by Vernon's men. As narrated elsewhere, the colonies were invaded by a second English team promoted by the well known trio of Lillywhite, Shaw, and Shrewsbury, who had given Bobby his first opportunity to visit Australia in 1884–85. The captain of this second combination was C.A. Smith, the future Sir C. Aubrey Smith, now remembered not so much for his prowess on the cricket field as for his portrayal of the archetypal English gentleman according to the conception of the Hollywood film industry. Both teams contained some good names, and the cricket they played was of a high standard, but the inevitable outcome of two sides vying with each other for the patronage of the Australian public was a serious financial loss and an end to the promotion of cricket tours by Shaw and his partners.

Bobby, of course, was not concerned with the politics nor the financial side of the awkward situation besetting his superiors. As usual, he concentrated his attention on the action of the cricket field, and in so doing he established himself as one of England's leading all-rounders, a position from which he scarcely looked back throughout the remainder of his career. In "odds" contests he once again took a stack of wickets, including one match analysis of twenty-four for 52, and he made some hefty scores, among them one knock of 119. Taking part in nine first-class matches, he came second in the batting averages (449 runs at 34.53) and second also in the bowling table (50 wickets at 16.44). His greatest triumph occurred at Sydney, on February 10, 11, 13, 14, and 15, 1888, when England, represented by the best players drawn from the two touring teams, defeated Australia by 126 runs. He did nothing with the bat – single figures in both innings – but he exacted more than ample revenge with the ball. Play was out of the question on the second and third days, and on a rain-affected pitch he bowled unchanged with George Lohmann in the first innings and throughout most of the second, securing ten wickets for 58 runs (5–18 and 5–40) – his best match performance in Tests in Australia. Another member of the England side was his rival Briggs, whose run aggregate on this occasion was only two more than Bobby's. The Lancastrian, however, was denied the opportunity to atone for this failure, since his services as a bowler were never required in the whole match!

Fresh from his triumphs down under, Bobby continued to ride the crest of the wave during much of the summer of 1888. Sandwiched between an average amount of sunshine in early May and September lay a prolonged spell of uncertain weather producing the pitches most favourable to his type of bowling. His batting, it must be confessed, showed a marked decline from the more heady days of 1887. As a bowler, however, he was superb, and it might be claimed with justice that the spectre of Ted Peate was finally exorcised for good and all, since his aggregate of wickets was doubled, rising to 171 at an average of 12.22. Such an achievement would be lauded to the skies today, turning his fellow trundlers green with envy, but in 1888 it could secure for him no higher place than sixteenth in the national averages!

There were many personal successes to warm the cockles of his heart. Fourteen times he claimed five or more wickets in an innings, the second highest tally of his career, while ten or more victims in a match were routed on four occasions. At The Oval, he recorded his best ever analysis in an innings for the Players against the Gentlemen – this was the match in which Johnny Briggs replaced him in the second innings – but his most startling performance occurred in the contest between Yorkshire and Nottinghamshire at Bramall Lane, on July 23 and 24, when the rain was his ally once again. Winning the toss, the visitors took first innings, but the ground dried out quicker than expected. Not a single batsman succeeded in reaching double figures, and the final total was 24. Bowling unchanged in partnership with Ted Wainwright, the medium-pace off-spinner, Bobby delivered 20.2 overs, of which thirteen were maidens, and conceded only 12 runs in capturing eight wickets! The treacherous pitch reduced the Yorkshire batsmen to a similar state of weak-kneed impotence, and they were dismissed for 46, with only one double figure (Peel 13!). There were some early hopes that Nottinghamshire might stage a minor recovery, piloted by the dead-block tactics of Will Scotton, who carried his bat through the innings for 17, but Bobby soon found the spot once more. With the aid of Saul Wade, dispensing off spinners with an extravagant break, he completed the humiliation of his opponents with six wickets for 21 runs, and the Yorkshire opening pair easily knocked off the deficit of 37. Any bowler today would be in raptures over a return of fourteen wickets for only 33 runs – a rate of about two and a-half per wicket – but in a later season Bobby would rise to even loftier heights.

The Australians were in England again in 1888, playing Test Matches at Lord's, The Oval, and Old Trafford, and the selectors picked Briggs and Peel for all three contests. According to the method then practised in choosing the England team, Briggs was virtually guaranteed a place at his home ground of Old Trafford, but Bobby, on form, could not be left out of the side. In the initial encounter at headquarters, ending in a victory for the tourists, he was the most successful member of the home attack, claiming eight wickets for 50 runs. Although Briggs carried much before him in Australia's first innings at The Oval (5–25), his Yorkshire rival still managed to lift five scalps as a contribution to England's victory by an innings. This result was repeated at Old Trafford, on August 30 and 31, with Johnny Briggs being granted only a minor though useful role in the proceedings. Exploiting the dampness of the pitch, Peel proved irresistible in the first innings, his full analysis being 26.2–17–31–7. This was his best performance in a single innings against the Australians and, with four for 37 the second time round, he recorded his best match figures in Tests.

A notable recognition of Bobby's performance in 1888 appeared in *Wisden* the following year. For the first time, the almanack included a photographic plate bearing portraits of "Six Great Bowlers of the Year" – a precursor of the section "Five Cricketers of the Year." Peel was one of the six, and another, almost inevitably, was Briggs.

With the pitches generally rather less to the liking of some of the bowlers in the summer of 1889, Bobby's success was not so spectacular as it had been in the previous season. Although he had no difficulty in claiming a place among the leading wicket-takers in the country, his tally of victims fell from 171 to 130, and his average rose to 16.39. For this superficially apparent deterioration of form there was ample justification, at least as far as county matches were concerned. Receiving barely adequate support from some of his team-mates, he was hugely over-bowled, "and considering that he had most of the work to do for Yorkshire, Peel deserves more credit than his figures would seem to warrant." Nevertheless, he had plenty of good days, achieving five or more wickets in an innings on eleven occasions and ten or more in a match four times. The unfortunate Sussex batsmen at Hove, on August 22, 23, and 24, were cast in the role of his chief sacrificial lambs of the season. Delivering far more overs than any other member of the Yorkshire attack, he accounted for seven opponents in the first innings and six in the second at a total cost of 118 runs. If this was one of the occasions Lord Hawke had in mind when his principal bowler betrayed no sign of elation at his repeated successes, it may also be conjectured that Bobby was seething inside and making strenuous efforts to preserve an outward appearance of equanimity. It was evident that his tally should have been more than thirteen. The Yorkshire fielding in 1889 made a dismal contribution to the County's poor record for the season, and in this match it descended into horrifying depths of abysmal incompetence, even though the outcome was a rare victory for Hawke's men. Catch after catch was grassed, the principal sufferer being Bobby, and one estimate suggested that as many as twelve chances went to ground off his bowling!

Although the statistics of his bowling were slightly less favourable in 1889, Peel's batting showed an enormous improvement. With an aggregate in all matches of 991 runs (average 22.02), he fell agonizingly short of the double. Many a knock of intrinsic merit, including five half-centuries, was inscribed in the score books, but against Middlesex at Lord's, on June

20, 21, and 22, he breached the three-figure barrier for the first time in his first-class career. Dismissed for three in the first innings and proving ineffective with the ball (for him an unusual match return of 1–160!), he won back his stripes in Yorkshire's second innings. There is some doubt about the length of his occupation of the crease, which was certainly over three hours. Apart from the possibility of nearly giving a hot return catch, he played a serene, chanceless innings, striking twenty-two boundaries, slightly more than half of his final score of 158.

By comparison with the previous season, Bobby's all-round performance assumed a kind of see-sawing movement in 1890: he scored fewer runs but took more wickets. With an aggregate of 817 – a significant retrogression from his total of 1889, though he played more innings with more not outs – his average slid below the twenty mark to 18.56. No century came his way, his best effort being a "splendid 83," taken off the menacing Nottinghamshire bowling at Trent Bridge, on August 7, 8, and 9, but as usual he played his part with some solid contributions from the middle of the order. His tally of wickets rose to 171, the same figure he attained in 1888, at little more than thirteen runs apiece. A sterling performance was registered in the contest against Surrey at Bramall Lane, on June 30, July 1 and 2, designated as a benefit for the Yorkshire stonewaller, Louis Hall. Unfortunately for the latter, the match was ruined by excessive rain, but Bobby, revelling in the condition of the pitch, romped through the visitors' first innings to plunder eight wickets for 60 runs. He would doubtless have had more victims, but the appalling weather prevented Surrey from batting again. It is some measure of his domination of Yorkshire cricket at this time that the other four bowlers should share one wicket between them. When looking back on the events of the season, one of the cricket annuals devoted considerable space to Bobby's achievements, asserting that his all-round success "was distinctly the most noteworthy feature of Yorkshire cricket in 1890." While paying a brief tribute to the value of his batting ("Always reliable, particularly at a pinch, when other batsmen have failed"), the writer expatiates in glowing terms on the outstanding merits of his bowling, characterized succinctly in the judgement that "On certain wickets he has always been unplayable, and for precision and ability to keep down the runs he has had, and still has, few if any superiors."

The Australians, captained once more by W.L. Murdoch, were on tour in England again in 1890, with three Test Matches featured in their programme. In the first, at Lord's, on July 21, 22, and 23, England won by seven wickets, with Bobby the most successful bowler (match figures of 6–87). There were some changes in the side for the second Test at The Oval, on August 11 and 12, the same dates as the fixture between Yorkshire and Middlesex at Bradford. This was the occasion

A. E. Stoddart

mentioned elsewhere when Mr A.E. Stoddart's decision to play for his county incited Lord Hawke to retaliate by claiming Peel and Ulyett for Yorkshire. While England were scrambling to a narrow victory, Bobby captured eight wickets, including Stoddart's in both innings (for 7 and 0), with the third day lost through rain. Not a ball was bowled in the final Test, scheduled to take place at Old Trafford, on August 25, 26, and 27, but in any case the local committee had plumped for their own man, Briggs. While Johnny sat idle in the dressing-room, Bobby was picking up a few wickets for Yorkshire at Maidstone.

There was a certain tinge of *déjà vu* about Peel's record in 1891, somewhat reminiscent of the season of 1889. Once again he came within striking distance of the double, only to fall short in both departments this time – 971 runs at 24.27 (fifteenth in the national averages) and a frustrating aggregate of 99 wickets at a cost of 17.35 each. Although this might suggest that his bowling had lost a little of the keenness of its edge, there was no sign of any deterioration in his batting, and his doings included two splendid centuries. The highest (150, including one 6 and twenty-two 4s) occurred in the contest between L. Hall's Yorkshire Eleven and M. Sherwin's Nottinghamshire Eleven – virtually an authentic county match – at Bradford, on July 20, 21, and 22, and it was reported that "Peel's success was very popular." Later in the season, at Hove, on August 17 and 18, he was Yorkshire's top scorer with 128.

In the winter of 1891–92, Bobby set off on his third tour of Australia as a member of the side led by W.G. Grace. He maintained his reputation with the bat in all fixtures, but not so much with the ball. For this last he could hardly be considered responsible, since he was in competition with four other bowlers, George Lohmann and J.W. Sharpe of Surrey, Attewell, and his perpetual rival Briggs, and in some respects he was a bit of an also-ran when it came to bowling. The programme consisted of nineteen "odds" contests and eight first-class matches, including three Tests. Although Bobby opened the bowling in the first at Melbourne, on January 1, 2, 4, 5, and 6, 1892, and captured five wickets in the match, W.G. showed himself more inclined subsequently to entrust the attack to the other members of the team. In the second Test at Sydney, a month later, Peel was given a spell only in the second innings (1–49), while in the final contest, in which Briggs achieved match figures of twelve for 136, the Yorkshireman's services were not called upon at all. The table of the Test bowling averages puts Bobby in third place with six wickets at 21.33 each, and the first column shows that he delivered fewer overs than Briggs and far fewer than the other three bowlers. This comparative neglect of his talents may not have been much to Bobby's taste, but at least he had a productive tour with the bat, averaging slightly over twenty-five runs per innings. Such admirable consistency was also reflected in his performance in the Tests. Fourth in the table, immediately after W.G., he scored 134 runs at an average of 26.80. His absence from the bowling line-up in the last Test at Adelaide, on March 24, 25, 26, and 28, was counterbalanced by his role as a batsman. Number six in the order, he shared a run-making stand with Johnny Briggs and remained at the wickets for about three hours, notching 83, with eight 4s, and giving only one chance. This was his highest score in Test Matches.

By 1892, Peel was becoming almost a veteran in years of service with Yorkshire, and his name was ascending towards the top of the list in terms of seniority. His all-round performance following his return from Australia and in the next season showed a slight subsidence from the higher standards he had achieved in earlier years, particularly in his batting. He still retained much of his old skill with the ball, and even though the state of the pitches tended to favour the batsmen on the whole, he captured more than a hundred wickets in both seasons. The Australians were in England yet again in 1893, and Bobby was picked as the slow left-hander for the first Test at Lord's, on July 17, 18, and 19 – a drawn match abandoned on the third day. It was a disappointing affair from Bobby's point of view. He scored 12 and 0 not out and performed rather indifferently with the ball. The Australians were restricted to only one innings, and A.E. Stoddart, deputizing for the injured W.G., chose Bobby to open the England attack. He was reasonably parsimonious in conceding runs – 36 in 22 overs, with 12 maidens – but he failed to take a wicket. It was doubtless partly as a consequence of this somewhat lack-lustre performance that he was omitted from the side for the remainder of the rubber. His replacement was Johnny Briggs (who else?), who celebrated his return to the team by capturing ten wickets at The Oval and six more at Old Trafford.

The season of 1894 marked a time of extra responsibilities for Bobby Peel. As senior professional in the Yorkshire Eleven following the retirement of George Ulyett, he took over the captaincy on one or two of those occasions when Lord Hawke was unable to play. He was fulfilling this onerous and largely unfamiliar role in the home fixture against Derbyshire on July 30, 31, and August 1, within a few days of his benefit match against Lancashire. J.A.H. Catton, a sporting journalist short of stature but never lacking in self-assertiveness, was intent upon arranging an interview with Peel, who agreed to meet him at Bramall Lane on the first day of the Derbyshire game. A sense of inferiority, perhaps, rather like his nervousness over signing his name, made Bobby extremely reluctant to abide by his promise. The opening gambit in his delaying tactics was to decline to fix an actual time for the talk until he had tossed for first innings, which could hardly be called unreasonable. He won, elected to bat, and then excused himself on the plea that he would wait until he had taken his innings – again, not unreasonable, all things considered. I suppose he was feeling rather jittery, what with the unaccustomed burden of captaincy and Catton's persistent badgering for the dreaded interview, for he was soon back in the dressing-room with only a couple of runs to his name. Seemingly more anxious than ever to avoid the importunate journalist, Bobby fled after making an appointment to meet him at a certain seat in the pavilion after luncheon.

Catton took up his position and waited – in vain. A search for his quarry in the immediate area proving equally fruitless, he bad-temperedly resumed his seat and continued to wait upon Peel's pleasure. Just as he was lighting his pipe to calm his jangled nerves, Catton became aware that somebody had taken a seat near him and was coughing to attract his attention. The stranger identified himself as one Fred Tempest of Morley – Bobby's place of residence – announcing that he was Peel's secretary (Peel, of all people, with a secretary!). Since his "employer" didn't like being interviewed and had little to say, Tempest added, "You can interview me on behalf of Peel. I can answer any questions."

In the more modern idiom, Catton instantly blew his top. Venting the full blast of his wrath upon the unfortunate Fred Tempest, the infuriated newspaper man rejected the proposal ("I don't want an interview by proxy") and declared his intention of concocting one, based on his knowledge of Peel's record and doings on the cricket field. Catton kept his word and took particular pleasure in wickedly inserting in his piece the comment that "Peel was a pleasant man and delightful to converse with!" He was, of course, on safe ground in the certain conviction that the interviewee would not dare to contradict him. One wonders how many interviews with sporting celebrities of today have a basis equally divorced from reality.

There was another interesting aspect to this bizarre episode. Catton had also undertaken to write an article on Johnny Briggs at the same time, and the reactions of England's two slow left-handers constitute a fascinating cameo on their contrasting characters. Bobby Peel, daunt-less on the cricket field, was almost tongue-tied and afraid of showing himself up under an interrogation by a journalist; the outgoing Johnny Briggs felt no such inhibitions and was only too willing to win a little publicity.

Henry Ainley, one of the darlings of the theatre-going public in bygone days, worshipped at the shrine of his own idol in the world of cricket – Bobby Peel. Throughout his life, the great Thespian loved to recall how he had given tangible proof of his devotion by insisting on carrying Peel's bag from the station to the ground at Bradford on the occasion of Bobby's benefit match against Lancashire, on August 6, 7, and 8, 1894 – a few days after the aborted interview with Catton. Yorkshire were the winners by 117 runs and, from the financial standpoint also, the affair was a great success, contributing largely to the £2,000 that Bobby eventually received, which was a very large sum in those days. The beneficiary did nothing startling as an individual, taking five wickets all told and scoring 16 and 17, succumbing to catches. The same bowler accounted for him in each innings – Johnny Briggs!

There was a slight improvement in Bobby's batting average in 1894, but it was well under twenty, which was rather low for one of England's leading all-rounders, and he had to be content with a highest score of 48. Apart from his debut in 1882, this was the first time he had failed to obtain a half-century in an English summer. His aggregate of wickets rose, however, to 145, at an excellent average of 13.44.

In the autumn of the same year, Bobby set sail as a member of A.E. Stoddart's team for what was destined to be his final visit down under. There were plenty of high jinks aboard the ship as well as after the party had landed, with Peel fulfilling his usual role as the principal perpetrator of practical jokes on his unsuspecting team-mates. He liked to get up early in the morning to watch racehorses being taken out for their first gallop, and he always enjoyed a few hours of shooting, though if you were prudent, you usually kept well out of his way, since Bobby tended to be rather indiscriminate in his aim, blazing away at anything in sight and claiming everything that fell. His most famous exploit in this line occurred not in Australia but back in England when, having wounded a hare which limped off beyond the boundary of his host's property, he proposed to pursue it. The gamekeeper's protests were of no avail. Declaring that they paid no heed to that sort of thing in Yorkshire, Bobby vaulted over the stile and finished off the hare.

The cricket on Stoddart's tour was at times sensational, with heavy scoring to the detriment of the bowlers' averages, no more so than in some of the five Test Matches. England won the first two at Sydney and Melbourne but were comprehensively defeated in the third and fourth at Adelaide and Sydney again. Came the final contest at Melbourne, in which Jack Brown, a fellow Yorkshireman, played his famous hurricane innings of 140, and Bobby had the honour of scoring the runs to secure the rubber for England. His record as a batsman in the five most important fixtures of the tour was curiously inconsistent, though in the end he managed to reach a half-way position in the batting averages with 18.66. England's second innings in the second Test at Melbourne, straddling New Year's Day 1895, was that occasion when he scored a slow and very patient 53, reminding his long-suffering opponents of the barn-door methods of Will Scotton. His best performance occurred in the fifth encounter at Melbourne, on March 1, 2, 4, 5, and 6, when he made a solid 73 in the first innings, sharing a partnership of 162 with Archie MacLaren. These two half-centuries were in sharp contrast to his ill-success at Adelaide, on January 11, 12, 14, and 15, and Sydney, on February 1, 2, and 4. At a low ebb in the third contest, the England batting was an even worse failure in the fourth, and in one sense Bobby's performance was a fitting symbol of this woeful decline. Put out for a "pair" at Adelaide, he suffered the same fate in the next match at Sydney, a victim in both innings of the same mode of dismissal (st A.H. Jarvis b C.T.B. Turner).

It may be conjectured that Stoddart, an habitual sufferer of the wiles of the Yorkshire left-hander back in England, held a high opinion of his conqueror's skills. Although Johnny Briggs and W.H. Lockwood were also in the side, the England captain chose to open his attack in all five Tests with the combination of Tom Richardson, the Surrey fast man, at one end, and Peel at the other. These two achieved the greatest success of the England bowlers, though their wickets were bought at – for those days – considerable expense. Richardson had thirty-two at 26.53, and his partner twenty-seven at 26.70.

Bobby's best performance in an innings, indeed his best ever in Tests in Australia, was recorded in the first encounter at Sydney, on December 14, 15, 17, 18, 19, and 20, 1894. Winning the toss, the home side batted first and gave the England bowlers some merciless stick in amassing a total of 586. Bobby, a martyr of the dentist's chair not long before the beginning of the match, was evidently far below the top of his form, since his two wickets cost 70 runs apiece! What would normally be considered a reasonably respectable total of 325 was not sufficient to save the follow on, but England exacted some vengeance in their second innings to the tune of 437, yet this left Australia with the seemingly simple task of scoring only 177 to win. By close of play on the penultimate day, the total stood at 113 for the loss of two wickets, Giffen and Darling both not out and going well, with merely 64 runs still required.

George Giffen, the first of the great Australian all-rounders, went to bed in a contented frame of mind. Relishing no doubt the prospect of an easy victory and the opportunity of adding a good score to his century in the first innings, he sank into a deep, untroubled sleep. Elsewhere, it is alleged, Bobby Peel was one of the England party to seek ample solace in the flowing bowl. Dead to the world throughout most of the hours

George Giffen

J. McC. Blackham

of darkness, he overslept and in fact was late in arriving at the ground the next morning.

Giffen, rejoicing at the hot sunshine streaming through the windows, went down to breakfast, only to meet his captain Blackham, "with," as he quaintly but graphically described it, "a face as long as a coffee-pot." While Giffen and Peel had been sleeping the sleep of the just and the unjust, there had been a prolonged and heavy rainstorm during the night. Sixty-four to make on a sticky dog!

Andrew Stoddart was probably one of the most capable captains when it came to managing his favourite left-hander, both at bringing him up to the mark and encouraging him to still greater efforts. Sizing up the situation and realizing that the talents of Peel and Briggs would be vital to England's cause, Stoddart thrust the bleary-eyed Tyke under a cold shower. Revived and told of the condition of the pitch, Bobby is said to have made one of those remarks which have secured a permanent place in the folklore of Test cricket: "Gi'e me t'ball, Mester Stoddart, and Ah'll get t'boogers out before loonch!" It was a near thing, but the combination of Peel (6–67) and Briggs (3–25) won the match for England by ten runs. Later, when somebody blurted out that the rain had been the cause of Australia's defeat, Blackham mournfully replied, "No, it was the sun that did it."

Back home in England in the summer of 1895, Bobby showed no sign that his fourth visit down under would have any adverse effect on his form. On the contrary, he enjoyed the most successful season of his whole career with the ball. His batting, it must be confessed, was of the nature of being useful rather than outstanding (847 runs, average 17.28, highest score 78), but his bowling reached new heights of excellence. Achieving his greatest total of five or more wickets in an innings (16) and ten or more in a match (6), he also recorded his best aggregate of 180 victims at only 14.97 each. This brought him his highest ever position (sixth) in the national bowling averages.

It is surely permissible to linger over one of Bobby's exploits in his golden summer of 1895. From the standpoint of personal records, one of the most sensational matches of the season was the encounter between Yorkshire and Somerset at Headingley, on July 22 and 23. With a wicket "all in favour of the bowlers," the contest ended with a victory for the home side long before the close of the second day. Lord Hawke won the toss and elected to bat. Yorkshire were soon in trouble and were put out for only 73. The damage was done by two bowlers – E.J. Tyler (slow left-arm) and Captain W.C. Hedley (right-arm fast-medium). The latter, later Sir Walter Coote Hedley, had migrated to Somerset from Kent, where Lord Harris had disapproved of his bowling action. In the years to come, his delivery would be universally condemned, and, curiously, his partner Tyler would be no-balled for throwing.

Hedley was the man who tore the Yorkshire batting to shreds, claiming his best ever analysis in a single innings (8–18). I can think of few things more galling than taking eight wickets so cheaply and still coming off second-best in the eyes of statisticians. Somerset, with only 69 runs in the book, fell just short of Yorkshire's effort. The failure of the visitors to secure a lead on the first innings can be attributed largely to Yorkshire's champion bowler, Bobby Peel, whose return of nine wickets for 22 runs was unsurpassed in his whole career. Hedley, I suppose, girded his loins, at any rate metaphorically, for the home side's second innings, when Yorkshire managed to cope more competently with the difficult conditions, thanks largely to David Denton, who contributed 60 to the total of 163. In devastating form once more with six wickets for 52, Hedley recorded match figures of fourteen for 70. His splendid efforts were nullified when Somerset were dismissed for 64 (Peel 6–28). So, at one and the same time, Bobby registered his most outstanding performance in an innings and a match.

Having achieved new records as a bowler in 1895, Bobby went on to set the seal on his prowess as an all-rounder the next summer by completing that double, which had eluded him in previous seasons. Only five cricketers had accomplished the feat in England before 1896: W.G. Grace was the first, in 1874, and in six subsequent seasons; C.T. Studd in 1882 and 1883; Wilfred Flowers, the Nottinghamshire and MCC professional, also in 1883; G.A. Davidson, Derbyshire and MCC ground staff, in 1895; and the fifth, the Australian George Giffen, in 1886 and 1893. There was a repeat performance by Giffen in 1896, and two English all-rounders kept him company. In his final appearance of the season, George Herbert Hirst marked the first of his fourteen doubles. He was beaten past the post by his senior team-mate. In all matches, Bobby Peel scored 1,206 runs (average 30.15) and took 128 wickets at 17.50 apiece, becoming the first Yorkshireman to reach the target, and it may be added that he also achieved the double in Yorkshire matches alone.

By comparison with the previous year, his performance with the ball was more steady and sober – though "sober" is not necessarily the word that springs immediately to mind, when you're talking about Bobby Peel. Most trundlers, however, would confess to a feeling of blissful contentment in contemplating a seasonal record of five or more wickets in an innings ten times and four instances of ten or more in a match. His most outstanding exploits occurred late in the season, both at Scarborough, when a South of England Eleven were defeated by Yorkshire (Peel 8–27 in the second innings, his best of the year).

Immediately afterwards, on August 31 and September 1, he bowled C.I. Thornton's Eleven to an innings victory over the Australians with seven scalps for 53 runs at the first attempt, followed by five more for 43 in the second innings.

Of a certainty, however, 1896 was Peel's special year with the bat. Thrice he passed three figures, two of his centuries being taken off the Sussex bowling – 111 at Bradford, on May 18, 19, and 20, and 106 at Hove, on August 20, 21, and 22. These were preceded by the most famous innings of his career, which occurred in the contest between Warwickshire and Yorkshire at Birmingham, on May 7, 8, and 9. A perfect wicket boded no good for the bowlers, and, having won the toss, Lord Hawke had no hesitation in deciding to take first innings. The home side had a miserable time in the field on the first day, and at close of play Yorkshire had scored 452 for the loss of seven wickets, but there was still more to come. Doomed to a second day of leather hunting, the unfortunate Warwickshire team suffered under another remorseless glut of runs, until stumps were drawn with the long awaited conclusion of the visitors' first innings. The match ended in a draw, of course, with Warwickshire completing their first innings and starting their second.

The Yorkshire total amounted to the – for Warwickshire – stupendously horrifying figure of 887, which is still a record for county championship matches. Alfred Law was the only member of the home side not put on to bowl, and the most successful analysis (4–184) was achieved by H.J. Pallett. There were four centurions in the Yorkshire innings, the first Mr F.S. Jackson with 117, and the second Ted Wainwright, run out for 126. Their capital efforts were eclipsed by the exploits of Bobby Peel at number seven and Lord Hawke at number nine. Coming together not long before play ended on the first day, they extended their partnership far into the second, until the captain was dismissed for 166. This stand, worth 292 runs, remains to this day in the annals of Yorkshire cricket as the record for the eighth wicket. Peel continued serenely on his way and was undefeated when the last man was out. His final score, which included one 5 and sixteen 4s, was 210 not out – only the second double century in Yorkshire's history and just beating Ephraim Lockwood's 208 against Kent in 1883. If the tales about Bobby's addiction to strong drink be true, then you can only assume that on this occasion he might have temporarily signed the pledge. To remain at the wickets for nearly seven hours and see 548 runs scored was nothing short of a marathon performance, particularly when you remember that Bobby had reached the somewhat venerable cricketing age of thirty-nine.

On tour over here once again in 1896, the Australians contended against the might of England three times at the usual venues of those days. For the first encounter, played at Lord's, on June 22, 23, and 24, the home side took the field without a slow left-hander, the main attack being entrusted to the Surrey pair, Tom Richardson and George Lohmann, supported by J.T. Hearne of Middlesex and MCC. Since this trio took nineteen wickets between them – the other was run out – and England won by six wickets, the policy of the selectors was justified. Lohmann was compelled by an unfortunate injury to miss the next contest at Old Trafford, on July 16, 17, and 18, and his place was taken by Briggs. The latter, with match figures of three wickets for 123 runs, scarcely added to his laurels, while Jack Hearne failed completely. In spite of the Herculean efforts of Tom Richardson (13–244), England went down to defeat by three wickets.

Before even play began for the decider at The Oval, on August 10, 11, and 12, there was turmoil in the England side. From time to time over the previous twenty-odd years, there had been complaints by some of the professionals over the emoluments paid under the guise of expenses to certain amateurs, especially W.G. Grace. This was one of two grievances aired in August 1896. The other concerned the amount of the match fee for representing England, and five of the professionals originally selected demanded that their pay should be doubled to £20. After this had been rejected by the Oval committee, three of the "malcontents," all Surrey men, were prevailed upon to withdraw their demand and resume their places in the side. One of the two failing to make his peace with the authorities was George Lohmann, and the selection committee called upon the services of Bobby Peel.

George Giffen (0 and 1, and only two wickets to his name) had some bitter memories of the event ("That last wretched match played in the mud at The Oval was a farce"). The pitch, already drenched by heavy rain on the two previous days, was subjected to a further downpour, which delayed the start until late in the afternoon of the 10th. W.G. won the toss and chose first innings. Coping with a slow wicket and variable light, England did well to reach 69 for the loss of only one wicket. In fact, from the batsmen's point of view, these were the most favourable conditions of the whole contest, since the remainder of the match was played out largely on a sticky wicket. Australia, needing 111 for victory, were eventually defeated by 66 runs.

And Bobby's part in this, his final appearance for England? In spite of his triumphs on the county circuit, he failed to improve on his batting average on this occasion. For the third time in Tests he collected a "pair," and for the second time suffered an identical dismissal in both innings (b H. Trumble). Nor did he distinguish himself particularly in the Australians' first innings. Unable for once to find his length, he had to settle for only two wickets for 30 runs and the role of playing second fiddle to Jack Hearne (6–41). By the time the tourists came out for their second innings, the conditions were perfect for Bobby. Once again, it has been alleged, he approached his captain with one of those pleas of the "Gi'e me t'ball and Ah'll soon get t'boogers out" variety. W.G., however, decided to give the honour to Tom Richardson. He soon found he was wrong, since Tom could not get a proper footing, and on came Peel to partner Hearne. This combination eviscerated the opposition (total 44), and Peel, with an analysis of 12–5–23–6, went out in a blaze of glory. So delighted was F.S. Jackson with his team-mates' performance that he presented both bowlers with "a small gold replica of a cricket ball in the form of a watch chain attachment." Bobby, it may be added, wore his watch fob with pride for many years to come. This unique trophy, like Billy Bates's, seems to have vanished beyond all ken.

The three "pairs" told heavily against Peel, when you consider his batting record in Test Matches. In twenty appearances he scored only 427 runs at an average of 14.72, which was rather mediocre, even by the standards of his time. Briggs did rather better as a batsman, with an aggregate of 815 runs at 18.11, highest score 121. As a bowler, Johnny's tally in all matches (33) amounted to 118 wickets at 17.74 apiece, but it must not be forgotten that his statistics enjoyed the benefit of twenty-one cheap wickets captured on the tour of South Africa in 1888–89. His record against the much more formidable opposition provided by the Australian batsmen was not quite so impressive – 97 victims at 20.55 each. Peel, on the other hand, claimed 102 wickets with an average of 16.81, all of them exclusively in encounters with the Australians. He was, in fact, the first England bowler to reach a hundred wickets in Test Matches against Australia.

Throughout most of the season of 1897, the pitches were generally more suited to run-getting than wicket-taking, but for good cause Bobby Peel fell well below the aggregate of 1,000 runs and 100 wickets. He had usually managed to escape being disabled on the cricket field in previous years, but his luck deserted him in the match against Lancashire at Bradford, on July 19, 20, and 21, when he was so badly injured that he was unable to bat a second time and was subsequently incapacitated for about three weeks. He resumed his place in the side for the fixture with Middlesex at Bramall Lane, on August 16, 17, and 18. Always popular with the Yorkshire crowds, he was given a splendid reception when he went in to bat at number seven. He rewarded his admirers with a well played innings of 40 and claimed the bowling honours in the Middlesex first innings with five wickets for 71 runs. Then, for Bobby, everything went awry, and "Circumstances

. . . induced the committee to leave him finally out of the County team."

The details of Peel's dismissal have been handed down from one writer to another over the years, but one of the best known versions in print appears in A.A. Thomson's book, *Hirst and Rhodes*, based on Hirst's own recollections of the sad event. Perhaps George Herbert's memory had become clouded with the passing years and, in looking back, he fell into the not unusual trap of magnifying one's own part in a particular incident. The possible location of the match is given as Chesterfield, that is to say against Derbyshire, an error that was repeated beyond Thomson's book. Hirst described how his breakfast in the professionals' hotel was interrupted by the sudden appearance of Bobby Peel reeling into the room in "a proper condition." After persuading the culprit to go back upstairs, Hirst managed to undress him and put him to bed. As soon as he had arrived at the ground, he informed Lord Hawke that Peel was ill. Having lost the toss, the Yorkshire captain called for the twelfth man and led his team into the field. To Hirst's dismay, there were twelve fielders, including Peel "in an even 'properer' condition than before!" Appalled at this distasteful sight, Lord Hawke thundered at Peel to leave the field immediately, but Bobby declared he was in fine form and attempted to demonstrate his fitness by bowling a trial ball. As luck would have it, he chose the sight-screen rather than the stumps for his target. Thomson was rather hazy about what happened next, but he imagined that Peel was led away with a minimum of fuss, and few if any of the spectators realized what was going on – which, if you think about it, is a somewhat optimistic assumption. This, or something like it, might be termed "the authorized version" of the incident. A subsequent accretion to the tale was the allegation that the miscreant had given additional offence by urinating on the pitch – an act you would scarcely expect to see reported in the press of the day!

At the risk of being accused of spoiling a good story, I have to say – as implied in an article published some years ago – that this excellent example of a kind of black comedy is riddled with errors and implausibilities. As noted above, the venue of the match, and thus the identity of Yorkshire's opponents, are given incorrectly, though it is only fair to add that these particular mistakes were amended in some later accounts, but by no means all. Then there is the matter of the toss. Actually, it was won by Lord Hawke, who elected to bat, and Bobby, as we have seen, was in fine fettle up to the end of the second day, when Yorkshire had begun their second innings. The episode of the noisy invasion of the breakfast room followed by the forcible putting to bed could only have occurred on the morning of the final day. And if it, or something like it, really happened, how come Hirst failed to see Peel getting changed in the dressing-room? It might, of course, be argued that the latter arrived late at the ground, as he did at Sydney in 1894, and certainly he had not batted again when the Yorkshire innings was declared closed. Perhaps, on the previous night, he had been celebrating his successful return to first-class cricket and was suffering from a hangover, which, in Hirst's eyes, was "a proper condition." There was sufficient time, by the way, for Middlesex to score 219 for 2 before the match ended in a draw.

Above all, we must not forget the extraordinary incident of Bobby's trial ball. Common sense dictates that it is pure fiction. Put yourself in Lord Hawke's place. Supposing you saw your principal bowler was in such an advanced stage of inebriation that he mistook the sight-screen for the wicket, would you have chosen him to open your attack? No, of course you wouldn't, but what actually happened? For the first half-hour or so the bowling was entrusted to Mr F.S. Jackson and Peel! The captain tried eight bowlers in all, and the fact remains that Peel's analysis (7–1–15–0) was better than that of Mr F.W. Milligan who replaced him (14–1–39–0), or Hirst's (7–0–30–0), or Haigh's (4–0–18–0). That being said, it has to be admitted that Bobby did not perform up to his usual standards; he was seen to slip and fall, once when he was bowling and once when he was fielding, and this is when the trouble probably started. Lord Hawke, convinced apparently that his senior professional was in no fit state to play, strode off into the pavilion, rounded up those members of the committee present, and held an extraordinary meeting. The upshot of their deliberations was the suspension of Peel for the remainder of the season.

Brief references to the culprit's alleged misconduct on the field appeared in the sporting press, and in future years we have been regaled with the particulars of "the authorized version." The details of the trial ball at the sight-screen and the unorthodox method of watering the pitch continue to exert a special fascination. While England's cricketers were engaged in their disastrous tour down under in 1990–91, an interview with the Australian Prime Minister was televised, during the course of which he referred to both these events, though, if I remember correctly, without naming the offending bowler.

Was Bobby ever given the opportunity to present a case for the defence? As a matter of fact he was, but his explanation has been accorded such little publicity that in all fairness it should be taken into consideration. Shortly after the tragic events had occurred at Bramall Lane, a reporter from a Yorkshire newspaper called at his home in Morley and asked him for an interview. On this occasion, Bobby was only too ready to oblige by running over the salient features of that fateful day. First, the matter of being unfit to play as a result of being intoxicated. Before going to the ground he had imbibed two small glasses of gin and water ("Ah doan't bloosh to say it"), but this was all, and he asserted that he did not touch alcohol during the luncheon interval. If his claim be true, the two small, diluted gins would hardly have been sufficient to make him lose his footing. And was there any word of complaint or remonstrance when he was taken off, asked the journalist? None, was Bobby's reply, and he then continued by offering a perfectly plausible explanation for his two falls. From the bag containing his cricketing gear he produced the left shoe he claimed to have been wearing at the crucial time. Turning up the sole for the reporter's inspection, he pointed out that three of the spikes were missing and another one was bent. This mishap, which caused his first fall, occurred during the time he was bowling, and it was the same defective shoe which made him stumble and drop on one knee later, while he was fielding ("no proper bite o' t'ground"). He was adamant that nobody, not even Lord Hawke, uttered a word of complaint to him at the time of the incident, nor was he ever called upon to appear before the committee. The unpleasant task of informing him of his fate was given to the secretary, J.B. Wostinholm. At the end of the match, the latter handed him his wages, saying, "Peel, I am sorry to tell you that your services will not be needed any more this season." Bobby was flabbergasted, and the secretary went on with the assertion that his play had not been satisfactory. This was not good enough for Bobby, so, by way of explanation, Wostinholm added, "You have had a glass too much."

Bobby's version of the events at Bramall Lane was ignored, and his claim that he could call upon "a number of persons" to testify that he was perfectly sober fell upon deaf ears. For a time, the deposed senior professional harboured a burning sense of injustice, which even found its way into the 1898 edition of *Wisden*, whose contributor felt that there must have been a good reason for the dismissal, but noted at the same time that "Peel complained that he had been harshly treated." He was excluded from the Scarborough Festival at the end of the season but participated in two matches at Hastings, without any particular success. Any hope that Yorkshire might relent and recall him to the side in 1898 was soon stifled, when his place was filled by Wilfred Rhodes, a greater all-rounder and a man of much more temperate habits. Bobby's first-class career came to its final end in 1899, when he appeared in two matches, neither of them connected with Yorkshire. The second of these took place at Truro, on July 7 and 8, when he assisted an England Eleven against the Australians. Behind the stumps on this occasion was A.F.A. ("Dick") Lilley, the current England wicket-keeper. Dick was a little hazy about the statistics when recalling this contest in his memoirs, but he did not hesitate to assert that Bobby's "powers were still apparently unimpaired . . . His bowling retained all its old qualities." Before moving on to another topic, Dick added that the Yorkshireman "was a very sociable fellow, full of good-humour, and with a fund of anecdotes."

Perhaps Bobby was too sociable for his own good. It was claimed that he had been warned more than once about his "lack of self-control" before his personal tragedy was played out at Bramall Lane. Lord Hawke, it may be postulated, was not the most sensitive of men. In his autobiography, largely composed by somebody else, the Yorkshire captain maintains that nothing gave him so much pain as the necessity for dismissing Peel for the sake of discipline, adding:

> I did not care for the fact that, by dispensing with our foremost all-rounder, we were losing the Championship. What hurt me was publicly censuring a valued comrade and a real good fellow. Peel thoroughly proved he was loyal, for he never bore me malice for my decision to dismiss him. We have met as friends many times since . . .

I do not know if Peel ever read this statement – the book was published in his lifetime – but it is not easy to swallow it whole without question, especially the remarks about loyalty and bearing no malice, and there may be some who would feel a slightly bitter taste in the mouth from studying this declaration. Was Lord Hawke over hasty or not in his knee-jerk reactions at Bramall Lane? Nobody would argue over the necessity of maintaining discipline for the sake of the team and the state of cricket in general, but perhaps the situation might have been handled with greater tact and skill by another more level-headed captain, such as F.S. Jackson or Andrew Stoddart.

So, at a time when he probably felt that there was still plenty of cricket left in him, Peel was compelled to seek employment in less exalted spheres. He had a coaching appointment with Essex, and he played for some years in league cricket. If his various engagements entailed longer absences from his home, this might not have proved too irksome to him, since it has been implied that he was not the most domesticated of men. A familiar figure at Yorkshire's home matches, he lent a hand in bringing on the rising generations, and when he had passed beyond the age of demonstrating the arts of bowling and batting, he was always ready to weigh in with some sound advice. At the age of eighty, he took on one side the future Sir Leonard Hutton, who was on the threshold of his brilliant Test career. The gist of Bobby's admirable counsel was that the youngster should concentrate on the immediate job in hand and ignore everything else. Above all, he must play himself in and not think about scoring quickly and, as Sir Leonard remembered it, Bobby concluded his advice in a manner that most Yorkshiremen would have appreciated: "We don't expect 'fireworks' from an opening batsman."

Outliving many of his contemporaries, Bobby Peel died at Morley, Leeds, on August 12, 1941, in his eighty-fifth year, which suggests that either he was blessed with a most remarkable constitution, or else the tales of an excessive addiction to alcoholic beverages might have been just a little exaggerated. At that time, England was in the throes of World War II, but his death was not allowed to pass unnoticed, and one of the tributes appearing in print came from Sir Stanley Jackson, his Yorkshire and England team-mate. Among other things, "Jacker" remembered that the last time he saw Bobby, the latter was wearing on his watch chain the small gold replica of a cricket ball the amateur had presented to him as a souvenir of his bowling feat against the Australians at The Oval, in 1896.

Peel left an enviable all-rounder's record behind him. Mentioned already were his feats of being the first Yorkshireman to achieve the double in all and in only Yorkshire matches, and the first bowler to capture 100 wickets for England against Australia, both in his last full season of 1896. With the bat in all first-class matches, he attained an aggregate of 12,191 runs (average 19.44), with seven centuries, and in the field he held 214 catches. As a bowler, he outstripped most of his contemporaries. He passed one hundred victims in a season eight times. His tally of wickets amounted to 1,776 (average 16.19), and he claimed five or more in an innings 124 times and ten or more in a match on 34 occasions.

Of Bobby's supreme value to any team in all departments of the game there can be no question, but what of his merits as a "team man?" A remarkable tribute, enough to gladden the heart of even the most exacting individual, was recorded by W.G. Grace:

> What I like about Peel is his plucky, willing, cheerful way, and on that account I would as soon have him on my side as any man in England. Never a grumble comes from him, and he is ready at a moment's notice to go anywhere in the field. Now and then a bowler begs to be let off, alleging that he is either a little bit tired or that the end does not suit him. Peel is never tired, at least he never admits it, and he does not care whether he bowls up-hill, down-hill, with the wind or against it.

I made a promise early in this sketch that evidence would be produced to prove that, no matter how modest were his attainments in elementary education, Bobby possessed at least the ability to write his own name. First, readers need only consult Richard Gorton Barlow's *Forty Seasons of First-class Cricket*. An admirable all-rounder at county and England level and a contemporary of Peel's, Dick Barlow was also a keen and industrious collector of cricket memorabilia, and a whole section of his book is devoted to the collection of autographs he painstakingly assembled during his days as a player and umpire. Turn to page 186, and you will find reproduced in facsimile the modest signature, "R. Peel." The same also appears on pages 42 and 228 of C.W. Alcock's *Famous Cricketers and Cricket Grounds 1895*.

There is, in addition, another piece of evidence to offer in support of my claim. In the early 1930s, I was one of a group of small boys avidly seeking autographs in the pavilion at the Scarborough cricket ground. There was a break in the proceedings out in the middle – it was, perhaps, the luncheon interval. From what was in those days the home side's dressing-room there emerged a small, elderly, grey-moustached figure wearing a trilby hat, a dark-blue, double-breasted overcoat, and carrying a walking-stick. After he had taken a seat on one of the benches reserved for the players, somebody near me, possibly an ageing adult, pointed at that solitary figure clasping the handle of his stick and said something along the lines of "That's Bobby Peel, who once played for Yorkshire and England. Why don't you go and ask him for his autograph?" Plucking up my courage, I approached this relic of a bygone age and made my request. He looked at me keenly and, to the best of my recollection, asked me if I knew who he was, or why I wanted his autograph. After I had recited my newly acquired information, he relinquished his hold on the stick and signed his name on a blank page – with his left hand, of course. Alas! where is that autograph book now?

NOTE.– The details of all the circumstances surrounding Peel's final match for Yorkshire have been adapted from my article, "You Have Had a Glass Too Much," *Wisden Cricket Monthly*, July 1982, 45–47.

Select Bibliography

The principal publications consulted are the following:

1. Collections of Scores, Annuals, and Reference Works

Bailey, Philip, Philip Thorn, and Peter Wynne-Thomas, *Who's Who of Cricketers* (Feltham: Newnes Books, 1984)
Cricket Scores and Biographies, 15 vols
First Class Cricket Matches 1864–1866, and succeeding volumes covering the period 1867–1897, comp. and pub. by the Association of Cricket Statisticians
Frindall, Bill, comp. and ed., *The Wisden Book of Test Cricket 1877–1984* (London: Guild Publishing, 1985)
——comp. and ed., *The Wisden Book of Cricket Records* (London: Guild Publishing, 1986)
A Guide to First Class Cricket Matches Played in the British Isles, and various county booklets, comp. and pub. by the Association of Cricket Statisticians
James Lillywhite's Cricketers' Annual
John Lillywhite's Cricketers' Companion (later *John & James . . .*, and finally *James Lillywhite's Cricketers' Companion*)
John Wisden's Cricketers' Almanack

2. Newspapers

The Argus (Melbourne)
The Australasian
Bell's Life in London
The Daily Telegraph
The Field, the Country Gentleman's Newspaper
The Huddersfield Daily Chronicle
The Huddersfield Weekly News and South West Yorkshire Record
The Illustrated London News
The Illustrated Sporting News
The Illustrated Times
The Leeds Daily News
The Leeds Mercury

The Leicester Chronicle and Leicestershire Mercury
The Leicester Daily Post
The Manchester Guardian
The Nottingham Daily Guardian
The Sheffield Daily Telegraph
The Sporting Life
The Sportsman
The Times
The Yorkshire Post

3. Journals and Periodicals containing articles and miscellaneous material

Baily's Magazine of Sports and Pastimes
Cricket: A Weekly Record of the Game
Cricket Chat
The Cricket Field
The Cricket Quarterly
The Cricket Statistician
The Cricketer
The Journal of the Cricket Society
Labour History
The Playfair Cricket Monthly
Wisden Cricket Monthly
The World of Cricket, 1914

4. Books

Altham, H.S., and E.W. Swanton, *A History of Cricket* (2 vols., London: George Allen & Unwin Ltd., 1962)

Alverstone, The Rt. Hon. Lord, and C.W. Alcock, eds., *Surrey Cricket: Its History and Associations* (London: Longmans, Green, and Co., 1904)

Ashley-Cooper, F.S., *Edward Mills Grace Cricketer* (London: Chatto & Windus, 1916)

——*Nottinghamshire Cricket and Cricketers* (Nottingham: Henry B. Saxton, n.d. [1923])

——*Cricket Highways and Byways* (London: George Allen & Unwin Ltd., 1927)

Barker, Ralph, *Ten Great Bowlers* (London: Chatto & Windus, 1967)

Barlow, Richard Gorton, *Forty Seasons of First-class Cricket* . . . (Manchester: John Heywood Ltd., n.d. [1908])

Bettesworth, W.A., *The Walkers of Southgate: A Famous Brotherhood of Cricketers*, ed. by E.T. Sachs (London: Methuen & Co., 1900)

——*Chats on the Cricket Field*, with Explanatory Notes by F.S. Ashley-Cooper (London: Merritt & Hatcher, Limited, "Cricket Office," n.d. [1910])

Birley, Derek, *The Willow Wand: Some Cricket Myths Explored* (London: Queen Anne Press, Macdonald and Jane's, 1979)

Bowen, Rowland, *Cricket: A History of Its Growth and Development throughout the World* (London: Eyre & Spottiswoode, 1970)

Brodribb, Gerald, *Hit for Six* (London: Heinemann, 1960)

——*The Croucher: A Biography of Gilbert Jessop* (London: Constable, 1985)

Brookes, Christopher, *English Cricket: The Game and Its Players through the Ages* (London: Weidenfeld and Nicolson, 1978)

Cashman, Richard, *The "Demon" Spofforth* (Kensington, NSW: New South Wales University Press, 1990)

Catton, J.A.H. ("Tityrus"), *Wickets and Goals: Stories of Play* (London: Chapman and Hall Ltd., 1926)

Coldham, James D., *Lord Harris* (London: George Allen & Unwin, 1983)

Coldham, James P., *F.S. Jackson: A Cricketing Biography* (Marlborough: The Crowood Press, 1989)

——*Lord Hawke: A Cricketing Biography* (Marlborough: The Crowood Press, 1990

Collins, W.E.W., *Leaves from . . . An Old Country Cricketer's Diary* (Edinburgh and London: William Blackwood & Sons, 1908)

Country Vicar, A. [R.L. Hodgson], *Cricket Memories* (London: Methuen & Co. Ltd., 1930)

——*Second Innings* (London: Hutchinson & Co. Publishers Ltd., 1933)

——*The Happy Cricketer*, 2nd ed. (London: Frederick Muller Ltd., 1947)

Crowley, Brian Mathew, and Pat Mullins, comp. and eds., *Cradle Days of Australian Cricket: An Anthology of the Writings of "Felix"* (T.P. Horan), (South Melbourne: MacMillan Company of Australia Pty Ltd, 1989)

Daft, Richard, *Kings of Cricket: Reminiscences and Anecdotes with Hints on the Game* (Bristol: J.W. Arrowsmith; London: Simpkin, Marshall, Hamilton, Kent & Company, Limited, n.d. [1893])

Frith, David, *"My Dear Victorious Stod": A Biography of A.E. Stoddart* (Guildford: Lutterworth Press, 1977)

——*The Fast Men*, rev. and up-dated ed. (London: Corgi Books, 1977)

——*The Slow Men* (London: Corgi Books, 1985)

Gibson, Alan, *The Cricket Captains of England: A Survey* (London: Cassell Ltd., 1979)

Giffen, George, *With Bat and Ball: Twenty-five Years' Reminiscences of Australian and Anglo-Australian Cricket* (London: Ward, Lock and Co., Limited, 1898)

Gordon, Sir Home, Bart., *Background of Cricket* (London: Arthur Barker Limited, 1939)

Grace, W.G., *Cricket* (Bristol: J.W. Arrowsmith; London: Simpkin, Marshall, Hamilton, Kent & Co., Limited, 1891)

——*The History of a Hundred Centuries*, ed. by W. Yardley (London: L. Upcott Gill, 1895)

——"W.G.": Cricketing Reminiscences and Personal Recollections (London: James Bowden, 1899)

Green, Benny, comp., The Wisden Book of Obituaries: Obituaries from Wisden's Cricketers' Almanack 1892–1985 (London: Macdonald, Queen Anne Press, 1986)

Harris, Lord, A Few Short Runs (London: John Murray, 1921)

Hawke, Lord, Recollections & Reminiscences (London: Williams & Norgate, Ltd., 1924)

Hawke, Lord, Lord Harris, and Sir Home Gordon, Bart., eds., The Memorial Biography of Dr W.G. Grace (London: Constable & Company, Ltd., 1919)

Hodgson, Derek, The Official History of Yorkshire County Cricket Club (Marlborough: The Crowood Press, 1989)

——, R.L., see Country Vicar, A

Holmes, The Rev, R.S., Surrey Cricket and Cricketers 1773 to 1895 (London: "Cricket" Offices, 1896)

——The History of Yorkshire County Cricket 1833–1903 (London: Archibald Constable and Co. Ltd., 1904)

Hutton, Len, Cricket Is My Life (London: Hutchinson & Co. (Publishers) Ltd, n.d. [1949])

Kemp, Jan, Cheerful Charlie: A Biography of C.P. McGahey (Great Wakering, Essex: The Author, 1989)

Kynaston, David, Bobby Abel, Professional Batsman, 1857–1936 (London: Secker & Warburg, 1982)

Lewis, W.J., The Language of Cricket, with Illustrative Extracts from the Literature of the Game (London: Oxford University Press, 1934)

Lilley A.A., Twenty-four Years of First-class Cricket, Recalling the Most Famous Cricketers and Their Methods, new ed. (London: Mills & Boon, Limited, 1914)

Lillywhite, Fred., The English Cricketers' Trip to Canada and the United States (London: F. Lillywhite; Kent & Co., 1860; rpt., Introduction by Robin Marlar, Tadworth, Surrey: World's Work Ltd., 1980)

Lodge, Harry, Lascelles Hall Cricket Club Centenary 1825–1925 (Huddersfield: The Author, 1925)

Lucas, E.V.. ed., A Hundred Years of Trent Bridge (Privately Printed for Sir Julien Cahn, 1938)

Lyttelton, The Hon. R.H., Cricket (London: Duckworth & Co., 1898)

Lyttelton, The Hon. R.H. and others, Giants of the Game: Being Reminiscences of the Stars of Cricket from Daft down to the Present Day (London: Ward, Lock & Co., Limited, n.d. [1899])

MacLaren, A.C., Cricket Old and New: A Straight Talk to Young Players (London: Longmans, Green and Co., 1924)

Midwinter, Eric, W.G. Grace: His Life and Times (London: George Allen & Unwin, 1981)

Mosey, Don, We Don't Play It for Fun: A Story of Yorkshire Cricket (London: Methuen, 1988)

"Old Ebor," *see* Pullin, A.W.

Pullin, A.W. ("Old Ebor"), *Talks with Old Yorkshire Cricketers*, 2nd ed. (Leeds: "The Yorkshire Post," 1898)

——*Talks with Old English Cricketers* (Edinburgh and London: William Blackwood and Sons, 1900)

——*Alfred Shaw Cricketer: His Career and Reminiscences*, recorded by A.W. Pullin ("Old Ebor") (London: Cassell and Company, Limited, 1902)

——*History of Yorkshire County Cricket 1903–1923* (Leeds: Chorley & Pickersgill Ltd, The Electric Press, 1924)

Ranjitsinhji, K.S., *The Jubilee Book of Cricket*, 6th ed. (Edinburgh and London: William Blackwood and Sons, 1898)

Read, W.W., *Annals of Cricket: A Record of the Game Compiled from Authentic Sources, and My Own Experiences during the Last Twenty-five Years* (London: Sampson Low, Marston & Company Limited, 1896)

Richards, C.H., *Nottinghamshire Cricket Scores and Biographies* (Nottingham: C.H. Richards, 1891, 3 vols in 1)

Rutter, Edward, *Cricket Memories: Rugby – Middlesex – Free Foresters* (London: Williams and Norgate, Ltd., 1925)

Sale, Charles, *Korty: The Legend Explained* (Hornchurch: Ian Henry Publications, 1986)

Shaw, Alfred, *see* Pullin, A.W. ("Old Ebor")

Sissons, Ric, *George Lohmann: The Beau Ideal* (Leichhardt, NSW: Pluto Press Australia Limited, in Association with J.W. McKenzie, Ewell, Epsom, 1991)

Steel, A.G., and the Hon. R.H. Lyttelton, and others, *Cricket*, 2nd ed., The Badminton Library of Sports and Pastimes (London: Longmans, Green, and Co., 1888)

Thomas, Peter, *Yorkshire Cricketers 1839–1939* (Manchester: Derek Hodgson Publisher, 1973)

Thompson, Flora, *Lark Rise to Candleford*, The World Classics 542 (London: Oxford University Press, 1975)

Thomson, A.A., *Hirst and Rhodes* (London: The Epworth Press, 1959)

Walmsley, E., *Cricket Celebrities of 1890* with a Complete Résumé of the Season's Doings (Manchester and London: John Heywood, n.d. [1890])

Warner, P.F., *later* Sir Pelham, *Cricket: A New Edition*, The Badminton Library of Sports and Pastimes (London: Longmans, Green and Co., 1920)

——*Lord's 1787–1945* (London: George G. Harrap & Co. Ltd., 1946)

——*Gentlemen v. Players 1806–1949* (London: George G. Harrap & Co. Ltd., 1950)

——*Long Innings: The Autobiography of Sir Pelham Warner* (London: George G. Harrap and Company Ltd, 1951)

West, G. Derek, *The Elevens of England* (London: Darf Publishers Limited, 1988)

——*Twelve Days of Grace* (London: Darf Publishers Limited, 1989)

Williams, Marcus, ed., *The Way to Lord's: Cricketing Letters to The Times* (London: William Collins (Willow Books), 1983)

——ed., *Double Century: 200 Years of Cricket in The Times* (London: William Collins (Willow Books), 1985)

Wood, Edward Allen, ed., *The History of Lascelles Hall Cricket Club: A Famous Nursery of Yorkshire Cricket, 1825–1968* (The Editor, 1969)

Woodhouse, Anthony, *The History of Yorkshire County Cricket Club* (London: Christopher Helm, 1989)

Wright, L.G., *Scraps from a Cricketer's Memory* (Derby: Derbyshire County Cricket Supporters' Club, 1980)

Wynne-Thomas, Peter, *Nottinghamshire Cricketers 1821–1914* (Haughton, Retford, Notts: The Author, 1971)

——*England on Tour: A Record of All England Cricket Tours Overseas, with Accounts, Results and Statistics* (London: The Hamlyn Publishing Group Limited, 1982)

——*The Hamlyn A-Z of Cricket Records* (London: The Hamlyn Publishing Group Limited, 1983)

——*"Give Me Arthur": A Biography of Arthur Shrewsbury* (London: Arthur Barker Limited, 1985)

Index

199